*Come Out from among Them, and
Be Ye Separate, Saith the Lord*

Come Out from among Them, and Be Ye Separate, Saith the Lord

Separationism and the Believers' Church Tradition

EDITED BY
William H. Brackney
WITH
Evan L. Colford

FOREWORD BY
James M. Stayer

The Acadia Centre for
Baptist and Anabaptist Studies

AND

◆PICKWICK *Publications* · Eugene, Oregon

COME OUT FROM AMONG THEM, AND BE YE SEPARATE, SAITH THE LORD
Separationism and the Believers' Church Tradition

Copyright © 2019 Wipf and Stock Publishers. All rights reserved. Except for brief quotations in critical publications or reviews, no part of this book may be reproduced in any manner without prior written permission from the publisher. Write: Permissions, Wipf and Stock Publishers, 199 W. 8th Ave., Suite 3, Eugene, OR 97401.

Published in cooperation with The Acadia Centre for Baptist and Anabaptist Studies, Acadia University, 50 Acadia Street, Wolfville, Nova Scotia, Canada B4P 2R6

Pickwick Publications
An Imprint of Wipf and Stock Publishers
199 W. 8th Ave., Suite 3, Eugene, OR 97401
www.wipfandstock.com

PAPERBACK ISBN: 978-1-5326-5943-0
HARDCOVER ISBN: 978-1-5326-5944-7
EBOOK ISBN: 978-1-5326-5945-4

Cataloguing-in-Publication data:

Names: Brackney, William H., editor. | Colford, Evan L., editor. | Stayer, James M., foreword.

Title: Come out from among them, and be ye separate, saith the Lord : separationism and the Believers' Church tradition / edited by William H. Brackney and Evan L. Colford ; foreword by James M. Stayer.

Description: Eugene, OR : Pickwick Publications, 2019 | Includes bibliographical references and index.

Identifiers: ISBN 978-1-5326-5943-0 (paperback) | ISBN 978-1-5326-5944-7 (hardcover) | ISBN 978-1-5326-5945-4 (ebook)

Subjects: LCSH: Protestantism. | Dissenters, Religious.

Classification: BX4817 .C655 2019 (print) | BX4817 .C655 (ebook)

Scripture quotations in the MacGregor essay are taken from The Authorized (King James) Version. Rights in the Authorized Version in the United Kingdom are vested in the Crown. Reproduced by permission of the Crown's patentee, Cambridge University Press.

Scripture quotations in the Goatley and van der Leer essays are from Revised Standard Version of the Bible, copyright © 1946, 1952, and 1971 National Council of the Churches of Christ in the United States of America. Used by permission. All rights reserved worldwide.

Manufactured in the U.S.A.   06/18/19

Contents

Foreword by James M. Stayer | vii
Preface | xiii
Acknowledgments | xv
The Contributors | xvii

Part I: Principles and Types

1 *Hoc enim est novam ecclesiam construere*: The Making of New Churches in Western Christianity, 1400–1600 | Martin Rothkegel | 3

2 The Genetic Separationist Trait Among the Baptists | William H. Brackney | 23

3 Born Again, Coming Again, and Going Out: The Significance of Believer's Baptism and Eschatology on Anabaptist Dissent | Colin Godwin | 38

4 Unifiers to Come-Outers: The Journey of the Stone-Campbell Restoration Movement | Douglas A. Foster | 51

5 "Without Spot or Wrinkle": The Tendency toward Separation in the Mennonite Tradition . . . and a Vision for a "Rhizomic" Church | John D. Roth | 66

Part II: The Principle Applied and Expanded

6 "Holy Living and Holy Dying": The Response of Some British Baptist Women to "Come Out" from the World | Karen Smith | 85

7   Making Room to Serve: Separation as a Strategy among African-American Baptists | DAVID EMMANUEL GOATLEY | 102

8   Union Overtures by Maritime Baptists and Disciples of Christ, 1903–1908 | RUSSELL PRIME | 117

9   Promiscuous Picnics: Newfoundland Pentecostalism as a "Come-Outer" Tradition | ALLISON S. MACGREGOR | 132

Part III: The Principle Writ Large

10 The Curse of Cults and the Scourge of Sects: Or a Come-Outing of New Religious Movements? | EILEEN BARKER | 157

11 The Past and Future of the Believers Church Conferences | TEUN VAN DER LEER | 189

Appendix: 17th Believers' Church Conference Findings Summary | 199

Bibliography | 203

Index | 229

Foreword

James M. Stayer

The Mennonite World Conference has instituted Renewal 2027 in its celebration of the 500th anniversary of the Anabaptist/Mennonite tradition. Together with other historical and current grounds for emphasizing the 1527–2027 anniversary, this confirms the view of John Howard Yoder, the great Mennonite spokesman of the past generation, that the Seven Articles of Schleitheim (1527) were "the crystallization point" of Anabaptism. Article Four, the keystone of the Seven Articles, declared "A separation shall take place from the evil and from the wickedness which the devil has planted in the world. . . . We have no fellowship with them, and do not run with them in the confusion of their abominations. . . . Now there is nothing else in the world and all creation than good or evil, believing and unbelieving, darkness and light, the world and those who have come out of the world, God's temple and idols, Christ and Belial; and none will have part with the other. . . . By this are meant all popish and re-popish works and idolatry, gatherings, church attendance, wine houses, guarantees and commitments of unbelief and other things of the kind. . . . Thereby shall also fall away from us the diabolical weapons of violence—such as sword, armor, and the like, and all their use to protect friends or against enemies."

The separation was to take place between true Christian baptized believers and "popish and re-popish works and idolatry." Certainly there was to be no separation from the Christian church, which was one, and divinely protected from division. Yet as John Roth acknowledges in his contribution, the historical consequence of the Protestant Reformation was a great proliferation of Christian organizations claiming to participate in the Christian church—or, in some cases, to be the exclusive embodiment of the Christian church. It has been part of Roman Catholic polemic against the Reformation that it created hundreds of churches where there had previously been one church founded by Peter. That, however, limits the focus on Christianity to Western Europe and its overseas expansions. In fact, since Paul of Tarsus created Gentile Christianity, with or without the approval to the Jewish Christian church in Jerusalem run by Jacob, brother of Jesus, the Christian church has had diverse expressions. The early Christianity of Egypt and Ethiopia was distinct from the Christianity organized by the Council of Nicaea (325) and that Christianity underwent a schism between its Eastern and Western components in 1054. So the Reformation was by no means the historical beginning of Christian divisions. In fact, it was not even the beginning of the separations in Latin Christendom, as Martin Rothkegel points out in the first essay of the collection. For a hundred years previously the Hussite movement in Bohemia and Moravia had generated divisions anticipating the German Reformation. Indeed, the beginning of separated Anabaptist brotherhoods in Mikulov, Moravia, in early 1528 was certainly an imitation of Hussite practice. John Roth suggests that the separation and unity of the church can be conceived as analogous to a biological rhizome: "Rhizomes are plants that propagate by sending out a profusion of roots laterally, parallel to the soil above. At various points, the interconnected roots of a rhizome develop nodes that send sprouts up above the ground in unpredictable places. From the surface it appears as if these sprouts are quite distinct entities. But underneath the soil, they are all joined together in a complex and interconnected web of horizontal relationships." Such an outlook would make separation compatible with the broadest and most ambitious ecumenism.

In fact, the Believers' Church Conferences in the past tended not to be broadly ecumenical. They were meeting places of Mennonites and Baptists (and related groups like the Church of the Brethren) who emphasized the baptism of believing persons who understood the meaning of the religious choice they were making. The distinction between "church" and "sect" was pioneered by Max Weber and Ernst Troeltsch—"churches" dispensed religious blessings to their members without making assumptions about the condition of their souls; the "sects" were according to Weber "communities of personal believers of the reborn and only those." This transformation of a formally pejorative term ("sect") at the beginning of the twentieth century did not deny that the churches and sects were each Christian in their different ways. In fact, it was intended to extract polemics from Protestant discourse. Troeltsch and Weber were responded to in 1923 by Karl Holl's "Luther und die Schwärmer," which undertook to reaffirm Luther's polemics against his Protestant opponents. A tradition of Protestant church historians in Germany and America extending into the 1960s and 1970s thereafter connected medieval mysticism with "bad religion," which was odd, because Luther's religious beliefs were also enriched by the medieval German mystical tradition.

The papers by William Brackney, Colin Godwin, John Roth, and Teun van der Leer fit the previous focus of the Believers' Church Conferences upon Baptists and Mennonites, applying the theme of separation. Brackney traces Baptist separations from sixteenth-century England through North America in the twentieth and twenty-first centuries. At first the division between Baptists who believed in freedom of the will and those who believed in predestination mirrored the differences between the Arminians and the orthodox Calvinists among the Dutch Reformed. In North America the presence or absence of slavery made a great difference between the tightly organized Southern Baptists, who became fundamentalists, and the congregational Baptists of the North, who were more typical mainstream Protestants. However, major Baptist personalities in the North tended to be disruptive presences, constantly on the lookout for doctrinal deviations. Colin Godwin writes about sixteenth-century Anabaptists, focusing on believers' baptism and eschatology. Truly, both were universal among early Anabaptists; but eschatological expectations were well-nigh universal in the age of the Reformation. John Roth highlights the spectacular expansion of the Mennonite/Anabaptist movement in the Southern Hemisphere; whereas there were 600,000 members in 1978, now there are more than two million. But the Mennonite Church USA, newly created from the union of the Old Mennonites and the General Conference Mennonites (2002), is already experiencing schisms as some congregations conduct same-sex marriages and others denounce them. General cultural changes do not let the Mennonites untouched—the Amish, while making adaptations of their own, continue less affected by the surrounding culture. Teun van der Leer's brief concluding paper is a retrospect on the Believers' Church Conferences. The *corpus christianum* of the pre-World War II European state churches is now gone. The individual congregation is the Body of Christ. It is obvious that believers' baptism was the norm in the New Testament. But amid the current wave of European secularism, are these concerns of a generation ago still relevant?

The papers by Douglas Foster and Russell Prime examine the collision between Baptists and Disciples of Christ, begun by Barton Stone and Alexander Campbell in the early nineteenth century. The Disciples practiced baptism by immersion, but it was not central to their message. They illustrate a different perspective on Christian primitivism, sometimes claimed to be the essence of Baptism and Anabaptism. They wanted to escape the world of competing denominations, and, guided by an Enlightenment outlook, to live as the New Testament apostles lived, rather than to quarrel over finer points of doctrine. Prime examines the failure of an attempted "organic union" between Baptists and Disciples in the Maritimes, 1903–1908. Both groups were immersionists, brought together by the Sunday School and Christian Endeavor Movements; but different views about congregational independence, and possibly fundamentalist vs. liberal riptides, prevented a merger.

The ecstatic, experiential, revivalist character of America's First and Second Great Awakenings tended to undermine churches that had become too dry and conventional. Allison MacGregor presents such an analysis of the rise of Pentecostalism in Newfoundland ca. 1925. The Methodists, of course, practiced infant baptism; but in an earlier generation they had stressed revivals with emotional conversions and sanctifying "second blessings." Now the immersionist Pentecostal leaders moved in, and Newfoundland Methodism "disappeared" with the merger that created the United Church of Canada in 1925. She acknowledges that similar lines connected Methodism with the rise of the Salvation Army in Newfoundland.

Most of the dissenting movements in the Reformation had a majority of women members. At the same time the women were enjoined by Paul to be silent during worship. Karen Smith argues, however, that, like Anabaptists, seventeenth- and eighteenth-century British Baptists had prophetesses among their female members, and that they made personal testimonies of faith before their baptisms as well as very noticeable death-bed testimonies.

David Goatley writes about black Baptist denominations. The need to create them, particularly in the Southern United States, was a product of the ingrained racism of slavery followed by segregation. They were not stable organizations, partly because of their inevitable political and social agendas. Virtually all black Baptist denominations outside the slave states in the United States and in Canada were abolitionist before the Civil War. After Reconstruction, and into the Civil Rights movement of the 1960s and 1970s, they divided into groups aimed at black power, and groups committed to accommodation between blacks and whites. Not unlike white Northern Baptist "prima donnas," charismatic black preachers were almost inevitably destructive forces in the organization of black Baptist denominations.

The longest and least typical chapter in the book is the contribution by Eileen Barker, described in the list of contributors at the end of the volume as "a sociologist of religion and an emeritus professor of the London School of Economics—widely regarded as the leading authority on New Religious Movements (NRM)," past President of the Association for the Sociology of Religion (2001–2002). The New Religious Movements she describes are decidedly not persons God has called out of the world to be members of Christ's church. They were in the past described as "sects" and "cults," but she prefers to class them as New Religious Movements, in order to make an empirical assessment about their character. From her standpoint these are by no means all objects of ecumenism, about which we can draw the "rhizomic" analysis suggested by John Roth. They include the People's Temple, famous for its collective murder/suicide in 1978 at Jonestown, the Branch Davidians, the Children of God, and the Church of Scientology, together with more conventional groups such as the Mormons and the Jehovah's Witnesses. She argues that the "brainwashing" and "programming" of which such groups are accused are, in fact, not distinguishable from the "conversions" of the nineteenth-century Great Awakening. She makes a good case that countries that legislate against them are in violation of the UN Declaration of Human Rights. Most readers would not want to place many of the groups Eileen Barker describes within the boundaries of the believers' churches. Put this way, some persons do separate from the world in order to do wicked things to other people who have not come along with them. Barker observes, probably correctly, that the fear of cults fits into American history between the Red Scare of the McCarthy era and current Islamophobia.

The Believers' Church Conferences have produced a heterogeneous collection of proceedings. They invite religious advocacy and/or critical scholarship from their contributors. This volume, particularly, reminds us that it is not always straightforward to distinguish the one from the other.

Preface

This volume contains the papers of the 17th Believers' Church Conference, held at Acadia University on June 22–25, 2016. The major sponsor was Acadia Divinity College, the Theological Faculty of Acadia University.

The late esteemed historian, Donald Durnbaugh, himself a founder of the conferences, helpfully defined the Believers' Churches. Durnbaugh considered nine factors: voluntary church membership, separation of church and state, performance of Christian works, high ethical standards, discipleship under discipline, benevolent giving to the poor, mutual aid, believers baptism, everything centered on the word, prayer, and love.[1]

The theme of the Acadia conference, as the title suggests, was Separationism, a noticeable tendency among the Believers' Churches since the sixteenth century. By separationism is meant a disposition or tendency to divide, separate or form a schismatic movement. As sociologists and historians have shown, this can be due to doctrinal, political, personal leadership, or ethnic reasons. The positive side of separationism is that it provides a renewing effect in a tradition and adds to the variety. The negative aspect is that fellowship is severed, mission impaired, and theologically the unity of the Body of Christ is broken. There are biblical foundations and theological rationales for separation, usually suggesting an unhealthy or unacceptable position in the main body, that will be improved upon, or "purified" in the successor groups.

The planners of the Conference sought to investigate the wideness of the phenomenon, which we perceived now extends far beyond the historic Believers' Churches even to New Religious Movements. Thus we include here early manifestations among European dissenters, the Baptists, Anabaptists, Mennonites, and the Restoration Movement. Special studies provide

1. Durnbaugh, *Believers' Church*, 32–33.

insights into the role women played, the nature of the Black Experience in the United States, and the modern Pentecostal Tradition. A major essay examines the New Religious movements who in many cases have "come out of" existing religious groups. As one essay indicates, the Believers' Churches are now a sustaining part of the experience and data of the Christian historical tradition. So far as we know, this is the first examination of the phenomenon among the Believers' Churches and it should become an authority in this generation.

William H. Brackney

Director, The Continuing Committee
for the Believers' Church Conferences
Spring, 2019

Acknowledgments

Many voices and hands went into the making of the Conference and the production of these papers. Within the Acadia community, the local administrator, the Rev. Ron Baxter kept us on track. The staff of Acadia Divinity College, particularly, Karen Cann, Trisha Urquhart, and Evelyn DeSchiffert, addressed many details energetically.

The overall theme and plan was approved by a voluntary affirmation of folk historically associated with the Conferences, including Marlin Jeshche, and John Roth.

Major financial backing came from Dr. Harry Gardner, president of Acadia Divinity College and the Baptist Foundation in Atlantic Canada.

A note of great appreciation is due the Rev. Evan Colford who arranged final copies of the papers to be delivered and provided extentesive and care editing of the final manuscript.

We are most grateful to Matthew Wimer, Daniel Lanning, Chelsea Lobey, and Zane Derven and the staff at Wipf and Stock Publishers for taking on this project.

Contributors

Eileen Barker is a sociologist of religion and an emeritus member of the London School of Economics. Widely regarded as the leading authority on New Religious Movements, Dr. Barker has published widely on various religious groups and is a Member of the Order of the British Empire (OBE) and President of the Society for the Scientific Study of Religion from 1991 to 1993 (the first non-American to hold that office), and President of the Association for the Sociology of Religion from 2001 to 2002.

William H. Brackney is The Millard R. Cherry Distinguished Professor Emeritus of Christian Thought and Ethics at Acadia Divinity College and Acadia University in Wolfville, Nova Scotia, Canada, where he also directed the Acadia Centre for Baptist and Anabaptist Studies. From 2018 he is the Pioneer MacDonald Professor of Baptist Studies and Ethics at Carey Theological College in Vancouver, British Columbia where he also heads the William Carey Centre for Excellence in Ministry.

Evan L. Colford is an MA student in Baptist Studies at Acadia University in Wolfville, Nova Scotia, Canada. He holds degrees from the St. Thomas University in Fredericton, New Brunswick, and Acadia University. He is working on a thesis in eighteenth century British-American Baptist thought and, with William H. Brackney, has previously co-edited *Maritime Baptist Old First Churches: Narratives and Prospects* (2017).

Douglas A. Foster is Professor of Church History in the Graduate School of Theology and Director of the Center for Restoration Studies at Abilene Christian University in Abilene, Texas. He served as General Editor for the *Encyclopedia of the Stone-Campbell Movement* (2004), as well as *The Stone-Campbell Movement: A Global History* (2013).

David Emmanuel Goatley is Research Professor of Theology and Black Church Studies and Director of the Black Church Studies Program at Duke Divinity School in Durham, North Carolina. He was previously General Secretary of the Lott Carey Baptist Foreign Mission Society, based in Washington, DC. He has served as chair of Mission, Evangelism, and Theological Reflection Division of the Baptist World Alliance and is widely regarded as an authoritative scholar of the African American Baptist tradition.

Colin Godwin is the Principal of Carey Hall and President of Carey Theological College, Institute and Centre in Vancouver, British Columbia, where he also teaches in historical studies. Previously he taught in theological schools in Europe and Africa. Dr. Godwin's doctoral dissertation on sixteenth-century Anabaptist mission, *Baptizing, Gathering, and Sending: Anabaptist Mission in the Sixteenth-Century Context*, was published by Pandora Press in 2012.

Teun van der Leer is General Secretary of the Baptist Union of the Netherlands and a doctoral student in the Vrie University of Amsterdam. He is currently working on an historical interpretation of the Believers Church conferences.

Allison S. MacGregor is professor of Bible and Theology at Master's College in Peterborough, Ontario and a doctoral student in Pentecostal Studies. She has also been adjunct professor in Pentecostal Studies at Queens Theological College in St. John's Newfoundland, Canada. She holds degrees from Master's College and Seminary and Acadia University.

Russell Prime is a practicing lawyer in Digby, Nova Scotia, with a keen interest in the Stone-Campbell and Baptist movements in Atlantic Canada. He has taught part-time at Saint Mary's University, Halifax, in Criminology.

John D. Roth is Director of the Mennonite Historical Library in Goshen, Indiana, where he also teaches in the Department of History. Dr. Roth is editor of the *Mennonite Quarterly Review* and has published widely in Anabaptist thought and life, notably *A Companion to Anabaptism and Spiritualism* (2011).

Martin Rothkegel is professor for Church History at the Teologische Seminar Baptistes (Hochschule) in Elstal, Germany. A linguist and historian, he is widely published in Reformation, Anabaptist, and Baptist studies. A Fellow of the Acadia Centre for Baptist and Anabaptist Studies, he also is editor of *Bibliotheca Dissidentium*.

Karen Smith is Honorary Senior Research Fellow of the School of History, Archaeology and Religion, at Cardiff University, and of the South Wales Baptist College in Cardiff, Wales. She is co-editor of the *Baptist Quarterly* (UK) and specializes in early English Baptist history and especially the role of women in Baptist life.

James M. Stayer is Professor Emeritus in History at Queens University in Kingston, Ontario. He previously taught at Bridgewater College, Ithaca College, and Bucknell University. A specialist in the German Reformation, he is the author of six books and numerous articles, including *Anabaptists and the Sword* (1972) and *The German Peasants War and the Anabaptist Community of Goods* (1991; 1994), both of which were ground-breaking interpretations.

Part I: **Principles and Types**

Chapter 1

Hoc enim est novam ecclesiam construere
The Making of New Churches in Western Christianity, 1400–1600

Martin Rothkegel

GERMANY IS PREPARING FOR the 500th Reformation anniversary. In the run up to 2017, the image of Martin Luther is omnipresent in public space, in the media, and even in nursery rooms as a toy figure—in spite of the fact that less than thirty percent of the population would identify themselves, in one sense or another, with the Protestant tradition. The German Reformation anniversary of 2017 will be a massive manifestation of public memorial culture, subsidized by the German state with several hundred million Euros. Why does a secular democracy so generously support the celebration of a religious symbolic figure?

The guiding idea behind the jubilee is that the Reformation is relevant not only to Lutherans, but to the society as a whole. It is perceived as one of the foundations of modern liberal, pluralistic, and democratic values. The programmatic document of the 2017 anniversary, published by the Council of the Evangelical Church in Germany under the title "Justification an Freedom," states:

> As an event of global significance, the Reformation brought changes not only to the church and to theology, but also to all aspects of private and public life, reshaping them in ways that can be felt to the present. It gave an impetus to education, it contributed to the development of the modern basic rights of freedom of religion and of conscience, it changed the relationship between church and state, it had a share in forming the

modern concept of freedom and the modern understanding of democracy, just to mention a few examples.[1]

This statement is obviously wrong and obviously true at the same time. Claiming Luther as the father of religious liberty or even democracy is absurd if you look at the persecutions of religious dissenters by Lutheran authorities in the sixteenth to nineteenth centuries or at the authoritarian political mentality that prevailed in German Lutheranism until the mid of the twentieth century. On the other side, it is obviously true that the Reformation, or more generally: the pluralization of Western Christianity, was one of the decisive factors that fueled the unique dynamics of Western civilization in the last five hundred years, eventually leading to the rise of civil societies that allow for the orderly and peaceful coexistence of diverse religious convictions.

If I was in Germany, I would probably face an audience that needs to be told that modern religious liberty was not exactly an achievement of the Lutheran Reformation but rather goes back to the radical visions of the non-conformist groups, the Anabaptists and Spiritualists of sixteenth-century continental Europe and even more directly to the British and North American Dissenters of the seventeenth century.[2] I think I can skip that section here in front of an audience that is sufficiently informed about the important role religious dissent played in "forming the modern concept of freedom and the modern understanding of democracy," to use the phrase quoted above.

This paper will rather focus on one very limited aspect related to this amazing, as painful as auspicious, story of religious pluralization: What gave religious nonconformists like the Bohemian Brethren, the Anabaptists or the Socinians the confidence and courage to leave the traditional churches into which they were born and to pursue their salvation in alternative communities? If all pre-modern Christians anxiously confessed that there is only "One Holy Universal and Apostolic Church," established and empowered by Christ himself as an instrument for the salvation of mankind, which arguments were produced to justify the formation of new groups that claimed to be church?

After a very short remark to Luther and the Lutheran Reformation—which is a complex topic of its own right—we will look at six examples that are all related to the rise of nonconformist movements and groups some of

---

1. Evangelical Church in Germany, *Justification and Freedom*, 7.

2. For a critique of the German Reformation Jubilee from believers' church perspectives see Roth, "How to Commemorate a Division?," 24–35; Strübind, "Erbe und Ärgernis," 71–88; Rothkegel, "Reformation, Nonkonformismus, Freiheit," 157–73.

which are can be regarded as early representatives of the believers' church type. We will see that these groups had a lot in common like: opposition to the papacy, minority situation, the experience of persecution, an emphasis on the authority of Scripture, and discipleship. But the arguments which these groups employed in order to legitimize their claims to be church were as diverse as their cultural contexts and their particular doctrines and religious practices.

The Absurdity of a Plurality of Churches

To most pre-Reformation Western Christians from Portugal in the West to Lithuania in the East, and from Malta in the South to Iceland in the North, the idea that there could be more than *one* Church would sound completely absurd. For sure, the various bishoprics and parishes could be referred to as *ecclesiae*, "churches" in plural, but they all formed the One Holy Church in communion with the see of Saint Peter in Rome, to whom Christ himself had entrusted his Church in Matthew 16 and John 21. Although the Oneness, Holiness, and Universality of the Church that was professed in the creeds was sometimes spoiled and beclouded by the shortcomings of the visible church and her clergy; and although the church provided wide space for a colorful variety of orders, brotherhoods, local and regional peculiarities: the uniform doctrine, the hierarchy, the Latin liturgy, and the uniform canonic law provided tangible evidence for the unity of the church. When Cardinal Cajetan was preparing for an interrogation of the querulent monk Martin Luther in 1519, he commented on one of Luther's controversial statements: "Hoc enim est novam ecclesiam construere [This means to make up a new church],"[3] which may sound ominous by hindsight, but in its original context, it actually did not mean much more than: "This is completely absurd."

Just one short remark to the popular perception of Luther as the Protestant church founder: In the dramatic course of events that followed the Augsburg interrogation, Luther never had the intention to found a new church. The local and territorial churches that embraced his doctrine in the course of the 1520s and after, employed the same buildings, to a large extent the same clergy and the same robes, and substantially the same liturgy as before, when they were still under the obedience of the pope whom they now regarded as "Antichrist." In their perception, *they* were the faithful children of the Church, and the pope was the alien intruder who had no right to dwell inside the church. Luther, so to speak, did not found a new church, but reclaimed the existing church for the rightful heirs. The Lutherans' claim to

3. de Vio, "Num fides ad fructuosam absolutionem."

be part of the church and to never have left it is the fundamental thesis of the Augsburg Confession penned by Philipp Melanchthon in 1530 which became the normative doctrinal statement of the Lutheran tradition.[4]

Unruly Claims of Being Church, 1400–1600

Secessionist Catholicity: The Hussite Utraquists in Bohemia

On 6 July, 1415, Jan Hus, a popular preacher from Bohemia and master at the University of Prague, was burnt on the stake after having been condemned as a heretic by the Council of Constance, which had primarily been convoked to reconcile the Papal Schism of Avignon. Instead of accomplishing the unity of the church and the effective suppression of heresy, the flames of Constance became the starting signal for the Hussite Revolution resulting in a new schism that would separate most Czech speaking Christians in Bohemia and Moravia from the Church of Rome for more than two centuries. Most of the Bohemian nobility, the University of Prague, most Czech speaking cities, and most of the Czech speaking clergy detested the judgement against Hus and refused to obey the Council and the pope. For their disobedience, the whole country of Bohemia was put under interdict. A crusade against the Bohemian heretics was announced, but the Bohemian rebels eventually remained undefeated in spite of five crusade campaigns between 1419 and 1434.[5]

While a minority fraction of the clergy remained faithful to the pope, observed the interdict, and suspended the celebration the mass, the rebel clergy would continue officiating. As a liturgical novelty, they introduced communion under both species to the lays instead of reserving the chalice to the priests, as it had been common in Western Christianity for centuries. Although John Hus had not directly been involved in the introduction of the lay chalice, the chalice became the symbol of the movement, along with the figure of Hus who soon was perceived of as a saint martyr.[6] And the chalice was more than a symbol: the vehement demand for communion under both species was motivated by the anxiety that those who do not

---

4. For a concise treatment of Luther's ecclesiology see Wendebourg, "Kirche," 403–14. An in-depth study of Luther's views of the continuity of the Church is Höhne, *Luthers Anschauungen*.

5. On Hus's life, work and significance see Fudge, *Jan Hus*. See also Šmahel and Pavlíček, *Companion to Jan Hus*.

6. On Hus as a martyr, see Haberkern, *Patron Saint and Prophet*.

eat Christ's flesh *and* drink His blood according to John 6 have no share in salvation, including infants to whom the eucharist was therefore administered immediately after infant baptism.[7]

Instead of the hereseological label "Hussite" used by their enemies, most of the Bohemian rebels would refer to themselves rather as "Catholic Christians that receive the Body and Blood of Our Lord Christ under both species," *sub utraque*, hence Utraquists. Not all Utraquists equally embraced the theology of John Hus, many tending to more moderate and traditional views, some to more radical doctrines than Hus himself. One can enumerate several factors that led to the Bohemian schism of the fifteenth century: Bohemia was one of the most densely urbanized regions of the Holy Roman Empire, with a growing tension between the Czech speaking majority and a relatively privileged German speaking minority. There was clearly an ethnic tension contributing to the schism. Religious life in Bohemia was intensified by a height of urban preaching culture that democratized religious knowledge and by the new custom of frequent communion that had become popular in Bohemia in the late fourteenth century, instead of the regular annual communion that most lay persons would observe in other regions of the Empire. Additionally, the writings of John Wycliffe became available in Bohemia as a result of dynastic connections between Bohemia and England. Around 1400, Hus was the most popular representative of the Bohemian Wycliffites.

Banned as heretics, the Utraquists sought for options to redefine their relation with the Roman church. Although not all of them shared the view that the pope is Antichrist, there was only a handful of prominent Utraquists who were ready for an abjuration and repentant return to obedience towards Rome. The most radical anti-Roman solution was represented by the Taborites who elected their own bishop who would ordain their priests, hence constituting themselves as an independent church.[8] The mainstream Utraquists, however, did not believe in the validity of the Taboritic priestly ordinations and adhered to the requirement of apostolic succession. Their urgent problem was that most of the time they had no clergy among their own ranks who possessed a valid episcopal consecration in order to perform priestly ordinations. Thus they were forced to send their candidates abroad to Roman or Eastern Orthodox bishops who would ordain them, often enough for bribes or under other strange conditions.

---

7. See Holeton, *La communion des tout-petits enfants*. Helena Krmíčková summarized her groundbreaking research on the introduction of the lay chalice in English in Krmíčková, "Utraquism in 1414," 99–106.

8. See Molnar and Cegna, *Confessio Taboritarum*; Zeman, "Restitution and Dissent," 7–27, esp. 17–20.

The odd love-hate relation of the Utraquists to the Roman mother church was more than a practical dilemma but was based on the Utraquists' conviction that they were part of the One Catholic Church. What they tried to achieve in their negotiations with the Council of Bâle in the 1430s was to be recognized as an affiliated Church, limited to the territories of Bohemia and Moravia, with a certain autonomy and with certain liturgical peculiarities like the lay chalice, on a similar basis like the Eastern Churches of the Byzantine ritual that had united with Rome. Although such a settlement was never officially confirmed to the Bohemians by the Roman curia, the self-perception as a national catholic church would be maintained by part of the Utraquist tradition even after the Reformation (when most Utraquists became Lutherans) until the Catholic Counter-Reformation made an end to the existence of the Utraquist church in 1629.

The most thorough English language account of fifteenth and sixteenth-century Utraquism by Zdenek David[9] strongly stresses an analogy with Anglicanism which sometimes tends to bias his interpretations. There is also an analogy with the early stage of the territorial Reformations in Lutheran Germany that claimed to be something like "liberated zones" within the existing church put under interim administration of the secular authorities, rather than establishing a new church. Significantly, the introduction of the Reformation to some German territories was staged as a public celebration of communion under both species by the ruler, with the Hussite tradition palpably serving as a point of reference.

Anti-Papal Successionism: The Waldensian Myth in the Fifteenth Century

Encouraged by encounters with the Bohemian Taborites, some mid-fifteenth-century German Waldensians claimed to represent the original Apostolic Church. Modern research has traced back the origins of the Waldensian movement to the figure of Valdesius, a layman from Lyon in South France, who initiated a group of lay preachers around 1170. Valdesius, in later sources sometimes called Peter by first name, possessed a collection of biblical texts in vernacular translation and felt a calling to preach, along with other men and women, the gospel in the fashion of the itinerant apostles of the New Testament. This was obviously not connected with claims to establish a separate church. When Valdesius and his companions failed to obtain a preaching license from the ecclesial authorities but would

---

9. See David, *Finding the Middle Way*.

not stop their preaching activities, they were eventually condemned as heretic in 1184.[10]

As a reaction to persecution, the Waldensian preachers went underground and build up networks of trustworthy people whom they periodically visited, preached to, and heard confessions. In most cases, the adherents would continue to take part in the sacraments and worship of the Roman church, and their affiliation with the itinerant preachers rather had the character of a complementary religious practice: they usually did not challenge the power of the local priest to perform baptism, eucharist and other sacraments, but they felt more sure about their salvation if they received additional pastoral care from the itinerant ministers.[11] Thirteenth and fourteenth-century inquisitors detected networks of this type in many regions of Europe, not only in the Southeast of France where the historical Valdesius had had the center of his activity, but also in Southern and Northern Italy, in the Alps, in Austria and Bohemia, and in other German speaking regions. All these networks were classified by the Inquisition as Waldensian, but in many cases it is hard to identify the historical connections to the original group in Lyon.[12] Especially in the regions north of the Alps, most Waldensians had never heard about Valdesius but were convinced that their group had existed since the time of the apostles.

A series of spectacular arrests and trials led to the detection and extinction of an extensive Waldensian network in Germany in the middle of the fifteenth century. At the center of this network was Friedrich Reiser, a merchant serving secretly as an itinerant minister to the scattered conventicles of the "Faithful Brethren," as they would call themselves. Around 1430, Reiser came in touch with the radical Taborite wing of the Hussite movement in Bohemia and was allegedly consecrated as a bishop. He himself would subsequently ordain other bishops, priests and deacons for the "Faithful Brethren" in Germany. He obviously had the idea to transform the loose networks of the "Faithful Bethren" into a proper underground church. Reiser and his disciples claimed to represent the true Apostolic Church in a direct line of succession from the Apostles to their own present.[13]

Drawing on a widespread medieval legend, they claimed that the Church of Rome had preserved the legitimate succession only to the time of emperor Constantine the Great. When Constantine fell sick and was miraculously

10. For the origins and development of the medieval Waldensians, see Audisio, *Waldensian Dissent*; Cameron, *Waldenses*.

11. See Audisio, *Preachers by Night*.

12. See Cameron, *Rejections*, 96–144; Segl, *Ketzer in Österreich*.

13. See Cameron, *Rejections*, 144–50; Lange and Tremp, *Friedrich Reiser und die*; Lange, "La fin tragique," 3–19.

healed upon the intercession of Sylvester, bishop of Rome, he bequeathed the western part of the Roman Empire to Sylvester and his successors. So far this is the motive so called Donation of Constantine. In the Waldensian version, the story continues that when Constantine gave the writ to Sylvester, a voice was heard from heaven: "Today poison was poured out into the Holy Church."[14] Since that time, the church of the popes had become the church of Antichrist, whereas true line of apostolic possession was preserved only underground, passed on by wondrous means to Friedrich Reiser who called himself "Friedrich by God's grace bishop of the faithful in the Roman Church who detest the Donation of Constantine."[15] However, the fifteenth-century German Waldensians' project of becoming church proper was only an ephemeral enterprise. Reiser was burnt in 1458 in Strasbourg, several of his disciples were executed in the following years. The last German Waldensians would join the Bohemian Brethren in the 1480s.[16]

The fiction of a legitimate apostolic succession of priesthood was preserved by the Bohemian Brethren (Unity of Brethren) who claimed to continue the Waldensian line. This myth would later even become relevant for North American church history. In 1749 the British Parliament recognized Count Nikolaus Ludwig von Zinzendorf's Moravian Brethren as a legitimate episcopal church in apostolic succession because Zinzendorf had been ordained as a bishop by the descendants of the Bohemian Brethren. By recognizing the validity of Zinzendorf's consecration, the Moravians, or the "Renewed Unity of Brethren," were licensed to do mission work in the British colonies—a decision of tremendous consequences for the subsequent history of global Protestantism.[17]

Detached from the concept of a sacramental succession of priestly power, a modified concept of succession became a standard argument of post-Reformation pre-critical denominational historiography and apologetics. All Evangelical groups that claimed to be based on the authority of Scripture alone (*sola scriptura*), and therefore rejected the authority of the ecclesiastic tradition, faced a serious theological dilemma: if the true faith is based on Scripture alone, and Scripture is self-evident, and Scripture has been there long before the Reformation, why were there no Evangelicals prior to the Reformation? Starting with the Lutheran theologian Matthias Flacius Illyricus, it became a pivotal concern of Protestant historiography to

---

14. On the Cathar origins and the Waldensian reception of the Sylvester legend, see Schäufele, »*Defecit Ecclesia*« 91–196, 197–247.

15. Köpstein, "Über den deutschen Hussiten," 1068–82, esp. 1082.

16. See Kurze, "Märkische Waldenser und Böhmische Brüder," 456–502.

17. See Podmore, "Bishops and the Brethren," 622–46.

demonstrate that there had always been witnesses of truth in all centuries from the Apostles to the present. In the narrative constructs the Protestants produces, the Waldensians were claimed as a proof that throughout the dark Middle Ages there had been true Christians whose faith was substantially identical with the Evangelical faith.[18]

The famous *Martyr's Mirror* published by Thielemann Jansz van Bracht in 1660/85 is a Mennonite adaptation of this construct. In order to emphasize the continuity, van Braght even claimed that the early Anabaptist martyr Michael Sattler (d. 1527) came from the group of Waldensians that had joined the Bohemian Brethren in 1481.[19] The British Baptists adopted similar successionist constructs in the eighteenth century, and some Baptist groups like the Seventh Day Baptists and the Landmark Baptists continued to cultivate such narratives well beyond the nineteenth century.[20]

Ecumenical Sectarians: The Bohemian Brethren (Unity of Brethren)

In the March 1467 believers from many places in Bohemia and Moravia gathered in a tiny village called Lhotka near Rychnov nad Kněžnou in Northeast Bohemia and constituted themselves as a church. The solemn event, which is described with varying details in a number of letters and treatises, part of which was composed by participants of the gathering, had been preceded by a long period of seeking.[21] Around 1453, a group of students at the Utraquist university in Prague started to meet for bible studies and prayer. Worried by the scandalous life style of many parish priests, they agreed to receive the sacraments only from trustworthy priests. In 1457, the group decided to withdraw from the capital and to move to the small village of Kunvald in Northeast Bohemia.

They were joined by likeminded men and women of various professions and backgrounds in other places. Their allegiance to certain sympathetic priests repeatedly resulted in the expulsion of these priests from their parishes. Less and less priests were ready to risk that. As the number of

---

18. See Cameron, *Reformation of the Heretics*, 247–57. On sixteenth-century Protestant historiographical constructs, see Schmidt-Biggemann, "Flacius Illyricus," 263–91; Pohlig, *Zwischen Gelehrsamkeit und konfessioneller Identitätsstiftung*.

19. van Bracht, *Het Bloedigh Tooneel*, 392, 454, s.v. "Waldensen."

20. See McGoldrick, *Baptist Successionism*.

21. The best work on the history of the Bohemian Brethren is still Müller, *Geschichte der Böhmischen Brüder*. See also Brock, *Political and Social Doctrines*; Říčan, *History of the Unity of the Brethren*; Atwood, *Theology of the Czech Brethren*.

local conventicles of brothers and sisters grew, they felt the need to have their own priests. One of the options they discussed was to send candidates for priesthood to churches that might have preserved an undefiled line of apostolic succession outside the Roman Church and have them ordained there, but they found out that the priesthood of the Greeks, Russians, Serbs, Armenians and even the Christians in India is no more trustworthy than that of the Roman succession. Not even joining the Waldensians seemed a trustworthy option to the Brethren. After many conferences and a period of prayer and fasting in which they arrived at certainty that God authorized them to take action, they scheduled the meeting of 1467. After examining the men that had been recommended as faithful by the local conventicles, they made a selection of nine candidates. Then they drew lots and thereby identified the three persons divinely appointed for priesthood.

The procedure that followed was the result of collective theological decision making in which the Brethren agreed on compromises between the sometimes contradictory positions present among themselves. They acknowledged that every believer, man or woman, who lives in unity with Christ is a priest in the spiritual sense because he or she participated in the priesthood of Christ. But for the sake of orderly ministry in the church, there should be a particular priestly office. Further, they believed that the three candidates identified by the lot had already been consecrated to the particular priesthood by God in the spiritual sense. But for the sake of orderly ministry in the church, there should be also an outwardly visible ordination. The Brethren believed that every gathering of true believers, and be it only two or three, has the power to perform this ordination. But for the sake of orderly ministry, they agreed upon a laying on of hands by a carrier of priestly succession.

This was performed by a priest called Michael who had joined the Brethren who once had been ordained in the Roman succession but additionally had been ordained by a Waldensian elder. As a carrier of these two lines of succession, Michael ordained one of the three candidates as a bishop and immediately after that renounced his Roman ordination. Then the newly created bishop ordained the two other candidates plus Michael to priesthood, and then they baptized the whole congregation. After this complicated procedure, the Brethren were confident that now they had an orderly clergy with the biblical offices of bishops, priests and deacons; that they were orderly constituted as a visible church; and that they now had the power to administrate sacraments and ordinances in a way that would be beneficial for salvation.[22]

22. For more on the first priestly ordinations of 1467, see Müller, *Geschichte der*

In spite of referring to traditional concepts like sacramental priesthood, three ranks of clergy, and episcopal succession, the Brethren relativized the significance of these ordinances in a remarkable extent. Although they paid respect to the anxiety of those in their midst who insisted on an orderly ordination of clergy, they challenged the idea that being church depends on succession but stated that ecclesiality results from *spiritual* participation in the One and Holy and Universal Church to which all elect in all nations and churches belong. In their own perception, the founding act of the Unity of Brethren (*Jednota bratrská*, Unity of Brethren) in 1467 was not the making up of a new church. Quite the contrary, they defended it as a manifestation of agreement with the One and Holy and Universal Church in an emergency situation in which the Romans and the Utraquists had obviously fallen short of being in agreement with that One and Holy and Universal Church.

In spite of periodic persecutions, the Unity of Brethren held her ground in Bohemia and Moravia. Gradually converging with the Lutheran and Reformed Reformation during the sixteenth century, the Unity remained a flourishing free church alternative to Roman Catholicism and magisterial Utraquism until the 1620s when all non-Catholic denominations in Bohemia and Moravia were violently extinguished by the Counter-Reformation. While their membership was just a small minority of the total population, the Brethren left a significant heritage to Czech national culture including the Bible of Kralice (1579/94) that remained the standard translation of Czech and Slovak speaking Protestantism to the twentieth century.[23]

The moment in which the early Brethren started to consider their community a church proper was the ordination of an own priesthood in 1467. The analytic sketch given above revealed that the strange sequence of solemn gestures performed at that occasion was the result of a compromise between two contradictory lines of thought: on the one hand the Brethren paid tribute (albeit in a peculiar way) to the traditional idea that there is no church without priesthood ordained in apostolic succession, on the other hand there was an awareness that a gathering of believers is entitled to ordain their own ministers by virtue of the priesthood of all believers.

The Bohemian Brethren's ambivalence between pre-Reformation and Evangelical ideas, and their concept of ecclesiality, according to which diverse empiric ecclesial bodies can be, and ought to be, manifestations of the One Church Universal, had an irenic or ecumenical potential and would later

---

Böhmischen Brüder, 1:113–48; Atwood, *Theology of the Czech Brethren*, 169–72. Sources on the ordination of the first Brethren priests in 1467 are accessible in original (Czech and Latin) texts and in German translation in Goll, *Quellen und Untersuchungen*.

23. See Just, "Kralitzer Bibel," 360–71.

enable them to recognize other Protestant churches as legitimate churches of Christ. Accordingly, the Unity of Brethren played an active role in inner-Protestant irenic settlements like the Sandomierz Agreement (1570), the Confessio Bohemica (1575), and the Colloquy of Thorn (1645).[24] Even after the expulsion from their home country when just a remnant of the Unity of Brethren continued in exile, Brethren bishops Jan Amos Komenský (1592–1670) and Daniel Ernst Jablonsky (1660–1741) had an impact far beyond the boundaries of their own community and emerged as champions of early ecumenism. It was the latter who imparted the episcopal succession of the Brethren to Zinzendorf.[25]

A Neo-Apostolic Sending: The Early Hutterites

What made sixteenth-century Anabaptists sure that the group they worshipped with was truly a church, or even the True Church, in contrast to all the false churches who made this claim in vain? Modern students of Anabaptism have stressed two aspects which, indeed, are often expressed in Anabaptist sources.[26]

The first is discipleship: most sixteenth-century Anabaptists would claim that discipleship makes the difference between a true Christian and a hypocrite. According to them, it is not enough to assert the truth of the Christian doctrine or of the Holy Scriptures. This would be only a historical faith that recognizes only the letter of the outward word, but it makes no Christian. The true Christian must be transformed by an inner spiritual experience that enables her or him to live a life of yieldedness to the will of God as expressed in the New Testament. While the world asserts that it is impossible to observe the words of Jesus about non-resistance, and about giving up one's will, possessions, home, and even one's own life, the true believer is enabled by the power of God to do this.

The second point is martyrdom: according to the Bible, the true believers will and must be persecuted by the world, especially in the period of tribulation that precedes the end of the world. The Anabaptists were not the only sixteenth-century Christians that tried to prove the truth of their cause by the martyrological argument: Ludwig Rabus, Jean Crespin, and

---

24. See Atwood, "Separatism, Ecumenism, and Pacifism," 71–90; Just and Rothkegel, "Confessio Bohemica. 1575/1609," 47–176.

25. See Wouter Goris et al., *Gewalt sei ferne den Dingen!*; Bahlcke and Korthaase, *Daniel Ernst Jablonski*.

26. On the state of research on sixteenth-century Anabaptism, see Roth and Stayer, *Companion to Anabaptism*.

John Foxe described Lutheran and Reformed identity as a story of suffering and martyrdom. Catholics perceived their co-religionists that fell victim to the ecclesiastic politics of Henry VIII or the Jesuit missionaries martyred in Japan as new saints added to the cloud of witnesses of early Christianity. What made Anabaptist martyrology more plausible than that of their Catholic Lutheran, Reformed contemporaries was the fact that the latter were, at the same time, persecutors themselves whose victims probably outnumbered their own losses.[27]

However, discipleship ethics and martyrdom do not add up to an answer why certain Anabaptist groups did not only claim that they were congregations of true Christians, but even dared to raise the claim that they are *the* true Church. This was obviously the case with the early Hutterites who often called themselves the "Church of God in Moravia." According to their chronicles, they believed that God, after a long time during which there was no true church on earth but only some zealous ones who had a partial knowledge of the truth, God started to gather a people for himself starting with the first Anabaptists in Zürich, continuing with the formation of a congregation in Moravia, and coming to full accomplishment with under the leadership of Jakob Hutter in 1533.[28]

Hutter's congregation, they believed, was the divinely authorized True Church restored at the end of times in the land of Moravia which was the Promised Land to which the elect must flee from all the sinful "Egyptlands" around. In some Hutterite texts, the end time Church of God in Moravia is identified with the woman clothed with the sun of Revelation 12 which withdrew to the wilderness where she had a place prepared by God to delivers her offspring, which is, the faithful believers. To fulfill this divine plan, the Hutterites made great efforts to send out their messengers to potential converts scattered in the surrounding countries.[29]

Werner O. Packull's monograph "Hutterite Beginnings" of 1995 directed our attention to the intensive debates on the issue of apostolicity among Anabaptists and Spiritualists around 1530. Caspar Schwenckfeld, Christian Entfelder rejected the claims raised by some Anabaptist congregations to be reestablished New Testament churches: it is more safe for salvation, argued the Spiritualists, to abstain altogether from the ordinances of the visible church unless God himself sends new apostles authorized to reestablish the true church. This context throws light on Jakob Hutter's

---

27. See Gregory, *Salvation at Stake*; "Anabaptist Martyrdom," 467–506.

28. See Hutterian Brethren, *Chronicle of the Hutterian Brethren*.

29. On Hutterite missions and community life, see Schlachta, *Hutterische Konfession und Tradition*; von Schlachta, *From the Tyrol*.

explicit self-designation as an apostle in his letters. Although the Hutterites never made it an article of faith that Jakob Hutter was a new apostle, their virtually exclusivistic ecclesiology was based on the assumption that Hutter was an apostle.[30]

Hutter's apostolic authority was manifested in a charismatic gift of speaking in biblical language which one may call "bibliolalia." Hutter's letters which consist of long torrents of memorized and reproduced biblical phrases document his claim for apostolicity in written form. After Hutter's death on the stake in 1536, there was no individual successor to the office of apostle. Instead, the Hutterite ministers, or "servants of the Word," were considered *collectively* as carriers of the "living word." Whatever that may have sounded like in practice, their preaching was perceived as divinely empowered in opposition to the preachers of other denominations who were only able to preach the dead letter. A careful reading of Peter Riedemann's "Account of Faith," the authoritative document of Hutterite doctrine published in 1545, and of the early Hutterite Bible commentaries confirms that being equipped with the "living word" gift (probably more than ethics and martyrdom) was perceived as the decisive difference between the ministry of the Hutterites and that of all rivalling groups.[31]

At the beginning of the Hutterian "Church of God in Moravia" was, in their perception, a divine intervention in history, a new dispensation of apostolic authority at the end of times. If this interpretation is correct, the early Hutterites' claim for ecclesiality was based on an argument quite different from those of the Utraquists, of "bishop" Friedrich Reiser and his fifteenth-century German Waldenses, and of the Bohemian Brethren, who were all convinced that being church required a legitimate priesthood linked with the apostles by succession. The Hutterite assertion of an apocalyptic divine intervention seems to be even more alien to the theologies of the sixteenth-century magisterial reformers. However, while the magisterial Reformers clearly rejected pretensions on direct inspiration or on directly imparted apostolicity, one must not underestimate the significance for sixteenth/seventeenth-century Lutheranism of the idea that Luther was prophet Elijah sent back to the world at the end of times to prepare the coming of the Lord.[32] Explicitly "neo-apostolic" arguments reoccur as legitimizing patterns, in various modifications, among the seventeenth-century Quakers, in the nineteenth-century Catholic Apostolic Movement in Britain (associated with Edward Irving), and in early twentieth-century

---

30. See Packull, *Hutterite Beginnings*.
31. See Rothkegel, "Living Word," 357–403.
32. See Dingel, "Luther's Authority in the Late Reformation," 525–39.

Pentecostalism—which, at present, has become the largest non-Catholic movement within Christianity.

Progressive Reformation: The Polish Brethren

Another way of positioning oneself in a divine plan of history and legitimizing one's separation from other ecclesial bodies can be observed among groups coming out of the post-Reformation Protestant tradition, starting in the second half of the sixteenth century. I have chosen as an example the Antitrinitarian Polish Brethren, a group which has no direct successors in the believers' churches spectrum of our time, while the modern Unitarians who sometimes claim the Polish Brethren heritage are not directly linked with sixteenth-century Antitrinitarianism and cherish religious convictions fundamentally different from the historical Polish Brethren.

The Polish Brethren resulted from controversies within the Reformed branch of Polish Protestantism. On a Reformed synod of 1556, the learned theologian Piotr z Goniądza (Petrus Gonesius) demanded a stricter application of the scriptural principle to practice and doctrine: instead of the non-biblical practice of infant baptism, believers' baptism should be introduced. Instead of the post-biblical doctrine of Trinity, a simplified Christology in a more scriptural terminology should be defined. Non-resistance ethics according to the Sermon of the Mount should be made obligatory for all baptized church members. This radical position found the support of a considerable minority among the Polish Reformed ministers and nobles. By the mid-1560s they formed a synod of congregations independent from the main branch of the Reformed communion.[33] In the end of the sixteenth century, the Italian exile Fausto Sozzini became their leading theologian, hence the appellation Socinians.[34]

In 1568, the Polish Brethren published jointly with the Antitrinitarians of Transylvania a programmatic book called "On the false and the true perception of the only God the Father, of the Son and of the Holy Spirit" ("*De falsa et vera unius Dei Patris, Filii et Spiritus Sancti cognition libri duo*"). The extensive work contains a historical sketch of recent church history according to which Luther was sent by God in order to start the work

---

33. For a detailed (though partially outdated) treatment see Williams, *Radical Reformation*, 1023–61, 1079–98, 1135–75. For a concise overview, see Balázs, "Antitrinitarianism," 171–94. Selected sources in translation: Williams, *Polish Brethren*; Brock, "Marcin Czechowic in Defense," 251–57; "Gregorius Paulus Against the Sword," 427–36; "Marcin Czechowic on the Via Crucis," 451–68; "Faustus Socinus Against War," 419–30; "Polish Antitrinitarian Against Nonresistance," 441–48.

34. See Szczucki, *Faustus Socinus and his Heritage*; Priarolo, *Fausto Sozzini*.

of unearthing the long beclouded biblical truth, followed by Melanchthon, then gradually progressing to Zwingli, Bucer, Calvin, and further to Miguel Servet and to the explicit rejection of the unbiblical doctrine of Trinity. With the formation of the church of the Polish Brethren, the light of biblical truth had regained its full brightness. The future development of mankind would see the victorius dissemination of their doctrine, culminating with the final abolition of false religion at the Second Coming of Christ.[35]

For a generation of theologians who had been born as Catholics, at some point of time identified with Lutheranism, turned Reformed and finally became Antitrinitarians, the "progressive Reformation" argument was especially suggestive. The "progressive Reformation" motif was later—in the seventeenth century—summarized in the famous distich:

> *Alta ruit Babylon: destruxit tecta Lutherus,*
> *muros Calvinus, sed fundamenta Socinus.*
>
> Proud Babylon has fallen: Luther demolished the roof,
> Calvin the walls, but Sozzini the foundations.[36]

Leaving aside other aspect of Socinianism including its seminal significance for the rise of the Enlightenment,[37] the Polish Brethren serve here just as a case example for the legitimiation rhetorics of a nascent denomination. As an argument for forming a new church, the progressive Reformation argument presupposes a Protestant context in which the Reformation is already perceived of as a past event and historical reality, in most cases with history understood as salvation history and with the Reformation localized in an end time stage of that salvation history. The Reformation was willed by God, and so is the additional refinement of doctrine or practice achieved since then. God wants the believers to proceed in the recognition of truth: hence separation from those who obstinately lag behind is mandatory.

Analogous progressive Reformation arguments were used in various post-Reformation contexts as a blank check for the legitimization of inner-Protestant splits and separations. One close analogy is the "further light" hermeneutic common among the earliest Baptists who understood the history of the century that had passed since the beginnings of the Reformation as a progressive recovery of pure biblical doctrine from Luther to Calvin, further to the Puritans, to the Separatists—culminating, for the time being,

---

35. Pirnát, *De falsa et vera unius*, 27f, 122–29, 207.

36. The distich is quoted in Fock, *Der Socinianismus*, 180. On Polish Brethren views on Luther, see Tazbir, "Die Stellung der polnischen Antitrinitarier," 438–50.

37. Recent contributions include Mulsow and Rohls, *Socinianism and Arminianism*; Salatowsky, *Die Philosophie der Sozinianer*; Daugirdas, *Die Anfänge des Sozinianismus*.

in their own insights.[38] In nineteenth-century liberal theology, progressive Reformation rhetorics were sometimes blended with the Enlightenment concept of progress as the teleological principle of history, whereas in Revivalist and believers' church contexts references the idea that the Reformation must be continued, finalized, or superseded, fueled the emergence of ever new denominations.

A Logic of Splitting: The Mennonite Divisions

Although Early Modern Catholic polemicists indulged in enumerating the manifold sects and splits of the heretics as a proof of their inconsistency and blindness, there were not so many group splits that one can compare with the Abolitionist come-outers of the nineteenth century or the splits between moderates and fundamentalists that became increasingly common by the twentieth century. The closest analogy with modern tendencies of denominational fragmentation may be the Mennonite divisions that started in the last years of Menno Simons's leadership before his death in 1561. In the 1540s, a significant part of the Anabaptist movement in the Netherlands began to form communions of local churches under the leadership of an order of elders. Conferences of elders made decisions binding for the whole communion, but also some individual elders like Menno Simons or Dirk Philips claimed authority to make decisions that would affect more than one local congregation.[39]

The elders were assigned the power to exercise the ban on church members who had committed transgressions in conduct or doctrine. Since the Christian ban is, according to the Rule of Christ in Matthew 18:18, binding in heaven as well as on earth, church discipline was perceived of as directly affecting eternal salvation. In case a local congregation refused to obey a ban issued by an elder, or in case another local congregation accepted a member previously banned elsewhere, this could result in the ban of a whole congregation, or even a whole fraction of the supra-local communion. By the 1560s, a complex process of splitting had started with fractions and sub-fractions, coalitions, mergers and new splits: There were parties called Frisians, Flemish, Waterlanders, High Germans, Old Frisians, Young

---

38. For the significance of the "further light clause" for the early Baptist movements, see White, *English Separatist Tradition*, 123; Coggins, *John Smyth's Congregation*, 117–20.

39. On the formation of denomaniational networks among the Dutch Anabaptistst, see Visser, "Mennonites and Doopsgezinden," 299–346.

Frisians, Old Flemish and several others.[40] The issues at stake in the splits were combinations of disciplinary matters, regional and ethnic differences, allegiances to elders, and theological disputes. Contemporary observers provided the hilarious detail that those congregations who accepted members that were banned by all others were called *Drekwagen*, or "dust-cart" churches.[41]

Contemporary anti-Mennonite polemics curiously registered the splits, sometimes mischievously triumphing that the Anabaptist Babel is dispersing and disrupting herself,[42] sometimes lamenting that like in the Greek myth of the fight with the many-headed Hydra, new heads would regrow for every head chopped off. The irritating grimness with which the conflicts were fought out resulted from the claims to be the True Church maintained by each group, sometimes mitigated by a spiritualist perception that the True Church proper is only the invisible Church Universal which may comprise scattered elect also in other or even in all denominations.

What makes the Mennonite splits different from the cases we have examined in the preceding paragraphs was that the Mennonite subgroups were not primarily worried any more with assuring themselves that they are, at all, a church empowered with divine authority—while the latter question had been the pressing issue behind the church founding scenario of the Bohemian Brethren or Jacob Hutter's claim for apostolicity. The Mennonite subgroups, instead, were raised rivalling claims for, and advocated rivalling interpretation of, a given pattern of being church, shared, and referred to, by the quarreling parties. This can in some sense be compared with the Dutch Reformed and Baptist schisms of the nineteenth and twentieth centuries with minority groups separating from the main body of the denomination by claiming to represent the regular and legitimate version of denominational identity.

In such a constellation, a doctrinal "downgrading"—a theological levelling of the controversial issues based on liberal or Revivalist hermeneutics—sometimes provided viable ways back to unity. Such was the case among British Baptists when most of their congregations overcame the century-long splits by joining the Baptist Union of Great Britain in the late nineteenth century. Even more effective was the reunification process

---

40. See Zijlstra, *Om de ware gemeente*, 270–315.

41. See Zijpp, "Drekwagen, de," 99.

42. E.g., Herman Faukelius, *Babel, dat is Verwarringe der Weder-doopeperen [!] . . . Met een cort verhael van den oorspronck, verbreydinghe, menigherley verdeelinghen ende scheuringhe der selven* ["Babel, that is, the Confusions of the Anabaptists . . . with a brief account of the origin, dissemination, subgroups, and schism among them"]. See Visser, "Mennonites and Doopsgezinden," 319f.

among the Mennonites in the Netherlands where all congregations of the Anabaptist tradition that still exist today are united in the *Algemene Doopsgezinde Sociëteit*, a denomination lacking any explicit statement of faith.[43]

The Contribution of the Church to Salvation

The preceding paragraphs offered a typology of rationales by which newly established communities of believers legitimized their claims on being church. In some cases, parallels between the historical examples and later cases of group formations, or denominational separations and splits, were suggested. It seems that today there is a growing tendency to a fragmentation of evangelical Christianity into non-denominational, non-cooperative individual congregations. Those who leave the traditional denominations and join post-modern, denominationally indifferent meetings sometimes refer to music styles or fellowship experiences as factors that motivated their decisions rather than anxiety for the salvation of their souls.

It seems that these post-modern dynamics of an ever-ongoing fragmentation of evangelical Christianity result from the assumption that the church is an optional addition to the believer's welfare rather than being instrumental for the individual's having part in Christ. This may go back to a type of Revivalist piety that perceived of salvation as something that can be accomplished in a completely individual and private way. The Church, in this perception, does not contribute anything to man's relation to God, but she is seen at best as a kind of training camp in which the individual practices her or his moral conduct, or, in the poorest case, as an opportunity to fellowship with like-minded persons.

There is a fundamental difference between this post-modern tendency towards a dissolution of denominational identities (or even any awareness of why supra-congregational unity of the believers is relevant) and the painful church formation processes that eventually pluralized Western Christianity in the Early Modern period.[44] The latter were, in each case, the results of anxious searches for a church that would administer the means of grace, the Gospel and the Ordinances instituted by Christ, in a way effective for salvation. The study of historical non-conformist ecclesiologies will probably not

---

43. For the transformations of the Mennonite tradition in the Netherlands from the sixteenth century to the present, see Hamilton et al., *From Martyr to Muppy*.

44. Volf, *After Our Likeness*, otherwise highly relevant for our topic, is probably imprecise by suggesting a parallel between the radical congregationalism of John Smyth's congregation founded in Amsterdam in 1609 and post-modern non-denominational congregations.

lead us to neat answers on modern questions. But maybe it helps to arrive at insights that are not so far from Article VII of the Augsburg Confession, a statement on the nature and foundation of the Church that deserves to be rediscovered by the believers' churches for its truly evangelical radicality and inclusiveness:

> Also they teach that One Holy Church is to continue forever. The Church is the congregation of saints, in which the Gospel is rightly taught and the sacraments are rightly administered. And to the true unity of the Church it is enough to agree concerning the doctrine of the Gospel and the administration of the sacraments. Nor is it necessary that human traditions, that is, rites or ceremonies, instituted by men, should be everywhere alike. As Paul says: One faith, one Baptism, one God and Father of all, etc. (Eph 4:5–6).

CHAPTER 2

The Genetic Separationist Trait Among the Baptists

WILLIAM H. BRACKNEY

SIXTY-FOUR YEARS AGO, FRANKLIN H. Littell[1] created a watershed in Anabaptist and Free Church historical and theological interpretation with the publication of his book, *The Anabaptist Vision of the Church* (republished as *The Origins of Sectarian Protestantism*, 1952; 1958; 1964). Following the traces of Kenneth S. Latourette, Roland Bainton, Harold Bender, Cornelius Krahn, and even further back, Ernst Troeltsch, Littell re-patterned the character of what he called "sectarian Protestantism." Among the traits he found among the sixteenth-century groups was that the church was understood to be a community of saints, exercising a strong band of ethical discipline and theological integrity, and significantly, separation from a great, apostate national church.[2] But, as Littell also noted, there is also a forward-looking side to separation, namely the desire to be part of a faithful church that restores the vision of a New Testament community. Many "believers churches" have emphasized this aspect and accordingly have followed a call of the Spirit.

Baptists are a leading category of the Free Church movement, and in the present era, the Believers' Churches. Throughout their four-century history, they have been characterized by separationism. Whether they inherited the separation trait from intermittent interactions with their Anabaptist

---

1. Littell was a Methodist whom Durnbaugh characterized as "an itinerant vigorously crossing the country with a gospel of the contemporary relevance of Anabaptist beliefs." See Durnbaugh, *Believers' Church*, 19.

2. Littell, *Anabaptist Vision of the Church*, 89–90. On separation, see also Durnbaugh, *Believers' Church*, 286–89.

forbears or came to it on their own,³ Baptists took "dissent" (an English equivalent for separation), Baptists stood against the great reputedly apostate Church of England and refused its sacraments and overlordship.

In some ways, Baptists have exhibited as much or more separation than other groups.⁴ So, there is a strange pride of place in this Believers' Church Conference that Baptists should present first. At last reckoning, there were seventy-one Baptist groups in the United States and twenty-two in Canada. Some are as small as a few congregations, while others embrace thousands of congregations. Beyond North America, the number of Baptist groups enlarges considerably with significant varieties of Baptist types in Russia, Ukraine, Britain, and India. How do we explain this great variety of Baptist groups in the tradition?

The thesis of this paper is that the separationist tendency is inherent in Baptist ecclesiology, that is the Baptist doctrine of the church. Proto-baptists (Separatists, Brownists, Barrowists) separated themselves from the Church of England, and later the National Church of Cromwell (Calvinists, Sabbatarians, General Atonement types). They also separated themselves from each other and self-defined their principles in contrast with other dissenters like Congregationalists (Independents), Quakers, Seekers, Diggers, Levellers, and Socinians. In his definitive book, *The Differences of the Churches of the Seperation* (1608), John Smyth wrote of the distinctions between a "true church" and a "false church," as "Christ in due tyme will bring his people out of Egypt though for a season they are kept in Antichristian captivity and greevous spiritual slavery."⁵ Similar is the wording of an article in the First London Confession (1644) about the church, "which Church as it is visible to us, is a company of visible Saints, called & separated from the world, by the word and Spirit of God, to the visible profession of the faith of the Gospel."⁶ Separation was inherent in the earliest Baptist ecclesiology: it was a calling, a sense of obedience to the call of Christ.

In order to make sense of the Baptist tendency toward separationism, I will introduce a typology that grows out of my reading of the history of Baptists: separation according to (1) theological; (2) ethnic/racial; (3) the need to bring about reform; (4) issues of polity; and (5) *prima donna* factors. As this conference suggests, any religious group is more (and less!) than its

---

3. There are those who espouse an Anabaptist kinship theory and those who connect Baptists with Brownists and Separatists in the Puritan movement. See Estep, *Anabaptist Story*, 215–30. Cf. White, *English Separatist Tradition*, xi–xiv.

4. As a denominational tradition, Methodists have a long history of schismatic behavior. See Barclay, *Early American Methodism*, esp. 62–71, 96–101, 357–61.

5. Smyth, "To the Lovers of the Truth," 3.

6. *Confession of Faith*, s.v. "Article XXXIII."

religious identity. Thus the reasons for separation involve social, political, economic, and complex leadership issues. Baptists are no exception.

Before we venture forth, a word about terminology. In Baptist history, the "mainstream" refers to the identifiable associations, conventions, and unions of congregations that possess organizational cohesion, a distinct theological/ethical consensus, membership accountability and leadership succession. The "mainstream" is the forward impulse of the movement, propagating and soliciting its ideals. Separation thus refers to any departure from the mainstream that begins within the mainstream or alongside as an alternative and that eventually morphs into its own enduring expression. In the history of Baptists, this has produced new subcategories of being Baptist, or in concrete terms, sub-denominations.

Theological Separationism

From their very beginning, emerging Baptists found pathways to obligatory separation. John Smyth published in 1608 a defining book, *The Differences in the Churches of the Separation*. Here was the classic stance of separation from what was perceived to be a great apostate church. In a next step, proto-Baptists distinguished themselves from Puritans and Brownists.[7] Within five decades, there was yet another example of practical separation: two major Baptist groups emerging from unique theological, social, and political circumstances that had little in common and rarely interacted with each other.

The first generation of Baptists in England were internally separated from each other within Dissent by deep theological issues. The earliest Baptists espoused a general atonement understanding of the work of Christ: namely that Christ died for all persons. Starting with John Smyth and Thomas Helwys, later to be carried forth in a General Assembly of General Baptists, these Baptists built upon Hebrews 6:1–2 and stressed human response to the Gospel, religious freedom, imposition of hands, and falling from grace.[8] These issues were clearly identifiable in confessional statements, treatises, and tracts.

---

7. In the Netherlands, three congregations ran separate courses: one associated with John Smyth, another with Thomas Helwys, and a third that coalesced around Leonard Busher. See my article, "Leonard Busher," 198.

8. The continuity was seen from Smyth/Helwys to Leonard Busher, John Murton, Edward Barber, Thomas Lamb, Matthew Caffyn, and Thomas Grantham. Some examples of this tradition, like Christopher Blackwood, exhibited both General Atonement and Calvinistic tendencies.

The second group of English Baptists to emerge was an outgrowth of the Brownist or Independent movement that represented a theological extension of the Puritan-Reformed tradition, the so-called Jacob/Lathrop/Jessey group.[9] These Calvinistic "Baptist Churches of Christ" rejected the charge of being "heretiques," "sowers of division," or "schismatiques."[10] They did not see themselves as outside the mainstream of Protestant Reformed Christianity. Rather, they identified themselves as "disciples," "chosen from the world," "good stewards of the manifold grace of God," "professors of the truth," and persecuted servants of Christ Jesus. Their theological tenets were announced in the First London Confession of Faith (1644), slightly amended two years later, and revised in its 1677/88 successor. There were limited interactions between the two streams, General and Calvinistic: crossover pastors, engagement in public disputations, and some confessional cooperation, as in the Midland Confession of 1655 and the Orthodox Creed of 1678.

This separation over theology was largely, though not completely, reconciled in the union of General Baptists and Particular Baptists in 1892. The "schism" was healed mostly by a cordial invitation from the Calvinistic mainstream to unite, displayed in a doctrinal statement that reflected both theological traditions.[11]

Theological variety from separationist roots was seen among Baptists in North America from the beginnings of the colonial era. In New England the separations of the Old Country were transplanted as the General Six Principle Baptists in New England and the Five Principle Calvinistic Baptists who ranged from Nova Scotia to Georgia. General Baptists, emigrating from Somersetshire, the Midlands, and Hampshire were found in Rhode Island, Massachusetts, Maryland, Carolina, and Virginia. Calvinistic Baptists from London, Bristol, and Wales were found in eastern Massachusetts, Rhode Island, Long Island, New Jersey, Pennsylvania, and in the southern backcountry and the Charleston region. Regionally, they lived in relative isolation from each other.

---

9. This group of seven London congregations by 1644 issued the [First] London Confession, described first as Calvinistic Baptists and later as Particular Baptists. See White, *Puritan Separatist Tradition*, 164–69.

10. The terms "heretiques" and "schismatiques" were used in the second imprint of the Confession of Faith (1646), "To the judicious and impartiall Reader," 1, and the term "sowers of division" was used in the 1644 first edition of the Confession, "To All That Desire," 1.

11. Even in this major national theological congruence, the tendency toward separation emerged again with the Strict and Evangelical Baptists and those in the train of C. H. Spurgeon.

The basic Calvinist/Arminian theological division remained a solid theological distinction among Baptists in North America, sometimes exhibiting a separationist tendency. The Freewill Baptists, originally of New Hampshire, demonstrate the separationism characteristic of the eighteenth century. Benjamin Randall, a self-taught sailmaker and itinerant preacher, presented his credentials to the Regular or Calvinistic Baptists of New Hampshire, disavowing the Calvinistic doctrines. He was roundly denounced by the Regular Baptist elders and Randall spun off a new movement, affirming "free grace, free will, and free communion."[12]

These two basic American streams of Baptists essentially merged in 1911 in the Northern Baptist Convention, with a continuing Freewill Baptist movement in the southern states. The northern states Free[will] emphases also had a pronounced impact on Canadian Baptists in the Maritime Provinces and Upper Canada. There a doctrinal statement adopted in 1905 blended both theological traditions.[13]

In the later nineteenth century, "liberal" Baptists became distinct from Conservative or evangelical Baptists. The liberal tradition actually had roots in the seventeenth century among English General Baptists, many of whom tilted toward Arian and Socinian positions.[14] Among university-trained ministers in the UK and US, similar tendencies were noticed at the turn of the nineteenth century.[15] Because of their openness on the atonement issue, Free Baptists were long considered liberal thinkers as were advocates of religious liberty as a primary tenet of Baptists. By the 1890s, Baptist ministers and educators who embraced scientific theories of geology and historical literary criticism of the Bible were labeled "Liberals."[16] In the twentieth

12. A similar seemingly unrelated movement in upstate New York, the Free Communion Baptists, rejected Calvinism and paid pews, and formed a regional body in 1841. It merged with the Freewill Baptists to form the Free Baptists. See Baxter, *History of the Freewill Baptists*.

13. On the Free Christian sect, see Renfree, *Heritage and Horizon*, 122–31. The 1905 doctrinal statement is still valid: see Renfree, *Heritage and Horizon*, 238.

14. A distinctly Socinian trend grew out of the teaching of Matthew Caffyn, a General Baptist messenger from Sussex and Kent. Disagreement over Caffyn's theological views led to a schism from 1693–1731 among the General Baptists, producing the General Baptist Assembly and the General Association of General Baptists. See Hayden, *English Baptist History and Heritage*, 31–34, 40–42.

15. Notably William Vidler in England, Elias Smith, Elhanan Winchester, Jonathan Maxcy, Asa Messer, Francis Wayland, and W. H. P. Faunce. Maxcy, Messer, Wayland, and Faunce were all associated with Brown University: Brackney, *Genetic History of Baptist Thought*, 256–69.

16. Four centers displayed these theological and philosophical orientations: Newton, Hamilton, Rochester, and Chicago. Chicago was devoted to the pursuit of untrammeled truth under the auspices of W. R. Harper, Shailer Mathews, S. J. Case, and G. B. Foster.

century, social gospel advocates[17] and those involved in ecumenical and interfaith activities, have been in the liberal tradition. It is the ongoing Liberal tradition among Baptists that has galvanized theologically conservative groups into separation, plus creating segments of the Baptist family that are closer to other Protestant denominations than evangelical Baptists, thus exhibiting a kind of separationism.[18]

The Liberal tradition thrived among Canadian Baptists as well. Acadia University educated a number of future scientific religionists, including social gospelers and higher critical approaches to understanding the bible. Brandon College in Manitoba became a center of the Social Gospel and McMaster University in Upper Canada was the deserved target of fundamentalist attacks on modernism, ecumenism, and the study of comparative religions. As in the US, these identities forced separation into liberal and conservative regional Baptist families.

Hyper-Calvinist theology has also provided the seedbed for Baptist separation, especially in the United States. In the early nineteenth century, among the most curious separated brethren were the Two Seed in the Spirit Double Predestinarian Baptists. Later, notable influences from Presbyterians brought forward purist forms of the old Particular Baptist identity: Sovereign Grace Baptists, Reformed Baptists, the Founders Movement, American Particular Baptists, and the Association of Historic Baptists.

Ethnic/Racial Separation

From the late seventeenth century, Baptists were ethnically diverse, but this did not always mean cordiality in relationships. London Baptists sought to evangelize the Welsh in the 1650s, spawning a Welsh-speaking union, and this followed with influences in the American colonial context. Eventually a Welsh-speaking Baptist union in Wales emerged, distinguished from the English-speaking Welsh congregations. In the 1660s John Myles and a scattering of Welsh Baptist emigrants settled in Massachusetts, with

---

17. Walter Rauschenbusch at Rochester Theological Seminary, William Newton Clarke and Nathaniel Schmidt at Colgate Theological Seminary, Shailer Mathews and Gerald Birney Smith at the Divinity School of the University of Chicago, and Milton Evans and Henry C. Vedder at Crozer Theological Seminary, defined the liberal tradition among American Baptists.

18. These include among Northern Baptists, the General Association of Regular Baptists and the Conservative Baptist Association, and from Southern Baptists, the Landmarker Movement, the Baptist Bible Fellowship, and the Southwide Baptist Fellowship.

other families moving to Rhode Island, the Delaware Valley, and Carolina.[19] They were distinct as to language, the practices of singing and imposition of hands, and self-identity. The Welsh Tract (Delaware) and Welsh Neck (South Carolina) congregations typify their presence.

As German, Swedish, Danish, Norwegian, and Italian immigrants came to the United States, the American Baptist Home Mission Society (founded 1832) commenced "domestic" missionary labors among them and the result was a series of separate associations or conferences, beginning in 1843. The Old World languages were continued in the worship and music traditions and institutions grew up among the separate language groups. By the 1920s clear separation was evident, with the several conferences making choices about great cooperation with English/American Baptists or complete separation.[20] Catalyzing factors toward separation were the growth of liberal social and theological perspectives and the desire to affirm cultural rootage.[21] Danish and Norwegian congregations were assimilated into the mainstream, while Germans, Swedes, and Italians separated and essentially formed "new" Baptist denominations: The North American Baptist Conference (1851), the Baptist General Conference (1856), and the Italian Baptist Association (1898). The reasons for separation were predominantly cultural.[22]

This form of Baptist separation crossed the border into the Canadian provinces, creating ethnic associations in Ontario, Manitoba, Saskatchewan, and Alberta, plus an identifiable, institutional life.[23]

Similar to ethnicity as a factor, separation based upon racial identity has worked both ways in the Baptist family. Of course, the most obvious separation was between Caucasian and Black Baptists. Beginning in the eighteenth century, when white southern preachers visited plantations and

---

19. The Myles story is recounted in Brackney with Hartman, *Swansea, Massachusetts*, xl–xlvii.

20. The Danish-Norwegian Baptist Conference merged with the American Baptist Convention in 1957, but the Italian, Polish, and Roumanian Associations continued a separate existence, sending delegates to the ABC.

21. As in worship services and hymns in the European languages, and fellowship meals emphasizing cultural heritage.

22. Woyke, *Heritage and Ministry*, 191–258; Olson, *Centenary History*, 153–73, 405–45, 483–99.

23. Ethnic missions in Canada commenced in the 1830s from the Upper Canada Baptist Missionary Society. The German Baptists started a bible college, and senior's home, and eventually the Swedes began a theological institute. Both were tied to US counterparts, the North American Baptist Seminary and Bethel Theological Seminary. See Woyke, *Heritage and Ministry*, 262–66, 384, 419–22; Olson, *Centenary History*, 478–81.

evangelized the slaves, the first black segregated congregations emerged in Virginia.[24] Before 1850, Black congregations were formed across the South. With passage of the Fugitive Slave Act in 1850, however, white tolerance became limited and in a few cases, Black congregations continued under a watchful eye.[25] In northern states like Illinois and Ohio, Black associations were formed in Free State territory. At the end of the Underground Railroad in Upper Canada and Nova Scotia, Black associations were formed.[26]

Following the Civil War, these early associations made several attempts to form national conventions, culminating in the National Baptist Convention in the USA. In 1895 it was ostensibly a Black association in the control of Black leaders.[27] David Goatley has provided a more detailed analysis of this movement in his paper, below in this volume.

The other prominent examples of racial separatism were among Hispanic and Asian Baptists. Hispanic Baptists were encouraged to form Hispanic associations and later conventions active in the Southwest, California, and Florida defined by Spanish language. In California, Oregon, Washington, and British Columbia, with the assistance of the Caucasian conventions, Asian associations were formed to meet the needs of the various immigrant communities brought about by immigrants from China, Japan, and IndoChina.

Here again, as with ethnic differentiation, Baptists separated for cultural and ethnographic reasons.

Seeking Reform in a New Direction

Some Baptists in North America have resorted to separation as a way to reform the mainstream movement. This has taken shape as a response to social and political concerns. Such separations include the Separate Baptists in the colonial period, Antislavery advocates, the Gospel Mission Movement, Cooperative Baptists, and the Alliance of Baptists.

At the heart of the eighteenth-century Baptist movement was the Philadelphia/Charleston tradition. It was urban, imitative of mainstream Protestantism and culturally accommodating. Smaller churches in the Piedmont and Appalachian backcountry, however, stressed religious experience

---

24. The first identifiable separate black congregation was on the plantation of William Byrd III at Mecklenburg, VA, in 1755. See Sobel, *Trabelin' On*, 102.

25. See the description of religious life in the slave community in Raboteau, *Slave Religion*, 219–31.

26. Fitts, *History of Black Baptists*, 44–64.

27. Washington, *Frustrated Fellowship*, 159–85.

and ethical strictness, and rose to call the mainstream to account. New strategies of evangelism following George Whitefield, coupled with believer's baptism and opposition to worldliness, gave shape to the Separate Baptist movement. These upcountry Calvinists stressed a "pure" form of the Baptist tradition: closed communion, biblical separation from churches and individuals whom they considered unorthodox, the need for a crisis conversion, believers' baptism, and the priority of preaching and church planting. Ultimately, as the Appalachian frontier closed, the Separates merged with the Regulars in the Union of 1801.[28] This reforming thrust in the South in fact led to a major cultural trait of future Southern Baptists and left its mark among New England evangelicals as well.[29]

In the nineteenth century, significant reforming movements arose in the northern United States over the issue of slavery and in the South in the next generation. Following the lead of one-time national advocate, William Lloyd Garrison, Baptists like William Brisbane, Albert Post, and Nathan Brown formed the American Baptist Free Mission Society, dedicated to bringing the northern societies to an abolitionist political position. Serious economic issues were at stake for Southern planters. After the Civil War, a reform movement in the South was active as the Gospel Mission Movement. Led by a former SBC missionary, Tarleton P. Crawford, these mostly lay advocates urged reform of strategies in the Foreign Mission Board, and opposed educational and humanitarian witness as priorities over personal evangelism.[30]

In the later twentieth century, social reform was a major thrust of progressive Southern Baptists who promoted women in leadership and as candidates for ordination; ecumenical engagement; and openness to alternative lifestyles and same-sex marriage. In 1987 many southern congregations joined the Alliance of Baptists, first dually aligned with the SBC, then separated completely from the Convention.[31] Later in 1991, 6,000 delegates, formerly Southern Baptists, formed the Cooperative Baptist Fellowship

28. A continuing Separate Baptist group in Kentucky remained out of the Union, the General Association of Separate Baptists in Christ, further illustrating the principle.

29. On the Separate Baptists in New England, see Goen, *Revivalism and Separatism*.

30. McBeth, *Baptist Heritage*, 416.

31. A contemporary example of this reforming tendency toward separation is the Canadian Association of Baptist Freedoms, chartered in 2012. It originated as the Atlantic Baptist Fellowship, a reforming influence movement within the Maritime Baptist Convention. In 1971, several pastors protested the newly-adopted requirement of believers' baptism by immersion for local church representatives to the Convention assemblies. As their influence within the Convention waned, the leadership moved to form a separate organization that affirms Baptist freedoms, ordains and validates ministers, publishes a bulletin, and holds lectures and annual meetings.

(CBF) in Atlanta, Georgia. The CBF has established state organizations that relate to the national organization and mirror its ideals.[32] Several historic Baptist institutions, plus a spate of new theological schools across the region, came to champion the broader social agenda. Superficially, lines were drawn between "evangelical" Baptists and the socially progressive-to-liberal Baptists.[33]

Polity Differences Create Separation

A third important form of separationism among Baptists is seen according along lines of polity or organization. Here one finds an early tendency among some English Baptists toward Sabbath-keeping. For theological reasons honoring the seventh day as Sabbath, mid-seventeenth-century Seventh Day Baptists conducted worship services on Saturdays, refrained from work and amusements, and restructured their congregational life accordingly.[34] They stood in marked contrast with both First Day Baptist groups.

Another evidence of separationism for reasons of different views on Baptist polity is opposition to the Baptist idea of the associational principle. From the epicenter of Philadelphia, the associational principle spread to the North, West, and South, creating a "Baptist America." It provided a standard confession, a church manual of procedure, standards of clergy ordination and discipline.[35] However, following the American Revolution, pockets of congregations in upstate New York, Pennsylvania, and Maryland began to resist the growth of associations on the comprehensive Philadelphia model, and after 1814 national organizations and state conventions.[36] They con-

---

32. See Durso, *Short History*.

33. In the reorganized or "Resurgent" Southern Baptist seminaries in the 1990s, intentional faculty appointments were made from among evangelical institutions like Trinity Evangelical Divinity School in Illinois, Gordon Conwell Theological Seminary in Massachusetts, Canadian Fellowship Baptists, and not necessarily Baptist, evangelical graduates of graduate schools like the University of St. Andrews in Scotland. The more liberal former Southern Baptist-related universities openly drew faculty from English and Scottish universities, Vanderbilt, Duke, and Emory Universities, and the former doctoral programs of the pre-Resurgent Southern Baptist Theological Seminary in Louisville, Kentucky.

34. Sabbatarian Baptists in America experienced schism themselves between the English and German speaking families, the latter centered in Ephrata, Pennsylvania. See my essay, "Hypocrites, Jews, or Nobodies," 201–25.

35. Shurden, *Associationalism among Baptists in America*; Gillette, *Minutes of the Philadelphia Baptist Association*, 60–64.

36. In New York State, the churches devoted themselves to the Old School Cause, in Pennsylvania it was the Primitive Baptist congregations, and in Maryland, those

sidered themselves "Old School" Baptists who held to the Old Confession of 1677/88. Demonstrably Calvinistic and resistant to Evangelicalism, they built a movement that found its strength in the local church and opposition to "gospel means." In the Ohio Valley and southwest, this separationism became in various forms, the Antimission movement; in Illinois and Texas it was manifested in Daniel Parker's "Two Seed in the Spirit Double Predestinarian Baptists" that opposed all human efforts in missions and education and spread geographically from Illinois to Texas. A major example of southern Primitive Baptist separationism organized as the Kehukee (Edgecombe County, North Carolina) Association in 1834.[37]

Perhaps the most striking example of separationism in this category is that of the US Southern Baptist Convention. Long thought to be an example preeminently of racial separation, historians of the Southern Baptist Convention have made a case for the conventions and associations in the Southland being of a different polity need and structure, thus explaining their separation from the northern Baptist societies. Robert A. Baker and H. Leon McBeth have argued that deep-seated organizational differences and regional needs were merely inflamed by the slavery issue. What Southern Baptists wanted—and created—was an integrated nationally-tiered organization of interlocking boards, associations, and conventions. Their separation in 1845 from the national Baptist societies was the most dramatic event in North American Baptist history.[38]

Not to be missed in the polity-generated separationism usually associated with Southern Baptists, is Landmarkism. This movement, otherwise known as "local church protectionism," began in New England and later emerged in Tennessee, Arkansas, and Texas as its epicenters. Based upon a strict interpretation of "landmark" Baptist principles, leaders like J. R. Graves, James M. Pendleton, and Ben M. Bogard, eschewed any congregations that were not organized according to the "Jerusalem principle," denying fellowship with them or their ministers. Banning conventions (esp. the SBC), alliances, and the ecumenical movement, the Landmarkers

---

churches that subscribed to the 1832 Black Rock Resolutions. See Hassell, *History of the Church of God*, 760–76, where Hassell gives an extended description of the character of Old School Baptists. Cf. Benedict, *General History of the Baptist Denomination*, 935–36; *Fifty Years Among the Baptists*, 101–8. A useful summary of this movement is found in Brackney, *Baptists in North America*, 57–59.

37. Hassell, *History of the Church of God*, 777–828.

38. What was left in its wake outside the North was a loose connection of societies for mission and education, and an annual "anniversary" meeting of Baptists from the northern states, the American Baptist Missionary Union (1846). See Baker, *Relations Between Northern and Southern*, 18–20; McBeth, *Baptist Heritage*, 381–82.

themselves coalesced under Bogard in the twentieth century to protect their polity in a national movement.[39]

The "Prima Donna" as a Cause of Separation

A *prima donna* is defined as a self-important person, possessing unusual gifts of personal charisma. Baptists have had their share. Single leaders, endowed with high self-esteem, coupled with a deep sense of religious vocation, have led to congregational and organizational separation among Baptists. The argument has been advanced that the fountainhead of nineteenth-century separationism among Baptists was the London pastor, Charles H. Spurgeon. Self-educated in the Puritan classics, gifted and insightful, Spurgeon built a powerful personal following from his London church. His departure from the Baptist Union over perceived theological liberalism, legitimated schism among fragile Baptist groups. If the Prince of Preachers could "come out," it must be theologically defensible. The result was "Spurgeonic Baptists," a new category.[40]

Among Black Baptists, about whom we shall hear much more in David Goatley's presentation, two examples stand out. The first was the schism surrounding the leadership of Richard H. Boyd. Boyd rose to prominence in the NBCUSA at the turn of the last century and came to control its Publishing Board. After an acrimonious debate with the National Baptist leadership, Boyd formed a new body, the National Baptist Convention of America, sometimes referred to as the "Boyd Baptist Convention."

The second example focused on Joseph H. Jackson. The pastor of a large Black Baptist Church in Chicago for over four decades, Jackson tightly controlled the presidency of the NBCUSA, creating in his image the policies of the denomination. Clashing in the 1960s with a younger generation including Martin Luther King, Jr. and Gardner C. Taylor, Jackson dominated the largest of the Black Baptist groups. The result was a 1961 separation from the NBCUSA to form the Progressive National Baptist Convention, led by L. V. Booth, King and Taylor.[41]

Prima donna-ism was also a factor in the emergence of several new movements in the South. While one could well argue the theological distinctiveness of fundamentalist Baptists, in fact it was a collection of megapastors who took the paths toward separation. In the great separation of the

---

39. Pratt, *Father of Modern Landmarkism*, provides a useful description of the movement.

40. Brackney, *Historical Dictionary of the Baptists*, 539–40.

41. The defining issues leading to separation are found in Avant Jr., *Social Teachings*.

1920s, vocal leaders and pastors emerged to coalesce congregations around their perspectives. Cortland Myers of New York City, J. C. Massee of Boston, R. T. Ketcham of Pennsylvania, and William Bell Riley of Minneapolis led groups that would evolve into separationist Baptist denominations. The results were respectively, the General Association of Regular Baptists (1932), the Conservative Baptist Association (1947), and the Conservative Baptist movement in Minnesota (1940s).[42]

Two decades later, a new generation of iconic personalities formed yet another set of separate Baptist denominations. These included J. Frank Norris, G. Beauchamp Vick, Lee Roberson, and John R. Rice. Cloaked in fundamentalist confessionalism, the leaders stood boldly against the evils of the mainstream and convention overlords.

Norris, an anti-saloon graduate of Southwestern Baptist Seminary ("Hebrew, SheBrew, the world's going to Hell on Home Brew"), gradually became critical of liberal theology and then the leadership control in the Southern Baptist Convention. In 1933 Norris founded the Premillennial Baptist Fellowship that he ran like a fiefdom. In 1950 a schism occurred within the Norris organization, a minority remaining with Norris, and the greater number following Norris's understudy, G. Beauchamp Vick. Vick was promptly elected the head of the new "Baptist Bible Fellowship" and the founder of Baptist Bible College, Springfield, Missouri. In the Southeastern states, Lee Roberson, pastor of a mega-church in Chattanooga, Tennessee, and John R. Rice, a fiery evangelist and editor of the *Sword of the Lord*, formed in 1950 the Southwide Baptist Fellowship, dedicated to the demise of Neo-Evangelicalism (and other moderate movements). Each created large, comprehensive congregations built upon the personality and charisma of the pastor.

Thomas Todhunter Shields of Toronto represents one example of the *prima donna* case among Baptists in Canada. From his base in Jarvis Street Church, Toronto, and influenced by US fundamentalists, Shields founded the Regular Baptist movement in Canada that flourished in Ontario and British Columbia. Further, he started a school and a mission organization.[43] In a later manifestation, after two schisms, this would become one stream of the Fellowship of Evangelical Baptist Churches, imitating the General Association of Regular Baptist Churches in the US.[44]

---

42. This was actually a hostile takeover of the Minnesota Baptist Convention, led by Richard Clearwaters, pastor of Fourth Baptist Church, Minneapolis for four decades.

43. The school was the Toronto Baptist Seminary and the mission arm was the Regular Baptist Missionary and Education Society.

44. In the Canadian Maritime provinces, in the 1940s, a regional *prima donna* movement coalesced around J. J. Sidey, a pastor in the Annapolis Valley in Nova Scotia. Sidey

Some Learnings from Baptist Experience

The tendency toward separation among Baptists is inherent in Baptist ecclesiology. It is a strong impulse. For most Baptists, the church must be an identifiable group of saints called to be the people of God. The earliest Baptists were emboldened by standing against what they considered to be an apostate national church. They were also prepared to stand alone as congregations and individuals who acknowledged Jesus Christ as Lord of the conscience. It was Christ who called them to separate.

Not wanting to be characterized as "schismatics," Baptists searched for a position that was defensible by scripture and history in definition of an unadulterated form of their tradition. The earliest generations of Baptists studiously avoided being classed as schismatics. Schism was seen as a sin against the mystical Body of Christ. The earliest Baptist confessional document was primarily a broadside against slanderous schismatic charges. Later Baptist separations recoiled at schismatic accusations, preferring to be seen as legitimate and pure extensions of historic ideals. In North America, this was at the foundation of Old School and many nascent reforming groups within the mainstreams.

The cultural and political ideal of religious freedom gave solace to frontier Baptists in North America who yearned for freedom from structural overlordship. In a religious application of the Frederick Jackson Turner Thesis, the open frontier of the eighteenth and nineteenth-centuries invited experimentation, strong leadership, and group loyalty to pastors and associations.[45]

Baptist separationism was also driven by environmental factors. These include social class, ethnicity, race, The clash between rural versus urban cultures, cultural modernization, and a desire to preserve traditions in contrast with rapid social transformation.

The English preacher Charles H. Spurgeon had a pronounced impact upon theologically conservative Baptist groups who sought separation from various forms of unorthodox belief and practice, like higher criticism of the scriptures and open congregational membership. An unwitting permission-giver, Spurgeon legitimated "come-outer-ism."

In the wake of Spurgeon, gifted pastors have influenced, particularly in the United States and Canada, a course toward separationism. Oratorical speaking gifts, a clear sense of vision and single-handed organization

---

was influenced by American fundamentalists and formed an association of churches, a bible college, and a mission organization, the International Christian Mission.

45. For an elaboration of this historic thesis, see Billington, *Westward Expansion*, 1–12.

skills not unlike those of a contemporary business executives, and an antagonism toward conglomerates, connect to provide *prima donnas* in every generation.

All Baptists harken back to the authority of the New Testament. A dominant hermeneutic of Baptists has been to identify the various congregations in the Acts and Paul's letters seemingly addressed to individual congregations. There they find a search for doctrinal and ethical orthodoxy *and* conflicts among apostles and elders that produced separation. It is not difficult for Baptists to find the tendency toward separation embedded in the context of New Testament Christianity.[46]

Some years ago, the eminent Baptist historian, Robert G. Torbet, cautioned against speaking of a Baptist "church" or "denomination." Instead, he thought of Baptists as a diffuse movement, each component of which claims authority from the New Testament. Torbet's own denomination, the American Baptist Convention (that included the oldest congregations and associations in North America), in 1957 declared in a promotional brochure, "We make friends—and some leave us" thus formally validating the legitimacy of separationism.[47]

---

46. This is the thesis of a recent general history of Baptists (Weaver, *In Search of the New Testament Church*).

47. Torbet, "Story of a People," 4.

CHAPTER 3

Born Again, Coming Again, and Going Out

The Significance of Believer's Baptism and Eschatology on Anabaptist Dissent

Colin Godwin

MANY FACTORS HAVE BEEN identified as instrumental to the formation of sectarianism. Trends in Anabaptist historiography since the 1970s have emphasized political, economic and sociological trends as instrumental in the separation of Anabaptists from the Catholic and Magisterial churches.[1] Earlier works, such as Franklin Littell's seminal study on *The Origins of Sectarian Protestantism*, underlined the importance of the rediscovery of the Bible and a primitivist missionary zeal to the formation of their dissident ecclesiology. Current views on Anabaptism draw both from the social sciences and from historical theology in an effort to understand the commonalities and distinctives of the Anabaptists.[2]

As we attempt to understand the movement towards Anabaptist sectarianism, two doctrines emerge as primary drivers for separation: believer's baptism and a belief in the Second Coming. These two tenets of faith moved Anabaptists toward dissent in two movements. First, through baptism they joined a new community, moving *away from* the multitudinous churches and the governments that supported them; second, through their

---

1. Stayer, *Anabaptists and the Sword*; *German Peasants' War*; Goertz, *Anabaptists*.
2. Snyder, *Anabaptist History and Theology*; *From Anabaptist Seed*; Littell, *Origins of Sectarian Protestantism*; Godwin, *Baptizing, Gathering, and Sending*.

expectation of the Return of Christ, they moved *towards* the ethic and imminent reality of God's new kingdom. I will examine each of these in turn.

Born Again: Baptism

It was believer's baptism that gave the Anabaptists both their name and their mission. Put simply, if the Anabaptists had confined themselves to a renewed spirituality and evangelical zeal, and had not stressed the water baptism of believers, they would never have developed into a unique dissident movement.[3]

Anabaptists of all declensions believed that baptism could only take place after teaching and believing, according to Matthew 28:18–20 and Mark 16:16. One cannot underestimate the importance of this sequence for their understanding of Christian faith. For the Brethren, the baptism of infants (before they could be taught or believe) led directly to the ineffectiveness and gross immorality of the established churches. In his 1526 pamphlet on baptism, Hans Hut explained:

> Christ said to go into all the world and preach the gospel of all creatures. Next he said, who believes, thirdly, and is baptized, will be saved. *This order must be kept* if we want to achieve a true Christian life and break the whole world to pieces. *Where this order is not kept there is no Christian community of God but only of the devil*, and the result is a world full of false Christians who champion what is not right in their perverted order.[4]

Hut's statement not only provides a clean diagnosis for the ills of the church, but also outlines the revolutionary impact that Anabaptists expected when they baptized only after the convert expressed a genuine and personal faith. True Christian life would result and the desired outcome would be "breaking the world to pieces." In his *Instruction on Beginning of a True Christian Life* (1527), Hans Schlaffer's dissenting view on baptism acknowledged the break not only from church practice, but from church tradition as well:

> It is a much surer and more true foundation to build upon Christ and his teaching than to rely upon the church fathers or councils. For on that final day, Christ will sit in judgment, not the popes, fathers or councils. It does not matter how old a

---

3. Snyder, *Anabaptist History and Theology*, 91, 305–26.
4. Hut, "On the Mystery of Baptism," 67. Emphasis added.

tradition may be. Christ and his word are older still, for he was the son of God from eternity and will remain so into eternity.⁵

The renewed emphasis of the Anabaptists on practical faith combined with their straightforward reading of Scripture led to a new theological formulation for the baptism of believers. One of the most important of these was Balthasar Hubmaier's 1525 *On the Christian Baptism of Believers*. In this work, Hubmaier cited Mark 16:16, Matthew 28:19, and John 20:20, noting that,

> From these words one understands clearly and certainly that this sending of the apostles consists of three points or commands: first, preaching; second, faith; and third, baptism.⁶

To such a clear directive of the Lord, Christian obedience was the only acceptable outcome, even if this meant upsetting the social, religious and political order of the day.

> Well, it is stated very clearly [in Mark 16:25]: (1) go, (2) preach, (3) he who believes, (4) and is baptized, (5) will be saved. Here you see a well-structured speech of which no single letter will fall. It must be kept as it is. Who then can change it?⁷

This Anabaptist concern for observing the correct order of preaching, faith and baptism is likewise echoed across Anabaptism in writers such as Hans Schlaffer, Hans Denck, Menno Simons, Peter Riedemann, and Dirk Philips.⁸

That this constituted a radical break with the sixteenth-century collaboration of church and state is evidenced by the reaction of the authorities. Anabaptist dissent, expressed through believer's baptism, was labelled as a crime. Instead of being content to advocate renewal in their local Catholic, Lutheran or Reformed parishes, the Anabaptists separated themselves from the protection of civil and ecclesiastical powers and invited their full sanction. The 1535 edict of Emperor Charles V, although not universally applied by the authorities, stipulated burning at the stake for all Anabaptists and their supporters who continued to,

---

5. Schlaffer, "Instruction on Beginning a True Christian Life," 107.
6. Hubmaier, "On the Christian Baptism of Believers," 114–15, 129–30.
7. Hubmaier, "On the Christian Baptism of Believers," 122.
8. Schlaffer, "Instruction on Beginning a True Christian Life," 107; Denck, "Concerning True Love," 119; Simons, "Foundation of Christian Doctrine," 120; Riedemann, *Peter Riedemann's Hutterite Confession*, 109; Philips, "Enchiridion (Handbook)," 73, 104, 110, 419.

Spread, sow and secretly preach their aforesaid abuses and errors, in order to allure a great number of men and women to their false doctrine and reprobate sect, to seduce them and to rebaptize some, to the great reproach and disregard of the sacrament of holy baptism, and of our edicts, statutes and ordinances.[9]

Anabaptists such as Menno Simons attempted unsuccessfully to persuade the authorities that their behaviour would not lead to another violent, immoral and ultimately tragic episode like the Münster debacle (1534–35). Instead of being given permission to practice believer's baptism as they understood it, their "disregard" for infant baptism led to persecution across Europe.[10]

Anabaptists risked exclusion, punishment and death because they believed that their adhesion to believer's baptism had ecclesiological consequences. A gathered church of regenerate believers required conscious belief at baptism. For them, the continued baptism of infants allowed unconverted Christians to linger comfortably in the pews of Reformed or Lutheran churches just as they had done in Catholic churches before the Reformation. Believer's baptism separated Christians into a new kind of church, an alternative community that sought to obey Christ's commands in a corrupt and violent world.

Believer's baptism formed the first movement of Anabaptist dissent, providing a clean break from state, society and the pedobaptistic churches. Once gathered into believing communities, they engaged in a second movement towards separation through their belief in the Second Coming of Christ.

Coming Again: Eschatology

The champions of Anabaptist reform were by no means unusual in their preoccupation with the Return of Christ. With the possible exception of Erasmus and Zwingli, the End was of great interest to all Christian writers of the period.[11] Depending on the writer, this almost universal sense of God's interruption of the human order had different degrees of imminence: the Second Coming could happen immediately, sooner or later.

Whatever the anticipated timing of the Lord's Coming, this future heavenly intervention produced very earthly expectations in terms of

9. Braght, *Martyr's Mirror*, 414, 438, 442.
10. Simons, "Foundation of Christian Doctrine," 129.
11. Klaassen, *Living at the End of the Ages*, xi.

church discipline, mission, society and politics. For Anabaptists, the End was near, and they needed to prepare for its coming. Signs of the End included the Turkish invasion of Europe (Vienna was under siege in 1529), social and economic injustices like the German Peasants' War (1524-25), and strange weather patterns and crop failures. For Anabaptists, further apocalyptic proof included the immorality of the clergy, the persecution of Anabaptists and the false doctrines of the multitudinous churches. Even some of the more moderate Anabaptists like Conrad Grebel saw incorrect doctrinal formulations around baptism and the Lord's Supper as proof that the churches that opposed them had fallen under demonic influences announced in the biblical book of Revelation.[12]

Long after the departure of the date-setting millennial prophets that emerged out of the German Peasants' War, Anabaptists continued to preach and write about the Return of Christ. This eschatological awareness directly fostered Anabaptist separatism in two ways. First, it promoted evangelistic activity, so as to bring more of the unregenerate into the church through baptism. Second, the Second Coming motivated a disciplined Christian community, separate and different from the world, so that believers would be ready for Christ's Return, whether this was imminent, sooner or later.[13] Local circumstances such as economic hardship, continued persecution or internal conflict in Anabaptist churches tailored the specific application of a belief in the Second Coming. Nevertheless, the twin separatist themes of evangelism and good conduct were present across the three streams of Swiss, South German and Dutch Anabaptism.

Hans Nadler was a disciple of Hans Hut who preached from his conversion in 1527 until his capture two years later. Nadler was an illiterate needle salesman who combined that vocation with that of itinerant evangelist after his conversion to Anabaptism. We have an insight into his theology thanks to his recorded testimony during his 1529 interrogation by the authorities. Hans preached the Second Coming, but refused to set a date for the event. When questioned about when it would happen, Nadler did not give a date and instead drove home the point about repentance, conversion and godly living,

> I do not know whether the spears are ready, whether he will come in twenty-three hundred or in two hundred or in a thousand

---

12. Littell, *Origins of Sectarian Protestantism*, 128; Klaassen, *Living at the End of the Ages*, 62–71.

13. Godwin, *Baptizing, Gathering, and Sending*, 221–52; Snyder, *Anabaptist History and Theology*, 201; Littell, *Origins of Sectarian Protestantism*, 127–35; Klaassen, *Living at the End of the Ages*, 113.

years. But the Scripture says: You are all to repent, forsake sin, and turn to God. All that is evil will be destroyed, but the devout and the godly he will take into his kingdom. "Therefore," says Christ, "Struggle to enter by the straight gate" (Matt 7:13).[14]

Balthasar Hubmaier was another Anabaptist who disagreed with apocalyptic date-setting but nevertheless preached the Second Coming of Christ as an inspiration to conversion and to holy conduct in an alternative Anabaptist community.

> We shall see our God and Savior face-to-face in his great glory and majesty, coming in the clouds of heaven. Then our carnal, sinful, and godless life will come to an end. Then each will receive the recompense for his works. They who have worked well will enter into eternal life, those [who have worked] evil, into eternal fire.[15]

In the Netherlands, although Menno Simons likewise rejected the calendarizing of the Hans Hut and the Münster radicals, the former priest also preached a message of conversion and holy living from the apocalyptic texts of the Old and New Testaments, likening the sixteenth century to the days of Noah and charging his readers to be ready for the wedding feast of Christ at his Return.

> Yes, we would sincerely watch for the coming of the Lord, give heed to the time of grace, and preserve our wedding garment.[16]

For Menno, the wrath of God would be poured out at Christ's Return, giving believers license even to "threaten" the unrepentant to bring them to salvation.

> He who lives according to the flesh will die, as the whole of scripture teaches. If people do not repent, nothing is more sure than your stern wrath. Therefore, beloved Lord, threaten, punish, admonish and teach them. Then perhaps they will regret their ways, recognize the truth and be saved.[17]

Dirk Philips, the former monk and more conservative colleague of Menno Simons, did not hesitate to use the Second Coming in his teaching to promote holiness and in his evangelism to encourage conversion

---

14. Nadler, "Declaration of the Needle Merchant," 147.
15. Hubmaier, "Twelve Articles in Prayer Form," 237.
16. Simons, "True Christian Faith," 345.
17. Simons, "Meditation on the Twenty-fifth Psalm," 250.

and baptism. The judgment of God was nigh. Women and men everywhere needed to convert and become Anabaptists or face God's wrath.

> May he [God] renew in us the inner person and keep us in his true way until the end. May we stand with joy before the judgement seat of Jesus Christ, when he comes again in power with the angels with the flaming sword of wrath, raised against those who have not believed in God nor were obedient to the gospel.[18]

Philips wrote extensively about the Anabaptist practices, which included the Lord's Supper, footwashing, church discipline, and, of course, believer's baptism.[19] Failure to teach and uphold these community practices would lead to punishment from Christ "on that final day."

> Therefore, anyone who refuses to follow Christ Jesus and is disobedient to his word, or who practices the ordinances and truth of Christ differently than Christ himself taught and practiced, does not fear God. He is being unfaithful and in opposition to his word. He shall not escape the punishment of God. Whoever despises Christ and does not accept his word will be judged on that final day by the words of his own mouth.[20]

Hutterite teachers were somewhat less literal in their apocalypticism than the Swiss and Dutch Brethren. However, they used the doctrine liberally to promote the separation of their communities from the surrounding churches, culture and government. Once new believers were baptised into the church and surrendered all their worldly goods to the community, Jacob Hutter sought to inspire faithful and separated Christian living through the Lord's Coming.

> What I fear most is that we will begin to say, as many people do, "Oh, my Lord will not come for a long time." And they eat and drink and associate with the godless and they beat and torment their fellow servants, as Christ said in the parable. But the Lord will come on a day and at an hour when they are not expecting or thinking about Him. Just when they think everything is peaceful and as safe as can be, destruction will suddenly come upon them. God grant that this does not happen to any of us. It is not for nothing that the Lord said He will come like a thief in the night, when everybody is fast asleep, and without a care in the world.[21]

18. Philips, "Concerning Spiritual Restitution," 246.
19. Philips, "Concerning the New Birth," 207–8.
20. Philips, "Concerning the New Birth," 210–11.
21. Hutter, "Letter 5," 95.

Because Christ was thought to be coming soon, Hutterite believers were to live holy lives in eager anticipation of the Return of their "Shepherd and King." At the Return, those faithful Hutterites who endured through trials and tribulations would be redeemed by Christ and be given peace and glory alongside the angels.[22]

Another influential Hutterite author, Peter Riedemann, used Christ's parable of separating the sheep and the goats at his Coming to remind his flock that the unconverted would be punished by Christ at the End. He writes,

> A place for the unbeliever is also already prepared, since he has presented to us the story of the last judgment. When the Son of Man comes in all his glory with his holy angels, he will sit upon his glorious throne, with all nations gathered before him. He will separate them as a shepherd separates the sheep from the goats, the sheep on his right hand, but the goats on his left.[23]

Indeed, the only way for women and men to avoid the judgement of God was to accept the Hutterite message, be baptized and give all possessions to the community to be shared. Believer's baptism functioned to separate the new believer from the corrupt churches and a hostile world. As these believers lived holy lives in Hutterite communities, they anticipated the Second Coming of Christ, where they would be rescued from the corruption of the age and set apart in eternity as a holy people in the eyes of God. As the Hutterites moved repeatedly across various lands and territories to escape persecution, the Lord's Return was used to encourage them to be faithful to the Hutterite message in times of hardship. In the words of Paul Glock to the Moravian Hutterites (1563), believers were to "wait for the revelation of our Lord Jesus Christ who will strengthen us to the end so that we may be blameless in the day of our Lord Jesus Christ."[24]

Across Europe, Anabaptists consistently preached the Second Coming of Christ. While this was not unusual in the sixteenth-century context of general apocalyptic expectation, the doctrine propelled the Anabaptists further into their dissent and separation. Anabaptists repurposed baptism from the gentle reception of infants by a welcoming Christian culture into a radical adult break from a hostile unbelieving world. Those baptized adults formed a dissident believing community. In parallel, they took the general apocalyptic expectation of Christian society and turned it into an impulse for separatism, where Christ's faithful Anabaptist minority would

22. Hutter, "Letter 8," 151; "Letter 5," 98.
23. Riedemann, *Peter Riedemann's Hutterite Confession*, 73.
24. Glock, "Letter to Loenhard Lanzenstiel," 325–26.

be rescued from the corruption and persecution of unconverted 'Christian' Europe. The combination of these two doctrines was a potent force for Anabaptist dissent and separation. They were called *out of* their churches and called *into* a community that looked *forward* to Christ's kingdom in the Age to Come.

Going Out: Separation

Because they held to radical conversion demonstrated by believer's baptism, Anabaptist belief in Christ's imminent Return motivated them to preach, baptise, and make disciples. Catholics, Lutherans, and Reformed believers did not need to change their ecclesial affiliation in order to allow their own eschatological expectation to produce better behaviour. For the Brethren, however, to become an Anabaptist one needed to be rebaptized and join a new church against the wishes of church and prince. Their dissident baptism enshrined their loyalty to the Kingdom of Christ, especially as described in the Sermon on the Mount, above all earthly kingdoms. Moreover, it placed their believers' church in opposition to the political and religious powers of Europe. Without the backing of a political ruler for their church, they developed a sectarian basis for their faith.[25]

The drive of any believers' church towards separation, will, almost by definition, encounter resistance from the accepted social and religious order that is being criticized by the separatists. Taking again the 1529 episode of the interrogation of Hans Nadler, the needle merchant, the response of the inquisitors shows that their primary concern was not fundamentally with the heretical doctrinal interpretations espoused by Nadler such as Anabaptist views of the Lord's Supper, baptism and original sin. They saw Hans as an ignorant man who had been beguiled by an itinerant preacher (Hans Hut). They suspected that he was basically harmless. What bothered them was the sectarian trajectory of his preaching and his capacity to influence others. In their conclusion to his interrogation, they note,

> But aside from [these erroneous doctrines] we cannot sense nor gather from any of the answers that he and his fellows might perhaps undertake any deed against the government, nor that they were ever, nor are now, minded to cause insurrection.[26]

They were concerned about Nadler' beliefs upsetting the social order and provoking another Peasants' War (1524–1525).

---

25 Williams, "Sectarian Ecumenicity," 159–60.
26. Nadler, "Declaration of the Needle Merchant," 153.

Still, it is a matter of concern that if such factions were to grow and daily gather strength, the devil might easily seduce and deceive them. By means of some misunderstanding of Scripture verses he might seduce them to the extent that disruption of the general peace and a *separation from common Christendom*, and in the future perhaps insurrection might come about under the pretense of destroying the godless.[27]

After they had tried unsuccessfully to correct his errant beliefs, they tortured and then exiled him, conveniently passing on the problem of a zealous Anabaptist rabble-rouser to the jurisdiction of another prince. What Nadler's questioners recognized was, in fact, the fundamental nature of Anabaptist dissent: on biblical and ethical terms, Anabaptists believed so strongly that the established churches displeased God that they rejected them and established their own alternative communities. They were, in fact, prepared to "disrupt the general peace and separate from common Christendom" as Nadler's inquisitors feared. Their community was founded on the separatist act of believer's baptism (by which they repudiated their infant baptism) and a belief in the final separation of the Second Coming (by which they repudiated the ethics of both their prince and the established church). These separatist beliefs were dangerous and had political overtones. They could fuel a wholesale disruption of the civil order, a breakdown in social values, a rejection of established hierarchy and even outright insurrection.

Baptism, Eschatology, and 'Coming Out' in the Twenty-first Century

In the twentieth and twenty-first centuries, there has been some movement for believers' churches to downplay both believer's baptism and the Second Coming. Membership rules have been changed in local churches to accept new members who did not follow the Anabaptist "order" of baptism. Believers' churches are making exceptions for those who were baptized as infants, feeling that those who have given strong testimony to their faith journey with Christ should not be required to be rebaptized. In some of these same believers' churches, there is little mention of the Second Coming. Preachers and teachers avoid this important doctrine, fearing that a simple presentation in layman's terms is almost impossible because of the intense eschatological debates that have flowed through believers' churches from the late twentieth century to the present.[28]

27. Nadler, "Declaration of the Needle Merchant." Emphasis added.

28. The writings of John Nelson Darby (1800–1882) and Hal Lindsey (1929–) come to mind.

Stuart Murray, in his exposition on contemporary Anabaptism, *The Naked Anabaptist*, attempts to articulate the essence of Anabaptism and its pertinence to twenty-first-century Christianity. Murray's list of attractional Anabaptist essentials was identified by a group representing the Anabaptist Network in the U.K. The list includes Jesus-centred discipleship, alternative faith communities, equality and the pursuit of nonviolence and economic justice. It also includes the baptism of believers. Murray explains, however, that believer's baptism almost did not make it as one of the essentials, largely because of the potential of this doctrine to be an obstacle for those who were investigating Anabaptism. Despite the objectionable nature of the doctrine, however, he explains that it was necessary to include it as part of twenty-first-century Anabaptist essentials because "the conviction that baptism is for believers is inextricably linked to fundamental beliefs about the nature of the church in the Anabaptist tradition."[29]

Other voices echo the importance for contemporary participants in the believers' church tradition to hold on to the centrality of believer's baptism. Rick Warren, commenting on the Anabaptist preoccupation with Matthew 28:18–20, writes "the Anabaptists baptized only believers, but baptism was far more significant than what would be considered adult christening. For Anabaptists, baptism was the most significant ordinance."[30] Believer's baptism may be under current pressure as an offensive and exclusionary doctrine, but it does not yet seem that contemporary Baptists and Anabaptists are ready to discard it.

At the same time, movements of adult conversions in the mainline churches and growth in Catholicism are prompting new thinking about the baptism of adults. Vatican II issued the new *Rite of Christian Initiation for Adults* in response to the increasing globalization of Catholicism and the need to support that growth with an evangelistic liturgy of adult conversion. While the post-Christian West grows in openness to adult conversion, Christians in closed countries risk incarceration or even death for participating in believer's baptism. This is a new day, with new (Southern) voices around the table and new challenges before the Christian churches. The time may be ripe for renewed conversations regarding the separatist and missionary impulse of believer's baptism.

The Second Coming of Christ has also been a complicated or even embarrassing doctrine for believers' churches. While not comparable to the excess of the Münster revolt, there has been ample calendarizing by evangelical Christians, Christian sects and other fringe movements in recent

---

29. Murray, *Naked Anabaptist*, 110–12.

30. Warren, "Anabaptists and the Great Commission," 95.

decades. The sometimes extravagant leaders of schismatic communities and the otherworldliness of doomsday cults make them memorable for media and society alike. For Christians located more firmly in the centre of the believers' church tradition, it can be difficult to hold on to the doctrine of the Second Coming amidst such bad press.

The sixteenth-century Anabaptists did not throw out the eschatological baby with the bathwater of excess. Without seeking to replicate the sixteenth century in the twenty-first, it may be helpful to reconsider their experience. They specifically rejected the extremism of the date-setters but nevertheless continued to proclaim the Lord's Return. Approximately one sixth of the collection of biblical texts in the *Biblical Concordance of the Swiss Brethren*, compiled between 1529 and 1540, refer to apocalyptic themes such as "Judgment," "The Day of the Lord," "Vengeance," and the "Reward of the Pious." The latter is the largest single section of the concordance, demonstrating how important the Second Coming was to inspire the faithfulness of believers who faced hardship or persecution.[31]

James McClendon is one Baptist theologian whose Christian and community ethic draws on the Anabaptist commitment to the Kingdom of God. He argues that the social and ethical separation of the church stems from the *discontinuity* of the Resurrection and the anticipated End with the world and its values. In essence, eschatological expectation fuels the dynamic of separation.[32] Citing the experience of Hans Hut and the context behind the writing of the *Schleitheim Confession*, McClendon notes that the *Confession* was simultaneously directed by the very real danger of political and religious threat and the notion that the Kingdom of God was invading the present order. Being centred on Jesus meant an eschatological awareness, an acknowledgement that the present is transitory and Christians need to root their behaviours in the Age to Come. In this way, the Christian belief in the *eschaton* is a continuation of faith in Christ's resurrection.[33] Baptism is, according to the first article of the *Schleitheim Confession*, for those who "believe truly that their sins are taken away through Christ, and to all those who desire to walk in the resurrection of Jesus Christ and be buried with Him in death, so that they might rise with Him." The cover letter to the *Confession* urges faithfulness "until the end."[34]

It may be that believers' churches find the twenty-first century ripe for a rediscovery and revision of their separation and dissent. There is a

---

31. Snyder et al., *Biblical Concordance of the Swiss Brethren*.
32. McClendon, *Ethics*, 1:251–53.
33. McClendon, *Ethics*, 1:248.
34. Yoder, *Schleitheim Confession*, 36, 34.

lot of discussion about the end of the world in contemporary culture. Each year produces a new onslaught of apocalyptic disaster movies, with some concoction of zombies, disease, aliens, terrorism or ecological disaster threatening the human race. In particular, the concern about environmental disasters has given rise to a vast array of scientific, political and social organizations that seek to take better care of the planet. Somewhat like how Christian eschatology functioned with sixteenth-century Anabaptists, today's apocalyptic ecological scenarios function to rally the convinced, convert the unpersuaded and cultivate an improved environmental ethic among all. In this context, Anabaptist concern for the End may discover new ways to understand the coming Kingdom of God and may encourage deeper belief in Christ's Return among members of believers' churches.

Together, believer's baptism and an expectation for the Second Coming worked to anchor Anabaptist faith and practice in the Kingdom of God, a set of values and expectations that existed *in opposition* to the world and its powers. Once they were baptized as believers, they were able to (imperfectly) affirm the new reality of the Kingdom of God in Christian community as they waited for the (perfect) expression of the Kingdom of God at the Return of Christ.

CHAPTER 4

Unifiers to Come-Outers

The Journey of the Stone-Campbell
Restoration Movement

Douglas A. Foster

The Stone-Campbell Restoration movement (SCM) that coalesced in the early nineteenth century had as its reason for being the visible unity of all Christians. The founding documents of the movement urged Christians in every locality to come together despite different doctrinal positions and practices, to work and worship as one. Over time, however, the call to embrace all who professed belief in Christ and manifested it in their lives as fellow Christians shifted to an impulse to separate from those not accepting "right" way.

This study examines the creation of the SCM's ecclesiology and its self-perception as an alternative to the separation of Christians they saw as an inherent part of what became known as denominationalism. It then briefly analyzes how the call to unity itself transformed into a "come-outer" separatist impulse. This shift resulted in, among other things, the extreme isolation of parts of the SCM and its ironic division into three major North American bodies.

The Unitive Impulse in the Formation of the Stone-Campbell Movement

The Stone-Campbell Movement began in North America in the early 1800s, one of several movements to "restore" Christian unity through adherence to a simple gospel. Leaders included Baptists Elias Smith and Abner Jones in

New England and Canada, Methodist James O'Kelly in Virginia and North Carolina, and Presbyterians Barton W. Stone in Kentucky and Thomas and Alexander Campbell in Virginia and Pennsylvania.[1]

In August 1801, Barton Stone organized the Cane Ridge revival marked by "religious exercises" in which hundreds accepted Christ and hostilities between denominations disappeared for a time. Strict Presbyterian leaders, however, opposed the exercises and the non-Reformed preaching that invited anyone to come to Christ. In 1803, Stone and his revivalist colleagues withdrew from the Synod of Kentucky to form their own Springfield Presbytery. Yet they were clear that though they were compelled to separate for their work's sake, they regarded their former colleagues as Christians and desired to maintain fellowship in every way possible.[2] The next summer, however, Stone and his colleagues disbanded the Springfield Presbytery in an attempt to remove all barriers to their association with all professed Christians. The "Last Will and Testament of Springfield Presbytery" of June 1804, the first founding document of the Stone-Campbell Movement, stated:[3]

> We will that this body die, be dissolved, and sink into union with the Body of Christ at large: for there is but one body and one spirit, even as we are called in one hope of our calling.
>
> We will, that our name . . . be forgotten, that there be but one Lord over God's heritage, and his name one.
>
> We will, that preachers and people, cultivate a spirit of mutual forbearance, pray more and dispute less.[4]

This Christian movement, begun in Kentucky and Ohio, eventually spread as far as New York and Iowa.

The second movement was begun by Thomas Campbell and later expanded by his son, Alexander. The Campbells were Irish, members of the Anti-Burgher Seceder "Synod of Ulster"—a faction of the Church of Scotland. Each division had to do with Scottish religio-political matters that were largely irrelevant to the Irish context, yet the divisions kept the groups in Ireland apart. Internal Presbyterian rivalry, disabilities imposed on Presbyterians by the (Anglican) Church of Ireland, and the constant

---

1. Haggard, *Address*; MacClenny, *Life of Rev. James O'Kelly*; Morrill, *History of the Christian Denomination*; Williams et al., *Stone-Campbell Movement*, 9–29.
2. Marshall et al., *Apology of the Springfield Presbytery*, 9–10.
3. Stone, *Biography of Eld. Barton Warren Stone*; Conkin, *Cane Ridge*.
4. Stone, *Last Will and Testament*, 17–19.

Catholic-Protestant conflict instilled in the Campbells a longing for peace and unity among all followers of Christ.[5]

After repeated failures to bring unity among Irish Presbyterians, Thomas Campbell departed for America in 1807. The leaders of his group there, the Associate Synod of North America, appointed him to serve congregations in Western Pennsylvania. But when he allowed Presbyterians not members of the Synod to take communion, a series of trials led to his separation from the Associate Synod in 1809.[6]

Campbell and his supporters formed what they named the Christian Association to promote simple evangelical Christianity and Christian unity, the same cause Campbell had pursued in northern Ireland.[7] To explain the purpose of the new group, Campbell produced in 1809 the second founding document of the SCM, *The Declaration and Address of the Christian Association of Washington, PA*. In it he contended that all Christians

> should consider each other as the precious saints of God, should love each other as brethren, children of the same family and father, temples of the same spirit, members of the same body, subjects of the same grace, objects of the same divine love, bought with the same price, and joint heirs of the same inheritance. Whom God hath thus joined together no man should dare to put asunder.[8]

Campbell was clear that unity could not be founded on precise intellectual agreement on doctrinal propositions.

> Although inferences and deductions from scripture premises, when fairly inferred, may be truly called the doctrine of God's word, yet are they not formally binding on the consciences of Christians farther than they perceive the connection . . . for their faith must not stand in the wisdom of men, but in the power and veracity of God. Therefore no such deductions can be made terms of communion.[9]

The Christian Association soon became a local church, and its members began to call themselves simply "disciples of Christ." Like Stone's choice

---

5. Richardson, *Memoirs of Alexander Campbell*, 1:41–45.

6. Campbell, *Memoirs of Elder Thomas Campbell*, 10–18; McAllister, *Thomas Campbell*, 60–95.

7. See material on Campbell and the Evangelical Society of Ulster in Thompson, "Irish Background," 23; Lester, "Form and Function."

8. Campbell, *Declaration and Address*, 17.

9. Campbell, *Declaration and Address*.

of "Christian," this was an attempt to use a generic descriptor that would not separate them from other Christians.

Though Alexander Campbell eventually concluded at the birth of his first child that immersion of believers was proper NT baptism, he never believed that those baptized as infants who manifested, in his words, "the image of Christ" in their lives were not Christians.[10] Furthermore, the Campbells never intended to work in isolation from other Christians, applying first for membership in the PCUSA, and when rejected by that body, becoming part of the Redstone Baptist Association and other such bodies for over fifteen years.[11]

As the Campbells' positions diverged from traditional Baptist teachings on matters such as Calvinist anthropology, the function of baptism, and the power of associations, however, Baptist Associations began to condemn and expel the Campbell reformers in the 1830s.[12] At the same time the Campbell movement was becoming acquainted with the Stone churches, which often existed in the same areas. Though both groups were committed to the visible unity of Christians based on their understandings of the "simple" teachings of Scripture, there were significant differences between them.

Stone and his movement were not Trinitarian; the Campbells were. Stone's churches practiced immersion but did not make it a requirement for membership or for taking the Lord's Supper. The Campbell churches insisted on it for church membership. Stone did not believe that Christ's death was to appease God's offense at human sin, but was to demonstrate God's absolute love. The Campbells held a traditional substitutionary view of the Atonement. Stone insisted on the name "Christian" while Campbell preferred "disciples of Christ." The Stone movement had a high view of ordained ministry, while the Campbell churches were populist and anti-elitist. The differences were not trivial.[13]

Yet both movements were committed to fulfilling Christ's prayer for unity in John 17 and had articulated visions for unity in the *Last Will and Testament of Springfield Presbytery* and *The Declaration and Address* based on shared faith in, and salvation through, Christ. Local congregations began to unite first in Kentucky at the beginning of the 1830s.[14] With no central

---

10. See especially the "Lunenburg Letter" articles, beginning with Campbell, "Any Christians among Protestant Parties," 411–14.
11. Richardson, *Memoirs of Alexander Campbell*, 1:324–30, 436–41.
12. Richardson, *Memoirs of Alexander Campbell*, 2:322–24.
13. See discussion in Holloway and Foster, *Renewing God's People*, 53–61.
14. Williams, *Life of Elder John Smith*, 447–58.

organization, congregations simply decided to unite in their own towns and did so, though not all congregations chose to do so. Over the next decades the Stone-Campbell Movement would become one of the ten largest Christian bodies in the United States, with an estimated membership of two hundred thousand by 1860 and over one million by 1900.[15]

Stone-Campbell Ecclesiology— A Vision for Visible Unity

Stone and the Campbells set about to destroy the system of "denominationalism" which they saw as inherently divisive. Ideally each local church would be made up of all Christians in that location, and would fully recognize every other such church, which would make visible the essential unity of Christ's body. Alexander Campbell wrote in his theology *The Christian System* in 1839, "faith in Christ and obedience to him [is to be] the only test of Christian character, and the only bond of church union, communion, and cooperation."[16] Their goal was not to create another denomination or sect, but to end all denominations and sects that separated and put Christians at odds with one another.

The SCM certainly drew from its Presbyterian Puritan heritage with its call to restore the church to its pristine purity. Yet previous advocates of restoration had understood it as a call to separate true Christians and churches from the corrupt visible church.[17] SCM leaders, on the other hand, saw restoration of the "simple gospel" as the only means whereby all Christians could be united. The strategy was to call all Christians to come together in every locality, which would lead to the collapse of inherently divisive ecclesiastical structures, leaving only free congregations of Christians no longer divided by denominational creeds, structures and loyalties.[18]

The early SCM leaders also drew from their Enlightenment context in their belief in a universal reason that would produce unanimity in essentials. While individual judgment concerning the scriptures could never be considered authoritative, the judgment of the common mind could not be mistaken. In all matters where the universal reason did not agree,

---

15. Garrison and DeGroot, *Disciples of Christ*, 324–29; Department of Commerce and Labor, *Religious Bodies*, 148.

16. Campbell, *Christian System*, xi.

17. Restoration (as well as restitution and religious primitivism) signifies a return to a perceived pristine perfection of the early church. Various forms can be traced through Christian history. See especially DeGroot, *Restoration Principle*.

18. Osborn, *Experiment in Liberty*, 97.

it was obvious that one was dealing with non-essentials, and freedom was required.[19] Christians were already agreed on the basic essentials of Christianity, Thomas Campbell insisted in his *Declaration and Address*. The basis of fellowship was not agreement on a detailed inflexible system of doctrine and church practice, but on the saving essentials of the gospel. Requiring adherence to human speculation beyond what were the universally recognized biblical truths was, he believed, responsible for all disunity.[20]

Thomas Campbell insisted in the *Declaration and Address* that the platform for unity was the New Testament, which he viewed as the authoritative source of the facts of the gospel. Campbell's view of "clear New Testament doctrine" must be viewed in light of the notion of the common mind—what all reasonable people already held as true. Unity in the truth of scripture was seen as a positive good since no church, no Christian, would have to surrender adherence to biblical authority to achieve the goal of visible Christian unity. All were already agreed on the essentials. They now had only to agree not to allow the non-essentials to separate and divide them.[21]

The early leaders shared the millennial conviction that it was in the God-prepared land of America that this goal could finally be accomplished. Stone and his colleagues confidently exclaimed, "We heartily unite with our Christian brethren of every name, in thanksgiving to God for the display of his goodness in the glorious work he is carrying on in our Western country, which we hope will terminate in the universal spread of the gospel, and the unity of the church."[22] Urging fellow ministers to take on the pursuit of visible Christian unity, Thomas Campbell affirmed, "The favorable opportunity which Divine Providence has put into your hands, in this happy country, for the accomplishment of so great a good, is in itself, a consideration of no small encouragement."[23]

The Grounds for Unity

In 1823, Alexander Campbell began publishing the *Christian Baptist*, a monthly journal that profoundly shaped the early thought of the SCM. In April 1824, he published an article titled "The Foundation of Hope and of Christian Union." After a dismal description of the state of religion in pre-Christian times, which he implied reflected the situation of his own day,

---

19. See discussion in Bergeson, "Plea for Christian Unity," 231–32.
20. Campbell, *Declaration and Address*, 10.
21. Campbell, *Declaration and Address*, 35.
22. Stone, *Last Will and Testament*, 22.
23. Campbell, *Declaration and Address*, 30.

Campbell explained the conclusion to which he and his father had come. A Christian is one who believes one fact and submits to one institution, and whose actions are in harmony with the system of morality and virtue taught by Jesus. "The one fact is, that Jesus the Nazarene is the Messiah. The one institution is baptism [immersion] into the name of the Father, and of the Son and of the Holy Spirit. Every such person is a Christian in the fullest sense of the word, the moment he has believed this one fact, and has submitted to the above named institution." These elements Campbell regarded as the "Gospel Restored," and he saw them as the only proper basis for the union of all Christians.[24]

This basis for union, perceived by Alexander Campbell to be quite broad, had actually moved considerably from the original platform of his father. He now advocated not simply a stand on the core beliefs on which all Christians already agreed, but he now deemed as essential a practice (immersion) upon which they were in agreement only with the Baptists. He still insisted that "Christianity consists infinitely more in good works than in sound opinions."[25] Still, Campbell had proclaimed a doctrine and practice to be universally clear to all reasonable Christians that was not, and made it central to his program for unity.

In 1825, Campbell began a series of thirty-two articles titled "A Restoration of the Ancient Order of Things" in which he explored the marks of the church he believed would restore it to its intended purity and unity. Although the theme of Christian unity is often implicit in Campbell's denunciations of sectarianism and the quest for the ancient order of things, no articles specifically on Christian unity appear after 1825 to the end of the journal in 1830. It was the means of achieving union—the restoration of the primitive church—that received his attention.

In 1823, the other major leader of the early SCM, Walter Scott, was chosen to serve as a traveling evangelist by the Mahoning Baptist Association, to which the Campbells then belonged. His enthusiastic, tireless and simple preaching resulted in the first major influx of converts to the Campbell movement. Scott epitomized the tendency to distill and simplify the message of Christianity. He developed what came to be known as the "five-finger exercise" as a condensation of the gospel: faith, repentance, baptism, remission of sins and the gift of the Holy Spirit. This Scott called "the Gospel Restored."[26]

---

24. Campbell, "Foundation of Hope," 220.
25. Campbell, "Foundation of Hope," 223.
26. Toulouse, *Walter Scott*, 55.

The term "Ancient Order" came to be used for the conclusions reached by Alexander Campbell in his articles on polity, worship, discipline, etc., especially his "Restoration of the Ancient Order" series in his journal the *Christian Baptist*. Scott came to call this double form of ancient gospel and ancient order the "true gospel," and it was this true gospel, he insisted, that was the basis for the unity of Christians.[27]

For Scott, the immediate goal was the universal spread of the "true gospel" which would, in turn, result in Christian unity. Christian unity was not something that could be pursued directly. Therefore, attention had to be directed toward the universal diffusion and acceptance of the true gospel. "The advocates of the primitive religion may hope to see union when by the uncorrupted gospel they conquer all perverted gospels and those that preach them: but not till then."[28]

Beginning in January 1830 with the inauguration of his new journal, the *Millennial Harbinger*, Alexander Campbell articulated an optimistic postmillennial vision for his movement. The efforts he was making toward restoring the ancient gospel and order were toward the end of the unity of all Christians, which would lead to the conversion of the world, which would in turn usher in the millennium. Only the restored church, or, as he began to call it, the "Millennial Church," could produce the unity in both church and society that was necessary for the millennial age.[29]

Even Thomas Campbell, now overshadowed by his more aggressive son, began to place a greater emphasis on the doctrinal and practical means to unity rather than unity itself. At the end of an 1839 article, in which he described sixteen marks of the primitive apostolic church, he stated:

> We make this appeal to the understanding and practice of the primitive churches, not to authorize our faith and practice, but merely to show, that we understand the apostolic writings upon these subjects, just as they were understood from the beginning. And this we think all true Christian unionists are bound to do; because it is only upon the belief of the apostolic doctrine, that Christ has proposed and prayed for the unity of his people.[30]

Despite this clear emphasis, the *goal* of the restoration of apostolic doctrine was still the unity of Christians, and the unity of Christians was the only essential element to the conversion of the world. "Neither truth alone, nor union alone is sufficient to subdue the unbelieving nations: but truth

27. Scott, *Evangelist*, 90.
28. Scott, "Union," 141.
29. Osborn, *Experiment in Liberty*, 26–27.
30. Campbell, "Christian Union," 164.

and union combined are omnipotent," Alexander Campbell would insist.[31] He saw restoration and unity as complementary and indispensable to each other and to the fulfillment of the ultimate goals of global conversion and the introduction of the millennial age.

While Campbell maintained that immersion for the remission of sins was the only viable basis for union, he, perhaps inconsistently, always rejected the conclusion that only immersed persons were saved. From the beginning his assumption was that committed followers of Christ who had received baptism by some other mode were Christians, though perhaps imperfect ones. Such Christians were the very ones the movement called on to unite!

> I do not substitute obedience to one commandment, for universal or even for general obedience. And should I see a sectarian Baptist or a Pedobaptist more spiritually-minded, more generally conformed to the requisitions of the Messiah, than one who precisely acquiesces with me in the theory or practice of immersion as I teach, doubtless the former rather than the latter, would have my cordial approbation and love as a Christian.[32]

But some in the movement came to insist otherwise. The logic seemed inescapable: if immersion into Christ is the means by which people are saved and enter the church, then those who have not been immersed are not among the saved. This tension revealed the seeds of the "come-outer" impulse present in the very call to unity itself.

For Barton W. Stone, the norm of unity did not rest on a perceived core of universally accepted beliefs and practices. It was the possession of the Spirit of Jesus by each individual Christian that was the essential basis of unity for Stone.

> But should all the professors of Christianity reject their various creeds and names and agree to receive the Bible alone, and be called by no other name than Christian, will this unite them? No: we are fully convinced that unless they all possess the spirit of that book and name, they are far, very far from Christian union.[33]

> I blush for my fellows, who hold up the Bible as the bond of union yet make their opinions of it tests of fellowship; who plead for union of all Christians; yet refuse fellowship with

---

31. Campbell, *Christian System*, 86–87.
32. Campbell, "Any Christians Among Protestant Parties," 412.
33. Stone, "Christian Union," 37–38.

such as dissent from their notions. Vain men! Their zeal is not according to knowledge, nor is their spirit that of Christ. Such antisectarian-sectarians are doing more mischief to the cause, and advancement of truth, the unity of Christians, and the salvation of the world than all the skeptics in the world. In fact, they create skeptics.[34]

Stone, like Thomas Campbell, had no objections to the use of creeds or to holding "non-orthodox" opinions, as long as they were not made mandatory on all Christians. In fact, he believed that all Christians should be constantly advancing and changing in their views on Bible doctrines.[35] Christians who in the spirit of Christ give up their opinions "as bonds of fellowship" would end strife and division.[36]

It is important to note that Stone's vision of unity, like that of the Campbells, was based not on institutional union, but on individuals who renounced party loyalties and divisive creeds to flow together into local communities of Christ.

> We have long been convinced that the sects, as such, can never unite. Every attempt has proved abortive, and must and will fail, till each sect give up its creed as authoritative, its name of distinction, its spirit of party, and feel willing to decrease that Christ may increase.[37]

Similarly, Alexander Campbell compared a uniting of "the sects" to an armistice between warring nations. "Christian union is a more intimate, spiritual, celestial sort of thing, into which we can enter only in our individual capacity and upon our own individual responsibility."[38] In 1825 he exclaimed,

> I have no idea of seeing, nor one wish to see the sects unite in one grand army. This would be dangerous to our liberties and laws. For this the Saviour did not pray. It is only the disciples of Christ dispersed among them, that reason and benevolence would call out of them. Let them unite who love the Lord, and

---

34. Stone, "Remarks," 180. See also Stone, "Union of Christians," 334; "Convention," 195.
35. Stone, "Reply to the Above Letter," 20.
36. West, *Barton Warren Stone*, 9.
37. Stone and Johnson, "Editors' Address," 1.
38. Campbell, "Elder William F. Broddus," 265.

then we shall soon see the hierling [sic] priesthood and their worldly establishments prostrate in the dust.[39]

In summary, all the early SCM founders condemned the system of denominationalism as divisive, yet acknowledged the existence of Christians in all groups—in fact, the plea was for Christians in all the sects to come together. For Stone, the key was a restoration of the spirit of New Testament unity, a spirit that was characterized by love, trust, forbearance and conciliation. The Campbells and Scott advocated restoring what they saw as the precise biblical pattern as the basis of union, with Scott's ancient gospel and Alexander Campbell's ancient order of things the only platform on which Christian unity could be achieved.

All believed that the "recovery" of the "simple gospel" and pattern for the church found in the New Testament scriptures would result in the union of all true Christians. No matter how much Walter Scott or Alexander Campbell insisted on the restoration of the ancient gospel and ancient order, that restoration was not itself the ultimate goal. It was, rather, the means of achieving the unity of the church, which would lead to the conversion of the world, which would inaugurate the millennium.[40]

When viewed in this context, it is clear why the SCM saw its mission as one directed primarily at divided Christendom rather than the world. Mission work to the "heathen" was largely useless in their eyes until those who already claimed to be Christians were united. It was necessary to convince Christians in all the sects of the reasonableness of the platform of the ancient gospel and order. Since they believed the truth of those ideas was self-evident, all reasonable people would eventually see and unite on that truth.[41]

The SCM experienced great success with its plea, as mentioned earlier growing from around 22,000 members in 1832, to over 200,000 by 1860.[42] Ironically, during a time of explosive growth between the US Civil War

---

39. Campbell, "Restoration of the Ancient Order," 173. See also Campbell, "Christian Union," 234–39. Yet, contrary to that sentiment, in 1839, Campbell proposed a "congress" of all Protestant groups, along with the Greek and Roman Catholic parties, with appointed official delegates. Representatives would identify the things that were universally accepted by all parties that would become the basis of union. He prefaced the suggestion, however, insisting that the union of sects would not be the union of Christians, though an effort to unite them might tend toward the unity of Christians. Campbell, "Union of Christians," 212.

40. Osborn, *Experiment in Liberty*, 26–27.

41. See for example, Stone, "Friendly Hints," 281–87. "We by sending missionaries to the pagans, are transplanting our sectarianism, our anti-christianity, in heathen lands."

42. McAllister and Tucker, *Journey In Faith*, 188.

and the turn of the century, the SCM itself became increasingly polarized internally. The ideal of modeling to the Christian world how believers could be visibly united in the midst of significant diversity became increasingly threatened. By the beginning of the twentieth century, the efforts of the SCM to eradicate division among Christians had produced a bitter division in its own ranks and planted the seeds of a second. The come-outer impulse would largely win the day.

The Shift to a Come-Outer Tradition

One of the inherent difficulties in the SCM's unity program was its insistence that it did not constitute a denomination. The *Declaration and Address* called individuals out of the denominational churches and looked forward to the complete elimination of divisive ecclesiastical machinery. The resulting "group" would be simply the church of Christ manifested in local congregations in full fellowship with one another without any denominational qualification.[43]

No matter how much they resisted the idea that they were a denomination, however, the fact was that the SCM was a distinct group among religious groups. The stress between the theory and the reality took some strange turns in the middle and later decades of the nineteenth century. As a feeling of group consciousness and organization grew, some desired to adopt models of mission and ministry that reflected those of other denominational groups (although continuing to deny they were a denomination), while others took on hardened sectarian views, insisting that the SCM was identical with the saved.

An exchange in the 1870 *Millennial Harbinger* between two writers identified only as "L." and "J. L." illustrates the two poles. In a September article titled "A Plea for Union," L.wrote:

> I presume that we are all agreed that our church, or our people, are a part or portion of the "Church of Christ." I believe more than this that all other bodies of professing Christians, who accept Christ as the Saviour and Redeemer, are also parts and portions of the "Church of Christ." I am constrained to believe thus when I remember that "Christ's Church" has existed and been in full and active operation since the day of Pentecost, and consequently long before   our people were ever known or heard of... I fear we do not rejoice as much as we should when we hear of conversions to Christ in other denominations—and

---

43. Kershner, *Christian Union Overture*, 35–36.

yet we should do so, without one shade of envy or regret that they did not join our own body.[44]

The next month a sharp reply came from J. L.:

> If we as a body cannot prove our identity with the Christian church of apostolic days: if we originated long after this, as "L." charges; and if our conditions are not the law of the New (Christian) Institution delivered by the Holy Spirit through inspired men, then let us hasten to shuffle off the unchristian coil, immolate it on the funeral pyre, and having consumed the unholy form, let us henceforth seek a purer, a higher and a more Christ-like existence. But if we are ready at all times to repudiate all that is shown to be merely human, and to accept all that is Divine, then we are in no sense a denomination or sect—a division from nor in the Body of Christ—but the glorious body itself, ruled and directed by its Divine Head.[45]

J. L. represented a substantial group, but even those represented by L. insisted that they were trying to build a church on the New Testament pattern and continued to urge all other Christians to do the same, rather than to create a new denomination.

Another inherent matter of tension within the SCM was the fact that the plea was directed at individuals, placing the burden on each person to break his or her denominational ties and come to the movement. Coupled with the above attitude, this appeared to many to be proselytization of the worst sort; the goal seemed to be to "sell" the SCM as the best brand of Christianity on the market.[46]

A third revolves around the understanding of restoration. What was essential, and what had to be restored that had been lost or perverted? Leaders consistently extolled both American religious freedom and a firm commitment to private judgment. But despite the notion of the "common mind" being a control on radical individualism, the strong impression was that every individual could define the essentials. Each Christian possessed the ability and the responsibility to discern the truth for herself or himself, and if done rightly, all would arrive at "the truth." Functionally, if someone concluded that a doctrine or practice was a matter of divine directive given in scripture, and therefore an essential element of the restored true church,

---

44. L., "Plea for Union," 524, 526.
45. J. L., "Remarks on L.'s 'Plea,'" 569.
46. Yoder, "Christian Unity," 239; Osborn, *Experiment in Liberty*, 107.

then all must accept it. If others placed the item in the realm of non-essentials or "human opinion," they had to be corrected or repudiated.[47]

Division became increasingly evident between those in the movement who emphasized a strict core of doctrinal essentials as the basis of unity and those who minimized the number of essentials and emphasized a unity in Christian fellowship.[48] All the groups continued to advocate unity, but on diverging bases and with different understandings of the nature of unity.

Specific issues of conflict included the use of instrumental music in worship, the legitimacy of extra-congregational organizations like missionary societies, and the use of one person as the settled pastor for a church. All were partly generated by tensions between upwardly mobile and educated members who held optimistic notions of progress and institutional maturity, and those who held to stricter views of simplicity and purity. These presenting issues reflected a complex mesh of socio-economic and sectional factors connected to the American Civil War, rural-urban tensions, and increasingly divergent theological commitments.

More profound differences in three areas made these presenting issues divisive. The first had to do with different views of the Bible. Many, like the Campbells and Scott, viewed the Bible as essentially a book of facts. This emphasized human intellectual action—we gather, organize, and master the data of the Bible. Another approach, reflected by Barton Stone, saw scripture primarily as a place where God's Spirit works on the human heart. Instead of being in scripture primarily to master facts, Christians must immerse themselves in the Bible so that God's Spirit would master them.

A second matter focused on differences over the significance of the silence of scripture. Reflecting clashes seen, for example, between Luther and Zwingli during the Reformation, some regarded silence as freeing, others as restricting. Those who opposed the missionary society and instrumental music argued that they were not authorized in Scripture. Those who favored them insisted just as strongly that they were merely aids to obey the explicit commands spread the gospel and to worship God.

Finally was how people understood the nature of Christian unity. By the late 1800s, harsh condemnations had produced so much hurt and alienation that each side retreated to its own "corner." On both sides many came to believe that the only basis of unity was agreement on doctrines and practices. The early vision of union based on shared faith in and salvation by Christ and humble submission to Christ and to one another was too

---

47. Garrison, *Christian Unity*, 210.

48. Rouse, "Voluntary Movements," 324.

distant. Cruelty on both sides created a separation from which there was no return—at least not then.

The radical congregationalism of the SCM and the lack of official denominational structures meant that division had to make its way through each of thousands of individual congregations. During early organizational work for the religious census of 1906, newly appointed Census Director S. N. D. North wrote David Lipscomb, publisher of the Nashville, Tennessee based journal the *Gospel Advocate*, to determine whether or not the Churches of Christ were a distinct religious group. Data collected in previous population censuses had listed simply "Disciples of Christ" as the designator for the entire SCM. Articles received in North's office from various SCM journals indicated that there had been a division, but a list of preachers published by the *Gospel Advocate* overlapped with lists from Disciples publications. Lipscomb replied that the Churches of Christ were indeed different from all other religious groups in name, work and rule of faith, explaining their separation from the Disciples or Christian Churches in terms of the latter's adoption of "human inventions." The first "official" recognition of the division of the SCM was the separate listings for Disciples of Christ and Churches of Christ in the US Census of Religious Bodies of 1906.[49]

Each of the groups held its own view of Christian unity as the authentic one. The hoped-for "unity in diversity" had given way to separatist "come-outer" attitudes on all sides. On a hopeful note, over a century after the separate listings in 1906, many heirs of the "come-outer" impulse in the SCM are reexamining the events and ideas that separated them and finding new ways of reclaiming the vision of visible unity among themselves and with all who profess Christ.[50]

---

49. See Foster, "1906 Census of Religious Bodies," 83–93.

50. See, for example, the documents of the Stone-Campbell Dialogue, begun in 1999, which brings members of the North American streams together in worship and efforts to serve the world together in the name of Christ. See Christian Church (Disciples of Christ), "Stone Campbell Dialogue."

CHAPTER 5

"Without Spot or Wrinkle"

The Tendency toward Separation in the Mennonite Tradition
... and a Vision for a "Rhizomic" Church

JOHN D. ROTH

Introduction

EARLY IN JULY OF 2015, nearly 4,000 pastors, delegates and lay people gathered in Kansas City, Missouri for the biannual churchwide assembly of the Mennonite Church USA. The weeks leading up to the event were surrounded by a great deal of anxiety. Indeed, some people stayed away altogether, while others attended with a sense of foreboding and dread, knowing that the battle lines had been drawn. At issue, not surprisingly, was an ecclesial controversy over sexual identity and same-sex marriage—a debate that has been unfolding in one form or another in the Mennonite Church USA since the late 1980s.[1]

The complex history of that debate and even the details of what unfolded at the 2015 assembly go well beyond the scope of this essay. But the arguments swirling around the issue of same-sex marriage—and the unraveling of the Mennonite Church USA that occurred in the months following the assembly—are a reminder that the central theme of this Believers Church conference is not simply of historical interest: they are a living reality in the contemporary church as well. Indeed, the "tendency toward separation"

---

1. There is an extensive literature on this debate. For a summary, see Johns, "Homosexuality and the Mennonite Church"; Grimsrud, "Logic of the Mennonite Church," 10–23. For substantive contributions to the theological debate among Mennonites, cf. Mennonite Church, *Human Sexuality in the Christian Life*; Swartley, *Homosexuality*; Kraus, *To Continue the Dialogue*; Grimsrud and Nation, *Reasoning Together*.

is very much alive today among both progressive Mennonite activists and more conservative traditionalists.

Taking the current controversy over sexuality within Mennonite Church USA as its starting point, this essay reflects on the themes of "discipline, separation, and authority" as they have found expression within the Anabaptist-Mennonite context, particularly in the context of church division. Following a brief description of the sources of current division unfolding in the Mennonite Church USA, the essay reviews the deeper historical roots behind the impulse, deeply embedded in the DNA of groups in the Anabaptist-Mennonite tradition, to resolve conflicts by dividing. It then concludes with a vision for ecclesial solidarity within the global Anabaptist-Mennonite church that remains true both to Anabaptist theology and to the biblical imperative for unity within the Body of Christ.

Sources Behind the Current Division

One way of understanding the current debate in the Mennonite Church USA over same-sex marriage, of course, is to situate it within a larger social context—particularly, the so-called "culture wars" that have deeply divided the social fabric of the United States along divergent perspectives on the authority of science, tradition, scripture, and personal experience, particularly as these differences are expressed in understandings of rights, sexuality, family, and the state.[2] In a significant empirical study called *Disquiet in the Land: Cultural Conflict in American Mennonite Communities*, sociologist Fred Kniss explored the origins of more than 200 conflicts in the Mennonite Church between 1870 and 1985.[3] A key explanation for the four distinct waves of conflict that emerged in the church during this period, Kniss argues, is their clear correspondence to times of particular cultural tension within the nation as a whole. Even groups like the Mennonites and Amish, who consciously seek to "separate" themselves from the world, cannot escape the profound influence of the culture around them.[4]

But the current unraveling of the Mennonite Church USA reflects internal tensions that go even deeper than the cultural wars of the broader society. From the beginning of the movement in the sixteenth century,

---

2. The classic text is Hunter, *Culture Wars*. Hartmann, *War for the Soul of America*, offers a very useful history of the "culture wars," especially since the publication of Hunter's book.

3. Kniss, *Disquiet in the Land*.

4. For a fine summary of this deep tension in the Anabaptist-Mennonite tradition, see Kreider, "Mennonite Ethics," 465–92.

groups in the Anabaptist tradition have consistently struggled over competing understandings of church polity. Some streams within the tradition have strongly affirmed the authority of the congregation in matters of faith and practice; others have looked to a regional conferences as a primary locus of ecclesial identity. Those conferences were originally understood to be gatherings of ministers seeking to harmonize church order—a tradition that lives on among the "ministers' meetings" of the Old Order Amish and in some Mennonite settings that have retained the "bishop board." Today, however, conferences generally function as representative bodies made up of delegates from individual congregations; and their primary authority resides in their oversight of pastoral credentials.[5] Along the way, Mennonite denominations in North America have emerged as "covenants" of these regional conferences.

Making matters more complicated during the second half of the twentieth century was the emergence of several powerful church-wide institutions—focused on such things as mutual aid, missions, education, health, service, publications—which often acted in the name of the denomination, though they were not directly controlled by denominational leaders. These church-wide agencies came to assume an informal authority that tended to eclipse the relevance of both the conferences and the denomination itself. In recent years, however, this concentration of authority in church-related institutions has been steadily eroding, with the reassertion of a much deeper bias in the Anabaptist-Mennonite tradition toward congregationalism. Current debates over same-sex marriage have been intensified by these competing understandings of the locus of authority.

Another long-standing debate within the Anabaptist-Mennonite tradition has focused on differing understandings regarding the place of confessional statements. Mennonites often like to claim that their identity is rooted more in "ortho-*praxis*" than in "ortho-doxy"—that is, in shared understandings of ethical behavior (or *Ordnung*, or church disciplines) rather than in doctrinal uniformity or shared statements of belief. There is an element of truth to this. In reality, however, confessions of faith have always been an important part of Mennonite identity.[6] The most recent confessional statement among North American Mennonites—"A Confession of Faith in a Mennonite Perspective"—was formally approved in 1995 by the two largest Mennonite bodies in the US and Canada in the hopes that it

---

5. Cf. Mennonite Church, *Shared Understanding of Church Leadership*.

6. Dutch Anabaptists formulated a long series of confessions of faith in the seventeenth and eighteenth centuries in an effort to bring about great unity among their fragmented groups, and the descendants of this tradition—Prussian, Polish, and Russian Mennonites—also have a rich confessional tradition.

could serve as a catalyst for church unity and the foundation for organizational integration. The 1995 Confession emerged out of a decade-long, collaborative process that included a series of public theological conferences and listening sessions, followed by numerous drafts and revisions that responded to written reactions from congregations and conferences. The statement that eventually emerged is relatively short, consisting of 24 articles, whose language draws heavily on biblical texts.[7]

Although both groups formally adopted the Confession, a significant debate unfolded almost immediately about its authority—particularly in regard to Article 19, which defined Christian marriage to be "between one man and one woman." In 1999 the General Conference Mennonite Church, the more progressive (or, depending on one's perspective, the more acculturated) of the two Mennonite groups, affirmed the merger. The General Conference church had a long tradition of a congregationalist polity, and a relatively low view of the authority of confessional statements. However, representatives of the larger group—the so-called (Old) Mennonite Church—did not affirm the merger. A significant source of concern focused on the lack of clarity regarding the authority of the 1995 confession within the new denomination, particularly on questions surrounding sexuality and marriage.

In 2002, the merger finally went forward; but only after a joint delegate body approved a new set of "membership guidelines." Those guidelines, citing Article 19 in the "Confession of Faith in a Mennonite Perspective," clarified that pastors in the newly-created Mennonite Church USA would not be permitted to officiate at same-sex weddings and they affirmed the statement "homosexual genital activity is sin" as the "teaching position" of the new denomination. Not surprisingly, however, neither the 1995 Confession of Faith nor the membership guidelines resolved the differences, not least because both groups had also issued resolutions calling their members to "ongoing dialogue" on the questions of sexuality and marriage.

In the years that followed, various individuals—appealing to these calls for "ongoing dialogue"—pressed the issue within congregations; and congregations, in turn, called for formal discussions within their conferences. At the same time, an increasingly vocal and visible group ("Pink Menno") advocated for changes at the denominational level. When traditionalist voices pressed back, and advocates on both sides began to weigh in on social media, fissures within the church deepened. Even as several conferences disciplined congregations and revoked pastoral credentials for

---

7. For a summary of the confession's origins, and its contested authority, see Susan Biesecker-Mast, "Genealogy of the *Confession of Faith*," 371–98. The entire October 2007 issue of *MQR* was devoted to the confession and its reception.

leaders who expressed public support for same-sex marriage, a significant number of conservative congregations, frustrated by the perceived lack of clarity among denominational leaders and church institutions, preemptively left their conferences . . . and sometimes the Anabaptist-Mennonite tradition altogether.[8]

Matters came to a head in the fall of 2014 when the Mountain States Conference—one of the twenty regional conferences that then constituted Mennonite Church USA—took a formal position that it would *not* revoke the credentials of a pastor who was in a committed same-sex relationship. Nor would it take action against pastors who, with the support of their local congregation, officiated at same-sex marriages.

In the spring of 2015, with the denominational assembly approaching, the urgency of the debate shifted from the conference to the denominational level: should the denomination, acting in the name of the other nineteen conferences, discipline or expel the Mountain States Conference, thereby honoring the covenant member conferences had made to uphold the authority of the *Confession of Faith* in its definition of marriage (Article 19)? Or would the denomination allow conferences greater freedom in these decisions, consistent with a polity that had always viewed the ordination and credentialing of pastors to be a prerogative of the conference?

In the end, the decisions of the delegate body, endorsed by denominational leadership, left all sides unsatisfied. On the one hand, 71 percent of the assembly voted in favor of a resolution on "forbearance" that explicitly acknowledged the lack of consensus within the church and called on members "to offer grace, love and forbearance towards conferences, congregations and pastors in our body who, in different ways, seek to be faithful to our Lord Jesus Christ on matters relating to same-sex covenanted unions."[9]

The same day, however, the same delegate body reaffirmed by a 60 percent majority the more restrictive membership guidelines that had been a condition of the merger in 2002. According to the second resolution, "the delegate assembly will not entertain changes to the membership guidelines

---

8. In addition to the questions of polity and confessional authority often cited by these congregations were a host of other differences regarding biblical hermeneutics and genuine unclarity about denominational policies: what exactly, for example, was implied by the "teaching position" of the church? Why was the focus of church discipline and the authority of the *Confession of Faith* applied only to questions of sexuality and not, for example, to church members who violated the church's "teaching position" by serving in the Armed Forces? What did it mean for a conference to discipline an entire congregation (as opposed to an individual pastor)?

9. For the text of the resolution, see Mennonite Church USA, "Forbearance."

for the next four years, in order to exercise forbearance on matters that divide us and to focus attention on the missional vision that unites us."[10]

Since then, the upheaval has only accelerated. During the past year, three regional conferences and numerous individual congregations—more than 600 congregations altogether—have formally left MCUSA, with others either contemplating a departure or actively seeking new forms of relating to the denomination. Where all these ecclesial refugees will ultimately land is far less clear, though a new body has since emerged—EVANA (Evangelical Anabaptism)—which may absorb at least some of them.[11]

This account of the divisions currently besetting the Mennonite Church USA is not unusual within the broader history of the Anabaptist-Mennonite tradition. "[The Anabaptists] have divided themselves over so many different things," wrote the German spiritualist Sebastian Franck in his *Chronica* of 1531, "that they now have almost as many teachings as they have leaders."[12] The same year, Heinrich Bullinger, Zwingli's successor in Zurich, denounced them in similar language. "[The Anabaptists] are divided into numerous sects," he wrote, "and each bans and denounces the other as if they were the devil."[13] Franck and Hubmaier were undoubtedly exaggerating; but their description of the Anabaptist movement as a confusing welter of competing groups was not entirely a figment of the polemicist's imagination.

Though scholars have not always agreed on the taxonomy, today there are no fewer than eleven Amish groups, ten Brethren groups, four Hutterite groups, fifty-three Mennonite groups, some seventy-nine regional conferences and at least 247 smaller independent congregations or alliances for a total of at least 409 discrete bodies in the US alone.[14] At the micro-level, the story gets even more complicated. The proliferation of alliances, fellowships, brotherhoods and independent congregations among Beachy Amish and Amish Mennonite groups, for example, defies all efforts at categorization.[15]

---

10. For the text of the resolution, see Mennonite Church USA, "On the Status." According to Ervin Stutzman, executive director of Mennonite Church USA, the Executive Board regarded the decisions "as a mandate to hold together the traditional stance of our church with an approach that grants freedom to congregations and area conferences to work things out in their own context" (Mennonite Church USA, "Frequently Asked Questions").

11. See Evana Network, "Home."

12. Franck, *Chronica, Zeitbuch vund Geschichsbibell*, 193b.

13. Bullinger, *Von dem unverschampten fräfel*, 1:viii.

14. See Kraybill, *Concise Encyclopedia*; Kraybill and Hostetter, *Anabaptist World USA*.

15. See Anderson, "Retracing the Blurred Boundaries," 361–412.

And a recent history of Old Order and Mennonite groups in Holmes County, Ohio enumerated more than thirty, mostly non-communing, Anabaptist-related groups in that settlement alone—making it a veritable game park of rare and exotic species that results from what Freud called "the narcissism of minor differences."[16]

Sources of Division within the Anabaptist-Mennonite Tradition

What accounts for this powerful tendency to division in the Anabaptist-Mennonite tradition? At least part of the answer is rooted in the very DNA of Anabaptist beginnings. Like all children of the Reformation, the Anabaptist movement was itself born of a division. Inspired by Luther's challenge to papal hierarchy, his rejection of tradition, and by his explosive appeal to *sola Scriptura*, the early Anabaptists—like all the reformers—came into being by rejecting traditional forms of authority.

But once the initial break with the church was formalized in the baptisms of 21 January 1525, they—like all the reformers—immediately faced a dilemma of their own creation: having broken free from the authority of Rome, how does one then put on the brakes of schism and relegitimate principles of authority and standards of church unity within one's own circle? The inability of Protestants to resolve this question is largely responsible for the estimated 15,000 different denominations in North America today (43,000 globally);[17] and it clearly has been part of the on-going struggle for identity within the Anabaptist-Mennonite tradition as well.

The challenge of church unity was compounded for Anabaptists, however, since they generally rejected strategies for church unity that other Protestant groups quickly developed in an attempt to put the lid back on the Pandora's box of ecclesial authority. Already in the 1520s, for example, Zwingli developed the *Prophezei*—a kind of seminary for the training of evangelical pastors to rein in the chaos inspired by the Anabaptist appeal to the "priesthood of all believers." By 1530, the Lutherans had agreed on the Augsburg Confession (and later, the Formula of Concord), which continues to serve as the theological foundation of Lutheran identity today. The Church of England retained the hierarchical authority of the episcopacy, grounded in a theory of Apostolic Succession. Calvin's *Institutes* became the anchor of a rigorously systematic approach to theology that has kept

---

16. Beachy, *Unser Leit*.

17. These estimates come from the Center for the Study of Global Christianity at Gordon-Conwell Theological Seminary, "Status of Global Mission, 2014."

Reformed groups in conversation with each other through the centuries. And when push came to shove, all of these children of the Reformation were willing to fall back on the authority of the state to enforce orthodoxy by means of the coercive power of the state if necessary. None of these "solutions" appealed to Anabaptist groups—for reasons they regarded as theologically sound. But the result was a much more complex, far less linear, understanding of church unity.

Several distinctive theological convictions have further complicated Anabaptist commitments to Christian unity. Through the centuries, most Anabaptists groups have insisted that the inner, personal experience of God's grace must be made visible in daily life. Ethical behavior, Mennonites have often argued—how one lives; what one does; what one says—is an inevitable, necessary expression of the gift of God's grace.

Moreover, Christians in the Anabaptist tradition are called not merely to be good people (honest, law abiding-citizens, for example); instead, they are called to be *transformed* people—part of a "new creation" in Christ who walk in the power of the resurrected Lord. And the standard for Christian discipleship is very high—nothing less than the life of Jesus himself!

Finally, when Mennonites talk about the "church," what they usually have in mind is a concrete, visible gathering of people—"set apart" by the voluntary commitment of each believer in the public act of baptism; united in a collective—not just individual—witness to the world; and accountable to each other for their actions. Thus, when Mennonites have conflicts they are not at liberty to shrug their shoulders and declare that "what you do is none of my business"—tempting though that response may be.

Mennonites have understood all of these convictions—a faith that is made visible in deed, modeled after the high calling of Jesus, and evident in the shared practices of the church—to be consistent with scripture and the witness of the apostolic church. But these same convictions have also been a source of persistent conflict in our tradition. After all, people of good will are inclined to interpret the ethical practices arising from the Gospel in different ways; the cultural context is constantly changing; and, not least, the church is always a clay vessel made up of imperfect people.

At its best, the Anabaptist-Mennonite tradition has struggled mightily with a kind of paradox. Precisely because the church is a visible witness to the world, we have insisted on the importance of holy living and unity within the body—hence the emphasis on the disciplined community. Yet the very depth of that commitment to Christ's pastoral prayer in John 17 for the visible unity of the church has led to a tangled history of conflicts and church divisions over the specific nature of that witness—groups in the

Anabaptist tradition have maintained the unity (or "purity") of the church by dividing.

At its worst, however, the propensity of groups in the Anabaptist-Mennonite tradition to divide is an expression of human sin that makes an idol out of the enculturated forms that particular groups have given to the body of Christ. If a gift of Anabaptist-Mennonites to the broader Christian tradition has been a strong emphasis on "the Word made flesh," their sin has been a stubborn tendency to reify particular incarnations of the faith in ways that result in worshipping the churches they have created, rather than the Creator. Like Cain, Mennonites bring their gifts to the altar; but instead of focusing on worship and the abundance of God's blessing, they anxiously compare their gifts with others and assert an identity of difference—the unique superiority of their own gift.

Such an identity, however, rooted in difference and separation is inherently unstable. And it will never find resolution since the enemy of "Otherness" always continues to rear its ugly face. The story is sometimes told of two Mennonites who survived a shipwreck on an isolated island in the middle of the ocean. When, at last, they were discovered it turned out that the two Mennonites had built three churches. Asked why, they answered: one attends the first church; the other attends the second church. Why then the third church? That's the church that neither of us attends.[18]

The reflexive alternative—a theme that also runs deep in the Anabaptist-Mennonite tradition—is a move toward Spiritualism or, ultimately, an affirmation of the invisible church. In 1660, to cite only one of many possible examples, the Mennonite church in the Netherlands became deeply divided when several young leaders in Amsterdam denied that any church could claim to be the "true" church of God. No one's conscience, they insisted, could be bound by the authority of those holding a church office—who were fallible human beings—or by doctrines formulated by humans, or by ordinances, which are always administered by humans.[19] The unity of the church could only be understood mystically as a unity of the Spirit. Their argument eventually prevailed. Thus, in 1811, when all of the various branches of the Dutch Mennonite church were formally united into one body, the basis of the union was a general appeal to the unity of the spirit and the explicit assurance that "every congregation kept its freedom to make

---

18. This same story is recounted in many other traditions as well—the impulse to divide is not unique among Anabaptists!

19. For a full recounting of the events, see Cate, *Geschiedenis der Doopsgezinden*. Unfortunately, the full details of this story are scarcely known to an English-speaking audience. The most accessible account is in Meihuizen, "Spiritualistic Tendencies and Movements," 288–91.

such decisions about doctrine as it wished, without the right to bind others to their convictions."[20] In the end, however, that same Spiritualist principle also prevailed within congregations—today the primary requirement of membership in the Dutch Doopsgezind church is that each individual compose a personal confession of faith.

Thus far I have tried to give a very general overview of the "tendency toward separation" within the Anabaptist-Mennonite tradition, beginning with the story of a current division and then situating that debate within a deeper historical, theological and ecclesiological context. In the second, more constructive, half of the essay I want to shift my focus from Europe and North America to the global church, highlighting a profound demographic transformation that has re-oriented the center of gravity of the contemporary Anabaptist-Mennonite fellowship to Asia, Africa and Latin America—the so-called "global south." The new, genuinely multicultural, character of the church, I argue, creates the possibility for a new vision of church unity, one that both honors the theological insights of the Anabaptist tradition while moving in the direction of increased solidarity and interdependence among our various bodies.

Unity in the Global Anabaptist-Mennonite Church?

From the perspective of a 500-year-old tradition, the Anabaptist-Mennonite fellowship today is currently in the midst of a profound demographic and ecclesial transformation. Forty years ago, in 1978, there were approximately 600,000 Anabaptist-Mennonites in the world—with the clear majority in Europe and North America.[21] Today, some four decades later, the church's membership has nearly quadrupled and its center of gravity has shifted decisively from North to South—a transformation that scholars like Philip Jenkins, Lamin Sanneh, and Mark Noll have insightfully documented for the larger Christian church.[22]

In 2015, the Mennonite World Conference identified 2.1 million baptized Anabaptists in 227 organized bodies, living in more than eighty different countries.[23] Of that number, approximately 500,000 (or 25 percent) are members of plain groups such as the Amish, Old Order Mennonites, or Old

---

20. Quoted in Meihuizen, "Spiritualistic Tendencies and Movements," 303.

21. See Shenk, "Mission and Service," 7–22, 10.

22. The literature on global Christianity is vast and growing rapidly. For a basic introduction see Jenkins, *Next Christendom*; Sanneh, *Encountering The West*; Noll, *New Shape of World Christianity*.

23. Cf. Mennonite World Conference, "World Directory."

Colony Mennonites. Diverse groups of Mennonites in Europe and North America account for another 250,000 or so. But the remainder—some 1.4 million; roughly 66 percent of the total—are church members in Asia, Africa and Latin America who represent the new face of the Anabaptist-Mennonite movement. In 2002, the Meserte Kristos church of Ethiopia surpassed the number of Mennonites in the US to become the largest Anabaptist-Mennonite national group—numbering some 375,000 baptized members—with Anabaptist groups in the Congo not far behind. Currently, the Mennonite Church USA, Mennonite Church Canada, and their Mennonite Brethren counterparts—groups who have long pictured themselves as the organizational, financial and intellectual centers of the Anabaptist tradition—constitute barely 7 percent of the global Anabaptist fellowship.

At some level, Mennonites in North America are aware of all this. At a time when church membership in North America is stagnant or declining, Mennonites are pleased to learn that "our numbers are growing" internationally. We hear these statistics; church papers are filled with stories about Mennonites in places like Congo, Zimbabwe, India, or Colombia; we increasingly recognize that the "real action"—especially in terms of spiritual vitality, numerical growth and renewal—is taking place in settings far from North America. Yet at the same time, many Mennonites in North America are genuinely bewildered about what this transformation means. What is the glue that holds this global Anabaptist fellowship together? When a new church emerges in Ghana or Chile that calls itself "Mennonite," what exactly do they mean by that term? Is it related in any way to what North American congregations understand when they use the word "Mennonite"? What, we ask, are the crucial markers that offer assurance that we are indeed part of the same family of faith? How do the bonds of trans-national ecclesial unity find expression? Lurking somewhere behind these questions are deeper concerns about marketing and identity—a desire to preserve the brand name of the franchise, and perhaps also an unspoken uneasiness about their own qualifications as heirs of the Anabaptist tradition.

No image for describing ecclesial relationships is perfect. The apostle Paul, of course, uses the metaphor of the body, highlighting on the mutual importance and interdependency of each specific part (1 Cor 12). Yet a body is not a body just because there are hands and feet, ears and eyes. It becomes a living body only if there is a constant vital flow of blood and neural impulses keeping all of these parts in a vital relationship with each other.

An alternative image to consider—one that might preserve certain crucial elements of an Anabaptist-Mennonite ecclesiology—is the biological metaphor of a *rhizome*. Rhizomes are plants that propagate by sending out a profusion of roots laterally, parallel to the soil above. At various points, the interconnected roots of a rhizome develop nodes that send sprouts up above the ground in unpredictable places. From the surface it appears as if these sprouts are quite distinct entities. But underneath the soil, they are all joined together in a complex and interconnected web of horizontal relationships.

Rhubarb, lilies, and bamboo are all rhizomes, as are aspen trees. Indeed, the Pando colony of aspens in Utah consists of nearly 50,000 trees extending over 105 acres; yet beneath the soil the colony is a single living organism. In fact, scientists have determined that damage done to trees in one part of the grove is "sensed" by other trees at a far distance.[24] One particular rhizome, the hosta, can even develop spontaneous mutations, called "sports," which appear on the surface as significant differences in color patterns; beneath the surface, however, the plants continue to share the same subterranean root structure. The result is a visible variety within the same living organism.

"A rhizome," writes the social philosopher Gilles Deleuze, "has no beginning or end. . . . It is always in the middle, between things. Rhizomes are always in relationships of mutual connectivity and in alliances with multiple entry and exit points."[25] The image suggests that the ecclesial identity of the Anabaptist-Mennonite fellowship might understood as a complex and unpredictable constellation of intertwining, unpredictable, and non-hierarchical relationships, many of them happening in settings outside of academic halls or church buildings—a vast inter-connected web of relationships whose character, like that of the Holy Spirit itself, is always exceeds our capacity to define, or grasp, or pin down.

To be sure, the metaphor has limitations. But imagining the church in such a way might encourage us in times of stress to resist the impulse to reassert hierarchies and external forms of ecclesial order, and to focus instead on the deeper, sometimes hidden, web of living relationships that connect us.

What does a "rhizomic" church actually look like? What mean for a congregationally-oriented tradition to embrace a commitment to promote rhizome growth? What sort of transformation of mind and heart—what kind of renewal—might such a vision require of those 7 percent of Mennonites in North America who are used to thinking of ourselves as being at the center of the church, rather than the periphery?

24. Grant, "Trembling Giant."
25. Deleuze and Guattari, "Rhizome," 7.

A Rhizomic Future?

The answer to those questions will undoubtedly take a variety of forms. One "rhizomic" expression of church unity in a global context can be seen in the work of Mennonite World Conference (MWC), whose self-understanding might be instructive for other groups—including the Mennonite Church USA—who are seeking to move beyond the logjam of internal divisions.

Mennonite World Conference traces its beginnings to 1925 when leaders from a diverse group of Mennonite churches in Europe gathered in Basel, Switzerland, not to promote unity in some abstract sense (indeed, leaders were assured that communion would *not* be celebrated!), but in a common effect to direct relief supplies Mennonites in South Russia suffering from famine and anarchy in the years following the Bolshevik Revolution. Those early efforts toward unity were profoundly disrupted by the events of World War II in which French, German, Russia, and Dutch Mennonite fought as combatants on both sides of that destructive war. But in 1948 MWC re-emerged as a crucial framework for mutual confession and reconciliation, with a strong emphasis on gathering every six years for a global assembly focused on singing, worship, and cross-cultural sharing.[26]

In recent years, however, MWC has become a significant symbol of ecclesial unity within the global Anabaptist-Mennonite community, not as "program-driven" institution, but as an organization committed to promoting "rhizome growth" among its 102 members in fifty-four countries. In contrast to many parallel organizations in other Christian communions, MWC's administrative footprint has remained very small—its central office, home to a staff of approximately five people, is located on the second floor of a non-descript building in the outskirts of Bogotá, Colombia. Instead, its primary emphasis has been on strengthening the relationships between and among its member groups, with particular attention to the global South. Those relationships have taken a wide variety of expressions:

1. Three of the last four global assemblies have taken place in the global south (Calcutta, Bulawayo, and Asuncíon), with local groups bearing the primary responsibility—often in the face of profound logistical challenges—of housing, feeding and creating a worship space for thousands of international guests.

2. The process leading up to the "Seven Shared Convictions" a statement of faith embraced by MWC member groups in 2006, was slow and arduous, shaped by input from numerous Anabaptist-Mennonite

---

26. See Lapp and Straten, "Mennonite World Conference 1925–2000," 8–45.

church conferences from around the world as well as by the insights of academically-trained theologians.[27]

3. For more than ten years, the Young Anabaptist Mennonite Exchange Network (YAMEN) has connected dozens of Asian, African, and Latin American young people with service assignments elsewhere in the global South, nurturing deep relationships among individuals, congregations and conferences from widely different cultural contexts.

4. The five-volume Global Mennonite History Series took nearly fifteen years to complete, largely because the project insisted on using local writers, many of them drawing on oral as well as written sources, who wrote in their own languages.[28] The narratives that emerge in the Global Mennonite History volumes are indigenous accounts, in which North American and European missionaries play relatively minor roles.

5. Virtually all of the publications in the Global Anabaptist-Mennonite Shelf of Literature—an effort to foster shared theological conversations through a series of books on specific themes, translated into multiple languages—are collaborative projects, linking authors from the global North and South.[29]

6. Music has long been a source of particular identity that can also be shared with others. Each of the recent MWC global assemblies has include significant blocks of time for singing together, learning the rhythms and harmonies of other people and cultures. The impact of the multi-lingual songbooks broadens as assembly participants introduce these new hymns in their home settings. Recently, while worshipping with a Mennonite congregation in South Korea, I joined in singing a Spanish song that I had first learned at the 2015 global assembly a year earlier.

7. Despite skepticism from some of member churches, MWC's active engagement in ecumenical conversations has reminded all it members

---

27. For the full text, see Mennonite World Conference, "Shared Convictions."

28. The Global Mennonite History Series consists of five volumes of history, one from each continental region. Writers from each region trace the origins, development and mission of the Anabaptist-related churches there, reflecting the experiences, understandings and perspectives of these churches. See Mennonite World Conference, "Global Mennonite History Series."

29. A great example of this sort of collaboration is Tshmika and Lind, *Sharing Gifts*. For more information on the seven volumes that have appeared thus far in the Shelflist (and the translations), see Mennonite World Conference, "Global Anabaptist Mennonite Shelf."

that the Anabaptist-Mennonite tradition represents only one small corner of God's kingdom. The possibility of deepening relationships with other groups in MWC is enhanced to the extent that we come to recognize the Spirit of Christ in the gifts of other Christian churches and learn to receive those gifts as a source of renewal.[30]

8. In a similar way, MWC has explicitly framed Renewal 2027—a ten-year series of events commemorating the 500th anniversary of Anabaptist beginnings—with a view toward ecumenical relationships. The annual events, which will rotate in two cycles within all five MWC regions, not only celebrate the shared identity associated with the Radical Reformation of the sixteenth century, but also the remarkable ways in which the Anabaptist movement has been enculturated today in settings far beyond Europe.[31]

9. The Global Anabaptist Profile, is the first systematic survey of demographics, beliefs and practices in the global Anabaptist-Mennonite church.[32] Launched in 2012, the survey—organized loosely around the MWC "Shared Convictions"—included twenty-four groups in eighteen countries and was translated into twenty-six languages. In July of 2015, leaders and research associates from the participating groups met for an intense four-day conversation about the results, comparing and contrasting the outcomes in light of their own particular cultural contexts and theological traditions. The final report will be published in early 2017.

10. The "Global Anabaptist Wiki," an open-access, on-line archive and repository of history and theological sources, embodies the rhizomic metaphor.[33] In contrast to encyclopedias, which rely on the wisdom of individual experts, the wiki model elicits information from the grassroots. Currently, the Global Anabaptist Wiki hosts an "Anabaptist Dictionary of the Bible," a major collection of resources that have emerged from ecumenical dialogues, a digital library of Spanish-language theological texts to support on-line classes, and rudimentary information

---

30. For a summary of the interchurch dialogues MWC has engaged in, along with the documents that have resulted from these encounters, see Mennonite World Conference, "Interchurch Dialogue."

31. For more information on Renewal 2027, see Mennonite World Conference, "Renewal 2027."

32. For more information on the project, see Goshen College, "Global Anabaptist Profile."

33. See Mennonite Historical Library, "Global Anabaptist Wiki."

on more 200 groups in the global Anabaptist-Mennonite church. Additional material appears on the site virtually every day.

11. In a related vein, the "Bearing Witness Stories Project," enables Anabaptist communities worldwide to share their stories of costly discipleship in ways that inspire greater faithfulness to Jesus Christ and strengthen the church's unity. The *Martyrs Mirror*—a massive martyrology of sixteenth-century Anabaptists that begins with Christ and moves through the history of faithful dissenters the Christian church—has been a formative text for European and North American. Yet the last edition of the *Martyrs Mirror* was in 1685. In the spirit of the *Martyrs Mirror*, the "Bearing Witness Stories Project" is actively gathering the stories of contemporary brothers and sisters in the Ukraine, Nigeria, Indonesia, Colombia, the Philippines who are living witnesses to that same narrative.[34]

In all these, and many other, ways, threads of relationships are reinforced and woven together across the distance of culture, history, and geography.

To be sure, the challenges of a "rhizomic" understanding of church unity are numerous. The exact number and character of these interconnected relationships is hard to quantify or assess; organizational flowcharts are messy and imprecise; beliefs and practices in the global Anabaptist-Mennonite have resisted reduction to a single confessional statement; and no central body claims ultimate authority in adjudicating questions of orthodoxy or heterodoxy. Nevertheless, in these many small points of connection, the presence of the living Christ is made real—often in surprising and unexpected ways.

Conclusion: Radical Patience

In a recent book, *The Patient Ferment of the Early Church*, Alan Kreider, a Mennonite missiologist and historian of the early church, argues that a crucial element of church growth in the first centuries—and, indeed, an

---

34. Indeed, leaders in the fastest growing churches in the Global South frequently identify precisely the criteria van Braght used for the *Martyrs Mirror* as the sources of their growth—namely, a voluntary church committed to daily discipleship, mutual aid, and a defenseless love for all people, including those who might be considered enemies. For more on the project, see Stories Project, "Bearing Witness." Recently, the project produced its first book: Moore and Keiderling, *Bearing Witness*. For more on the challenges and complexity of nurturing martyr memory in a context of both ecumenism and religious-inspired violence, see Roth, "Complex Legacy," 277–316.

essential quality of the early church's very identity—was the virtue of *patience*. It was not treatises on evangelism or a strategy for missions that enabled the church to thrive in the face of so many obstacles in the first three centuries. Rather, writes Kreider, "Christians believed that God is patient and that Jesus visibly embodied patience. And they concluded that they, trusting in God, should be patient—not controlling events, not anxious or in a hurry, and never using force to achieve their ends."[35]

A rhizomic church is a patient church. Because the unity we seek is ultimately anchored in real congregations and the embodied, concrete practices of worship and discipleship, the journey toward unity will inevitably be haphazard, nonlinear, and unpredictable. And it likely take a very long time—perhaps longer than most people in positions of leadership are willing to countenance.

Radical patience will resist declaring consensus in the form of documents and organizational flowcharts without being attentive to the long slow work of the Spirit in tending to the health of relationships. Radical Patience calls us to take a first, vulnerable step in the direction of the "opposition," without defining the outcome in advance and in the knowledge that the actions taken now may not bear fruit for several generations.

In the end, it is God who transforms hearts, God who is working His purposes out in history, and God who will establish the unity of the church, in God's own time. May it be so!

---

35. Kreider, *Patient Ferment*, 2.

Part II: The Principle Applied and Expanded

Chapter 6

"Holy Living and Holy Dying"

The Response of Some British Baptist Women
to "Come Out" from the World

Karen Smith

Although the story of their lives has not always made it into the annals of history, women have always been at the heart of Baptist life in Britain. Women were among the Separatists who left England and went to Holland in 1608 searching for religious freedom. Three years later in 1611, women numbered among the believers in Amsterdam who stated that "the church off Christ is a company off faithful people separated from the world by the word and Spirit off God."[1] Moreover, women featured among those who having declared their desire to "come out" from the world, returned from Holland to England and established a General Baptist Church (as it became known because of a belief in general atonement) on English soil at Spitalfields in London in 1612. Likewise, women were part of another group of Baptists in Britain who also grew out of Separatism, but were Calvinistic in theology, and emerged in England in the 1630s.

From their separate, but identifiable Puritan-Separatist roots, both General and Calvinistic (later Particular) Baptist congregations grew and eventually expressed their theological views in confessions of faith. The General Baptists published the *Orthodox Creed* in 1679 and Calvinistic Baptists published the *London Confession* in 1644, which was followed by the *Second London Confession* (1677/1689). Although only men signed these published confessional statements, and later men would primarily serve in leadership in the public sphere, women played a prominent role in early

---

1. "Declaration of Faith," 119.

Baptist life, though usually in ways that were considered culturally and socially acceptable.

There were, of course, women who seem to have assumed teaching roles in the church. In his vitriolic attack against Dissenters, entitled, *Gangraena* (1646), Thomas Edwards, claimed that Baptists were among those spreading "confusion and disorder in Church-matters both of opinions and practices."[2] He claimed: "swarmes are there of all sorts of illiterate mechanick Preachers, yea of Women and Boy Preachers!"[3] To support his accusation, he claimed that the Bell-Alley Church in London, led by the General Baptist, Thomas Lambe, was allowing a lace-woman, Mrs Attaway to speak publically.[4] Edwards gave a detailed account of Mrs. Attaway's involvement in public meetings and said that she had "offered a word of exhortation," though whether she or the members of the congregation would have claimed she was a preacher is a matter of dispute.[5]

Edwards's account was written during the tumultuous period of the Commonwealth, when it appears that there were women associated with Baptist congregations who claimed to have a word of prophecy. Curtis Freeman has described some of these "visionary women" among Baptists and collected their work in *A Company of Women Preachers: Baptist Prophetesses in Seventeenth-Century England* (2011). Those included are: Sarah Wight (1632–?), Anna Trapnel (1642–1660), Jane Turner (1653), Katherine Sutton (1630–1663), and Anne Wentworth (1629/30–1693?). As in the case of Mrs Attaway, whether or not such women saw themselves as preachers is debatable. Since some of the women had close ties to the Fifth Monarchy movement, their urgent prophetic call for change and separation from the world, seems to have reflected political, as well as theological motivations. After the Restoration in 1660, Baptist women no longer seemed to have "prophecies" and Freeman suggests that as "the Baptist movement became organized and institutionalized many of the egalitarian expressions of the early days dissipated."[6]

While there voices were not always heard in the public sphere, however, women remained in Baptist congregations. Though membership statistics are difficult to assess, from their seventeenth-century beginnings, it appears that in both Calvinistic/Particular and General Baptist congregations,

---

2. Edwards, *Gangraena*, 29.
3. Edwards, "Dedicatory Epistle."
4. Edwards, *Gangruena*, 30–31.
5. See Freeman, "Visionary Women Among Early Baptists," 260–83.
6. Freeman, *Company of Women Preachers*, 39.

women were for the most part in a majority.[7] The appeal of the Baptist way to British women, might be explained by arguing that Baptist ecclesiology, with its emphasis on the priesthood of the believer and congregational polity, offered women the opportunity to participate in church life. Rachel Adcock has suggested that women seeking 'greater liberty and purity of worship' may have been attracted by congregational order.[8] For example, Susanna Parr, who joined a congregation in Exeter in the early 1650s, claimed she had never before felt "a greater effusion of the Spirit, a more purity and holinesse, more union and communion, more liberty of Conscience, and freedom from that yoke of being servants unto men."[9]

Yet, while (in theory) Baptist polity allowed women, to have "a voice and a vote" within the congregation, this does not explain fully their willingness to embrace radical Protestantism.[10] Indeed, most congregations adhered to a literal interpretation of the injunction of 1 Timothy 2:11–12 which urged women to "learn with all submissiveness" and "keep silent" in the church and, therefore, did not encourage them to preach and to assume leadership roles. Hence, while "liberty of conscience" may have proved attractive to some, on the whole it would not appear that women embraced the Baptist way in order to be assured of freedom of speech.[11] To cite again the example of Susanna Parr, it seems that when she grew disillusioned with the congregation in Exeter it was not over matters of religious freedom. Rather, she seems to have complained about the spiritual state of the members of the congregation and claimed that they were not living out their commitment to Christ in the world. She wrote that she had "never heard or read in Scripture, or other history, that the Lord did make use of people of such an earthly, luke-warme, and indifferent spirit, in any publique worke of reformation" and that the people they had separated from were "more Godly than our selves."[12]

While the issues of freedom of speech and conscience were obviously important to early Baptists, it seems evident that the participation of women in Baptist life should not be equated with an imagined, nascent

---

7. Rachel Adcock claims that "given the fluid nature of mid-seventeenth-century congregations . . . it is not a straightforward matter to assert that women were more attracted to Baptist church membership than men" (Adcock, *Baptist Women's Writings*, 3).

8. Adcock, *Baptist Women's Writings*, 14.

9. Parr quoted in Adcock, *Baptist Women's Writings*, 14.

10. For the use of the phrase "Radical Protestantism" in relation to Baptists, see Durnbaugh, *Believers' Church*, 94–104.

11. Adcock, *Baptist Women's Writings*, 14, 70.

12. Parr quoted in Adcock, *Baptist Women's Writings*, 70.

seventeenth-century feminist movement. Women were not simply seeking the opportunity to preach. Nor were they seeking to be in leadership roles. Rather, it may be argued that both men and women believed they were called by God to share together in radical discipleship as a fellowship of believers. Baptist ecclesiology among both General and Particular Baptists was grounded on the idea that members of a congregation believed that they had been called together by God to live in fellowship with God and one another through a covenant relationship.[13] Significantly, covenant life meant that not only had they been brought together or "gathered" by God, but were called by Christ to separate from the world.[14]

The Commitment to Covenant Life

In recent years much has been said about covenant life as a seminal part of British Baptist life and spirituality.[15] By laying stress on the fact that the church belongs to God and was created by God, the language of covenant has been used to try to settle conflict, as well as to encourage cooperation and unity. For instance, in discussions held between the Catholic Church and the Baptist World Alliance between 2006 and 2010, a covenant emphasis featured strongly. A report of the conversations stated:

> 'Covenant' expresses at once both the initiative and prior activity of God in making relationship with his people through Christ, and the willing commitment of people to each other and to God. The church is a 'gift' in the sense that it is 'gathered' by Christ, and it 'gathers' in response to the call of Christ. The term ekklesia indicates an 'assembly' that is 'called out' by God. Calling the church a 'fellowship of believers' does not mean that the church is constituted only by faith: faith is always a response to the initiating grace of God. The fellowship or koinonia of the church itself is both a gift and calling, just as the unity of the church is both a gift of the Spirit and a task to be achieved.[16]

---

13. The term fellowship of believers was used by Ernest Payne in his discussion of Baptist ecclesiology. See Payne, *Fellowship of Believers*.

14. There has been debate over the terms "gathered" or "gathering" church. The phrase "gathered" implies the activity of God, but it also suggests that it is complete. While gathering church implies process, it implies a human dimension. Hence, the use of the phrase "being gathered by God."

15. See for instance, Fiddes et al., *Bound to Love*. See also, Fiddes, *Tracks and Traces*; "'Walking Together,'" 47–74.

16. "Word of God," 40.

While unity may be an important part of covenant life, early Baptists did not emphasize covenant relationship in order to stand against division among themselves. Rather, the idea of being "called out" by God to be in relationship with God and one another found expression in their belief that they were called to watch out for one another and to live in a way that reflected their commitment to Christ. This emphasis on being "set apart" or "called out" as God's people was expressed by General and Particular Baptists in the earliest confessional and covenant agreements in the seventeenth and eighteenth centuries. For example, the *Second London Confession*, (1677/1689) claimed that:

> The Members of these Churches are Saints by calling, visibly manifesting and evidencing (in and by their profession and walking) their obedience unto that call of Christ; and do willingly consent to walk together according to the appointment of Christ, giving up themselves, to the Lord and to one another by the will of God, in professed subjection to the Ordinances of the Gospel.[17]

Since Baptists believed that God created the church by calling out both men and women to be a "fellowship of believers" they believed that those who were part of the church should live lives that were holy and committed to God's ways. This call to "come out" from the world was expressed in covenant agreements in terms of guidelines or "holy duties" by which the community was bound to live. These duties included both personal conduct and care for one another and reflected the very evident way that they insisted on "holiness of life." For instance, in a covenant written by Benjamin Keach (1640–1704) and attached to his book, entitled *The Glory of a True Church and its Discipline display'd* (1697),[18] the first promise of the covenant stated:

> We do promise and ingage (sic) to walk together in all Holiness, Godliness, Humility, and Brotherly Love, as much as in us lieth to render our Communion delightful to God, comfortable to ourselves and lovely to the rest of the Lord's people.[19]

---

17. See "Assembly or Second London Confession," 286.

18. Keach had been in a General Baptist congregation in Tooley Street, Southwark, before moving to serve as pastor of a Calvinistic congregation in Horsleydown in London. He was also at the centre of the controversy over hymn-singing among Baptists at the end of the seventeenth century. Walker, "Benjamin Keach," 25–42. The church covenant written by Keach provided a pattern which was widely followed among many eighteenth-century and nineteenth-century Baptists, both in Britain and in the American colonies.

19. Keach, "Solemn Covenant of the Church," 72.

The second promise claimed:

> We do promise to watch over each other's Conversations, and not to suffer Sin upon one another, so far as God shall discover it to us, or any of us; and to stir up one another to Love and good Works; to warn, rebuke, and admonish one another with Meekness according to the Rules left to us of Christ in that Behalf.[20]

Other promises included the pledge to pray for one another, to bear one another's burdens, to bear with one another's weaknesses, failings and infirmities. They also pledged to meet together for worship and to support the minister in terms of sustenance and material provision.

At first hearing, covenant promises sound like little more than a set of rules and regulations for members of the congregation to live by, or else face censure. Yet, for early Baptists the pledge to observe the duties of membership was to be an expression of a desire to live for God. Indeed, the covenant duties were to be an expression of obedience to the call to holiness; they believed that to be "called out" meant that they were also "set apart" to be God's people. Similar to the purpose of monastic vows, the covenant promises of early Baptist men and women symbolized their desire to live for God within community, and reflected a desire to "come out" from the world.

While women and men were expected to be separate from the world and enter into covenant life within a congregation, they did not always share equally in the congregational life. With few exceptions, congregations seemed for the most part to adhere to the biblical injunction that women are to 'keep silent' in public worship. Some outspoken women challenged this view. For instance it was reported that Sister Anne Harriman of an early London congregation explained her absence from meetings by claiming that

> Bro: Naudin said He would not walk: with such as gave libertie to woemen to speak in the Church. For she could not walk where she had not libertie to speak. And therefore rather then (sic) Brother Naudin should withdraw, she would witb-draw.[21]

Apparently the church discussed the matter of whether "woemen may speak" and concluded that "a Woeman (Mayd, Wife, or Widdow) being a Prophetess 1 Cor 2 may speake, Prophesie, Pray, with a Vayl. Others may not."[22]

---

20. Keach, "Solemn Covenant of the Church," 72.

21. Burrage, "Trve and Short Declaration," 145–46. This article records the minutes of an early Baptist congregation formed in London in 1652.

22. Burrage, "Trve and Short Declaration," 146.

It seems obvious that even in congregations where women were allowed to speak, the conditions were tightly controlled. Patricia Crawford has pointed out that the fact that women were visited and questioned over their behavior by men demonstrates an expectation that women were to be submissive.[23]

Even in congregations where women were allowed to speak, the roles were carefully prescribed. In the *Broadmead Records* in Bristol it is stated that women were serving in the role of a deaconess, a recognized ministry in the church from 1662. While this was not a preaching role, they were certainly serving within the congregation in a recognized capacity. They had to be over 60 years of age and also to agree not to remarry. They were set apart by prayer and fasting to

> Speak a word to their soules as occasion requires, for support and consolation, to build them up in a spirituall lively faith in Jesus Christ.[24]

Evidence from church records in the seventeenth and eighteenth centuries implies that a theological emphasis on the church as a covenant people that had been called out by God provided a theological framework for the discipleship of early Baptists. Not only did church members seek to remind one another of the responsibilities of life together, but in many cases covenant promises provided a standard by which to measure the commitment of both men and women. While women usually served "behind the scenes" in ways that appeared to be traditionally and culturally acceptable,[25] they actively participated in the covenant life of the community and in so doing, by word or deed, reminded others of the importance of "holy living."

Holy Living: A Testimony of Faith

Although women were not, on the whole, recognized as "preachers" or even allowed to serve in the role of deaconess in every congregation, it is significant that from the beginning, women, as well as men, were encouraged to give a public testimony of their faith before the church. Indeed, willingness to give a public testimony to their faith was perhaps seen as the first indication that seventeenth-century Baptist women and men had responded to the call to "come out" from the world. Those who wished to be baptized and join with a congregation were required to "give in their experience," which

---

23. Crawford, *Women and Religion in England*, 150.
24. Hayden, *Records of a Church*, 87–90.
25. See Smith, "Forgotten Sisters," 163–83.

was a public verbal testimony of their experience with God. Although these testimonies varied in length and style, normally, they followed the pattern of Puritan conversion narratives.[26] While the point at which congregations began to expect potential members to give evidence of their faith is a matter of dispute[27], there is ample evidence in church books that early Baptist women, as well as men stood before the church meeting to offer a testimony of their faith.

In addition to offering testimony within a congregational meeting, some early Baptist women went so far as to have their testimony printed. Examining the writings of outspoken women or "Baptist prophetesses" Freeman suggests that the printed writings of these women fall into two different literary genres: oracles of speech and a conversion narrative. While neither category may be regarded as a sermon, it should be noted that both genres represent a testimony of faith that emphasized the importance being "called out" of the world. Anna Trapnel, for example, was a member of the congregation at All Hallows the Great Church in London, a stronghold for the Fifth Monarchy movement, and a regular meeting place among London Baptist ministers such as Henry Jessey and Hanserd Knollys. She claimed that after she was baptized in 1654 or 1655, her baptism led her to have the ability to prophecy. Trapnel declared:

> When I arose out of the water
> I beheld Christs sweet face;
> And he did smile upon me, as
> A token of his grace
> So that I was encouraged
> against the opposing foe.
> And enabled by my dear Lord
> Against them for to go
> So that I could declare, and I could speak

---

26. William Perkins (1558–1602) developed what may described as a morphology of conversion which included progressive stages moving from acknowledgement of sin, preparation and assurance, conviction, compunction, and submission, fear, sorrow and faith. Michael Watts has argued that "the process of conversion expounded by Perkins was upheld by English Evangelicals for three centuries as normative of Christian experience" (Watts, *Dissenters*, 174).

27. It has been argued that early Separatists did not require applicants for membership to be tested, but rather merely to give a confession which amounted to an intellectual understanding of faith. Edmund Morgan suggested that the idea of requiring members to give an account of their experience developed among non-Separating Puritans in Massachusetts and then spread back to England. See Morgan, *Visible Saints*, 63–68, 92–105, 109–10.

And for the King up stand
He gave me such instruction,
And brought words to my hand.[28]

While interest in Trapnel's exhortations has focussed mainly on her radical connections with Fifth Monarchists,[29] it is noteworthy that when she faced imprisonment for her prophetic ordinances, she wrote to the community of believers at All Hallows the Great and urged them to pray for her. She also spoke of her commitment to Christ:

> The Lord whom I serve hath from a child kept me, and still doth keep me as a Rememberer of him in his wayes, as well as rejoycing and working righteousness, and he meets me in all these according to his promise.[30]

Katherine Sutton, a member of Hanserd Knollys's congregation wrote, *A Christian Womans experience of the glorious working of Gods free grace* (1663). As the apostles received the Holy Spirit in Acts chapter 2, she believed that she herself had been given words of prophecy to be expressed in song. While many people were uncomfortable with women testifying in this way, Sutton clearly felt that God had given her this gift of speech. She claimed that her revelation came to her in 1655 when after a long period of struggle, she had assurance from God of her salvation. Again, it is noteworthy that her revelation was shared first within the community of faith and that her pastor, Hanserd Knollys, wrote a commendation to the reader in which he described her one of the Lord's "Handmaides"[31] Sutton's writings, while reflecting the millenarian ideas of the time, also highlight the need to be watchful and "to come out" from the world. In a testimony she claimed was given to her November 1656 she wrote:

> Oh! where shall I find now
> A people quickn'd still,
> That seek all times to live on God
> and eek[32] to do his will.

28. Trapnel quoted in Adcock, *Baptist Women's Writings*, 20.

29. She apparently fell into a trance in January 1654 and prophesied for twelve days while Vavasor Powell, the Welsh Baptist and Fifth Monarchist was being examined on charges of treason by the Council of State. See Freeman, *Company of Women Preachers*, 370.

30. Trapnel, "Letter to the Church at Allhallows."

31. Freeman, *Company of Women Preachers*, 592.

32. "Eek" is an Old English adverb meaning "also" (incorrectly transcribed in Freeman, *Company of Women Preachers*, as eck!).

> A people that deny themselves,
> And eek the cross up take,
> That doth delight in God alone,
> And eek the world forsake.³³

While Sutton wanted to sing her testimony, other women testified in different ways. The *Broadmead Records* recorded the outspoken witness of Dorothy Kelly, (later Hazard) (d. 1674):

> Mr. Kelly being some years deceased, his Widow persevered in godliness; and it might be said of her as of Ruth 3:11 (all the City did know her to be a virtuous woman). She was like a he-goat before the flock; for in those days Mrs. Kelly was very famous for Piety and reformation, well known to all, bearing living testimony against the superstitions and traditions of those days, and she would not observe their invented times and feasts, called Holy days. At which time she kept a Grocer's shop in High-street, between the Guilders Inn and High Cross, where she would open her shop on the time they call Christmas day, and sit sewing in her shop, as a witness for God in the midst of the city, in the face of the Sun, and in the sight of all men; even in those very days of Darkness, when, as it were, all sorts of people had a reverence of that particular day above all others. . . . She was the first woman in this City of Bristol that practiced that truth of the Lord (which was then hated and odious), namely Separation.³⁴

Taking a public stand for faith could not have been easy. But it appears that those who had been "called together" believed that they had a responsibility to witness and were willing to face scorn and ridicule in order to stand up for their beliefs. Having pledged their commitment through covenant statements, women did what they could financially, materially, and spiritually to contribute to the life of the congregation. It was reported, for instance that Elizabeth Poole, who had been a member of William Kiffin's church in London, stood and spoke in front of the general Council of the Army (1648–49).³⁵ Likewise, Ann Grave (Graves) was a woman of some means who lived among those associated with the congregation of William

---

33. Sutton, *Christian Woman's Experiences*.

34. Hayden, *Records of a Church*, 18.

35. I am grateful to Larry Kreitzer for drawing my attention to references of women in his sources on William Kiffen(in). In a discussion of Elizabeth Poole, Kreitzer notes that the stories regarding Kiffen's treatment of her and her dismission from the church cannot be substantiated. See Kreitzer, *William Kiffen and His World (2)*, 262–89.

Kiffin.[36] On one occasion it appears that she was one of a number of women who were arrested along with Kiffin when they met for worship in 1661.

Some women offered their homes as meeting places for congregations. In the Broadmead church, for instance, the records state that church met for a time at the house of Sister Griffen and then at the house of Mrs Nethway, a Bristol Brewer's wife. Nethway was described as "a woman who in her day was eminent for godliness," and as having "a good and great understanding in the fear of the Lord."[37]

Naturally, there is evidence in Church books of those who did not keep their covenant commitments. The Church book of the congregation meeting at Cripplegate in London describes a case in 1694 of Sister Cooke who:

> neglected her place in the church for 2 years at least. In which time . . . messengers had been sent to her from the church to speak to her but they could not find her to speak to her. . . . Also she was charged with dealing deceitfully with one Mrs Green.[38]

Those who did not keep their covenant vows were often denied fellowship in the church for a time or excommunicated altogether. Usually they were visited by members of the congregation and asked to give an account of themselves. For instance, in 1651, the Fenstanton congregation sent representatives to visit Anne Pharepoint. The stated reason for their visit was:

> The cause of our coming at this time is, to know whether you are willing to walk with the congregation in the practice of the ordinances of Christ, and those examples which Christ and his disciples left us to follow.[39]

She replied that she did. After conversation with her they apparently

> declared the care the congregation had over her, and how they did earnestly desire her welfare and increase in the knowledge of God. Then she said that she was very joyful, and did return thanks to the congregation, and declared that she would come to the congregation.[40]

At times, the result of such meetings were not always positive. Often they were dismissed for a time or excommunicated altogether. However,

---

36. See Kreitzer, *William Kiffen and his World (1)*, 149; *William Kiffen and His World (5)*, 63–116.
37. Hayden quoted in Briggs, "She Preachers, Widows, and Other Women," 339.
38. London Cripplegate, *Church Book 1689–1723*, 7.
39. Underhill, *Records of the Churches of Christ*, 24.
40. Underhill, *Records of the Churches of Christ*, 24–25.

the censure itself was a reminder to the person, as well as others in the congregation, that they, indeed, had been called together to be "called out" from the world. While discipline meetings were held when needed, censure was not meted out without due care and concern for circumstances, as was demonstrated in another case at Cripplegate in 1699 with the charge against Sister Hewett's daughter.

> A complaint by her husband that she had abused him with very uncivil and barbarous language . . . the whole being impartially examined it was found that she had been very badly and inhumanely treated by her husband. That deep distressing poverty had afflicted her through his incapacity or negligence to get a livelihood or subsistence whereby great provocation had given her to speak and act unadvisedly.[41]

Throughout the seventeenth and eighteenth centuries many Baptist congregations continued to insist that women and men had to give a public verbal testimony before the gathered church as a prerequisite of church membership. In the nineteenth century this practice was questioned and it was suggested that instead of asking for a testimony, in some congregations women could simply answer questions or be visited by several members of the congregation who could report their findings to the wider group.[42] Women, of course, had already found other ways of sharing their faith within Baptist life quite apart form verbal or written testimonies. For instance, some women wrote hymns, as a way of giving expression to their faith. Probably the best known hymn-writer of the eighteenth century was Anne Steele (1717–1778) who lived in Broughton in Hampshire. In 1760 her work *Poems on Subjects Chiefly Devotional* was published under the name *Theodosia*. Her hymns often picked up the theme of holy living. For instance, she wrote:

> Jesus, the spring of joys divine,
> Whence all my hopes and comforts flow;
> Jesus, no other name but thine,
> Can save me from eternal woe.
>
> In vain would boasting reason find
> The way to happiness and God;
> Her weak directions leave the mind
> Bewilder'd in a dubious road.

41. London Cripplegate, *Church Book 1689–1723*, 11.
42. *Baptist Magazine* 2, 388.

No other name will heav'n approve;
Thou art the true, the living way,
(Ordain'd by everlasting love,)
To the bright realms of endless day.

Here let my constant feet abide,
Nor from the heav'nly path depart;
O let thy Spirit, gracious guide,
Direct my steps, and cheer my heart.

Safe lead me thro' this world of night,
And bring me to the blissful plains,
The regions of unclouded light,
Where perfect joy forever reigns.[43]

Hymns such as this one focussed on the need to walk daily with God. Yet, it was not simply holy living that was important, but there was the whole matter of holy dying, too.

Holy Dying: Death-bed Testimonies and the Witness of Wills

Poor hygiene and lack of sanitation, as well as inadequate medical knowledge and treatment meant that up until the twentieth century, life was lived with the constant threat of death. If a person did not die of influenza or a pulmonary infection, life might be ended by cholera, typhoid, typhus, dysentery or small pox. While life expectancy varied according to social class, gender and region, it appears that by the mid-eighteenth century in Britain, the average life expectancy from birth was between thirty-five and fourty years.[44] While there are examples of women and men who lived to old age, owing to the risk of complication in childbirth, the mortality rate for women rose during the child-bearing years. Moreover, many women experienced numerous miscarriages before giving birth to a child who often lived only a few hours or days.[45]

The way people confronted death became an important indication of their piety and devotion to God. In recent years, it has been suggested that an examination of the distribution of personal property indicated in

43. Broom, *Bruised Reed*, 268.
44. Wrigley and Schofield quoted in Ottoway, *Decline of Life*, 21.
45. See Smith, "Baptists at Home," 105–10.

statements of the last will and testament may also be a sort of lasting testimony to personal faith and religious belief. Naturally, the testimony of a will is limited and does not give the full story of a person's religious beliefs or practices. Yet, the last will and testament of an individual certainly offers some insight into what was important in life and death. Hence it is noteworthy that wealthy Baptist women, as well as men, left money to ministers or members of the congregations. For instance, looking at the will of Susanna Hardy, who died in 1675, it appears that she bequeathed five pounds each to Baptist ministers: Lawrence Wise, Hanserd Knollys, Daniel Dykes and Thomas Hicks.[46] Likewise in the will of Ann Graves, money was left "Towards the maintenance of Eight poore and Aged and decayed ministers" namely, Hanserd Knollys, Benjamin Cox and Henry Forty and the other five ministers who were to be chosen by the executors, William Kiffen being one of them.[47] These examples of financial support for ministers serve as reminder of the serious way in which many Baptists took their responsibility to care for others, especially those in ministry. The support of women through wills may also have been viewed as a public expression of "holy dying."

The emphasis on holy dying was not unique among Baptists and may be seen as a long-standing concern for all Christian believers. Among Baptists in the seventeenth and eighteenth centuries, however, dying well was not only encouraged, but expected. So, not surprisingly, end-of-life stories became a tool for evangelism and a prompt to self-reflection.[48] By the nineteenth century, death-bed testimonies were often published and were used as an evangelistic tool, to educate other believers and, of course, as a means by which to encourage others to prepare to face death with faith. However, the practice of visiting the bed-side of the dying in order to extract a testimony of faith may be traced back to Puritan devotion.[49] For women, the death-bed became a pulpit, it was the place from which it was acceptable to preach to family and friends.

While the content of each testimony varied, as with conversion narratives, often there was a similar pattern to the death-bed scene. In printed accounts, the final days were depicted in high drama. Often the believer, was taken ill suddenly and confined to bed, was then visited by family and friends who posed particular questions to them regarding their faith. In answering the questions, the believer was able to speak with confident

---

46. Kreitzer, *William Kiffen and His World (5)*, 64.
47. Kreitzer, *William Kiffen and His World (5)*, 66.
48. See my article, Smith, "Preparation as a Discipline," 22–44.
49. Wakefield, *Puritan Devotion*, 146.

assurance of faith in Christ. For instance, when friends visited the deathbed of Sarah Miell they asked her if she wanted anything. She replied "I want everything, I want my dearest Lord. Asked about her state of mind, she replied, "I am happy, my mind is stayed on God."[50]

Of Mary Elyett, a member of the Salisbury congregation for nearly fifty-five years before she died in 1810, it was said her death-bed was a sort of "privileged station" by those who visited her. Asked about the meaning and significance of religion in the face of death, she answered "the same I have long thought, it is the one thing needful." Questioned about the fear of death she replied, "I am not afraid to die, for I can say, Thanks be to God, who giveth me the victory; but it is all through Christ." To another friend she quoted the hymn:

> He ever lives to intercede
>
> Before his father's face
>
> Give him my soul thy cause to plead
>
> Nor doubt the father's grace.[51]

While hymns were often on the lips of the dying in these accounts, the fact that there were some favourites which many seemed to quote leaves the impression that some of the accounts were highly stylized and perhaps shaped by those who published them. Esther Horsey of Portsea was described as a person who took seriously the importance of a holy life:

> She was not one of those professors to whom the bare name of a christian was satisfactory; nor one who was content merely because her state was safe: but her early and uniform attendance in the house of God, her regular and devout retirement, her conscientious regard to moral obligation, and the savour of holiness which marked her conversation, all declared her Christian indeed.[52]

She was also an example of someone who expressed holiness in death too. She offered advice to her grandson on "the importance of real and personal religion." Over a period of several days she spoke words of testimony to others who came to visit. At one point, when an attendant was about to adjust her pillow, she quoted part of a hymn that was often the testimony

---

50. "Sarah Miell," 136.
51. "Mary Elyett," 73.
52. "Mrs. Esther Horsey," 347.

of those who were dying: "Everybody thinks that I lie uneasy, but they are mistaken; no, Jesus can make a dying bed feel soft as downy pillows are."[53]

While recognizing that death-bed testimonies were often stylized, and taking into account that they were written so as to encourage, educate, and evangelize, they nevertheless provide insight into what Evangelicals as a whole believed to be a good death: a focus on Christ as Saviour, a denial of earthly concerns and a focus on the peace of heaven. For Baptists, attendance at the bedside of a believer by members of the congregation may have indicated something of the "priestly nature" of the church gathered.[54] Doreen Rosman has suggested that by the end of the nineteenth century, a death-bed testimony had an almost "sacramental function" in the evangelical experience as it provided an opportunity to speak of personal union with Christ.[55] While a death-bed testimony certainly served to witness to personal devotion, and an opportunity to stress commitment to holiness of life, there was also an opportunity to give testimony to the desire to be separate from the world. In fact, as Mary Riso has pointed out, the testimonies included "the basic tenets of evangelical theology (among them the necessity of conversion, the atonement, sanctification, personal experience of God and eternal life) which were and continued to be constitutive elements" of a Non-conformist view of death.[56]

For women, the death-bed testimonies were especially important in that they allowed women to be perceived as proclaimer/teacher and, furthermore, permitted women to transcend the normal church roles by allowing them to be viewed in the role of counselor/advisor.[57] Death-bed testimonies affirmed women as valued members of congregations, though they were also used a socializing force to maintain the traditional roles, behaviours and attitudes towards women in society and within the church, i.e., women

---

53. *Baptist Magazine* 2, 348–49. The hymn by Isaac Watts says:
   Jesus can make a dying bed
   Feel soft as downy pillows are,
   While on His breast I lean my head,
   And breathe my life out sweetly there.

54. Stannard, *Puritan Way of Death*, 87, describes the sacramental nature of the deathbed for Puritans.

55. Rosman, *Evangelicals and Culture*, 103.

56. Riso, *Narrative of the Good Death*, 14.

57. In the seventeenth century, Adcock claims that there was a denial by Nonconformist men that women were teaching or instructing from the bed when people gathered around them, though clearly this was the case. See Adcock, *Baptist Women's Writings*, 87.

should be quiet, useful, patient submissive, resigned.[58] While recognizing the stylized content of many of the death-bed testimonies it may be argued that such testimonies, like a last testament and will, allowed women to bear witness to a faith which demanded that they had "come out" from the world.

Conclusion

This overview of some British Baptist women in the seventeenth and eighteenth centuries, has attempted to show that the response to "come out" from the world was inextricably linked to their call to "come together" as a covenant community of faith. For early Baptists the idea of "coming out" of the established church and the world and forming churches was grounded in their understanding that they had been "called out" to holiness of life by God. They did not choose to be a congregation of believers, but insisted that God had taken the initiative and formed them into a fellowship. As a way of giving expression to their calling, many early Baptist congregations agreed on covenant statements that set out the privileges and responsibilities of church life. Although in the beginning Baptist women, on the whole, were not encouraged to preach, in the early period some women claimed prophetic utterances. Others, upon membership, gave testimonies of faith to the congregation. For many, their death-bed became the accepted place of proclamation. Later, as both church and culture changed, British Baptist women witnessed to their faith in other ways too: through preaching, hymnody, teaching, writing, as well as assuming roles in mission and social ministry.[59] At the heart of their response was the belief that life as a covenant people of God was best expressed in "holy living" and "holy dying," too.

---

58. Wilson, *Constrained by Zeal*, 156.

59. Smith, "Role of Women," 35–48; "British Women," 25–46; "Forgotten Sisters," 163–83.

CHAPTER 7

Making Room to Serve

Separation as a Strategy among
African-American Baptists

DAVID EMMANUEL GOATLEY

RACIAL PREJUDICE IS IN the DNA of the United States of America. DNA, or deoxyribonucleic acid, is the hereditary material found in nearly every cell in the human body. DNA stores the long-term instructions for the construction, reproduction, and replication of itself and of cells. In a sense, it can be considered to be the blueprint for an organism. Racial prejudice has been pervasive throughout the history of the United States. It did, and continues to influence the strategy of separation among African-American Baptists to make room for them to serve.

To assert that racial prejudice is embedded throughout the societal and structural fabric of the United States will be rejected by some who enjoy majority privilege and have not been on the painful receiving end of prejudgments based on the social construction of race. Because one has not experienced a thing, however, does not negate its presence. Influenza, for example, exists whether or not I am infected. I may not be infected because I have been immunized or because I have not been in close proximity to someone who is contagious. But the flu is real whether or not I am sick. Further, because one has not recognized the existence of something does not mean that the something is not real. Because one does not see rodents in the same building where one lives does not mean that rodents are not living in the same facility in great abundance.

Experience and recognition do not determine whether something exists or not. Consequently, someone who is part of a racially privileged culture may or may not realize that racial prejudice exists. Even if one sees racial discrimination, one may or may not recognize it. Implicit bias causes people to uncritically and unknowingly accept and advance unfairness and injustice unaware.[1]

Examples of Racial Prejudice

Racial prejudice is found in nearly every cell of the country's financial, educational self and continues to grow even among those with higher educational achievement. In 1980 white men with only a high school diploma earned 15 percent more than black men with the same academic achievement while white men with bachelors' degrees earned 5 percent more than black men with the same degree. In 2014, less educated white men earn 16 percent more than comparable black men. College educated white men, however, earned 18 percent more than college educated black men. Less educated white women with less than ten years of experience were paid 6.2 percent more than comparable black women, and college educated white women earned nearly 12 percent more than college educated black women.[2]

Educationally, the preponderance of data demonstrates convincingly that educational systems in the United States are failing black males. The Schott Foundation's report, *Yes We Can, The Schott 50 State Report on Public Education and Black Males*, shows that only 47 percent of Black males graduate from high school. This will contribute to a lifetime of lower income and anemic economic power. The report asserts that

> Black male students are punished more severely for similar infractions than their White peers. They are not given the same opportunities to participate in classes with enriched educational offerings. They are more frequently inappropriately removed from the general education classroom due to misclassifications by the Special Education policies and practices of schools and districts. By Grade 8, relatively few are proficient in reading and, finally, as a consequence of these deficiencies in educational practice, less than half graduate with their cohort.
>
> The great variation in these factors among districts and states indicates that the driver is not individual students, but the adults responsible for the policies and practices of the educational systems in which they study. In our democracy, a child's access to the resources necessary to have a fair and substantive

---

1. For information about how hidden biases affect decisions make about themselves and about society, see Banaji and Greenwald, *Blindspot*.
2. Guo, "Why Black Workers."

opportunity to learn should not depend on the zip code in which he resides.[3]

Governmentally, African-Americans have struggled for political enfranchisement since the abolition of slavery. The Thirteenth Amendment to the US Constitution abolished slavery in 1865. The Fourteenth Amendment granted citizenship to everyone born in the US or naturalized, including former enslaved persons. The Fifteenth Amendment granted African-American men the right to vote. The twenty-first century, however, has not yet brought full freedom recognized and protected by the government of the United States toward African-American people.

The United States Supreme Court scheduled cases in its 2016 term concerning issues of racial bias in the criminal justice system and the role of race concerning the drawing of districts for voting. Duane Buck was sentenced to death instead of life imprisonment following the testimony of an alleged expert witness that "the defendant was more likely to be dangerous because he is African American." A juror asserted that he doubted an alibi of Peña Rodriguez "because, among other things, he was an 'illegal,' even though he had testified at trial that he was a legal resident." The jury convicted Rodriguez. Additionally, "the high Court will also consider the role of race in our electoral system in two cases involving how states draw district lines for state and federal legislative seats. In both *Bethune-Hill v. Virginia State Board of Elections* and *McCrory v. Harris*, the Court is being asked to decide whether the use of a fixed racial quota to draw district lines violates the Fourteenth Amendment."[4]

African-Americans struggle to negate or negotiate ongoing issues of system racial discrimination. Racial prejudice has a long history in America.

A History of Racial Prejudice

Contemporary experiences of racial prejudice for African-Americans are not new phenomena. They are part of a long and painful journey of oppression that includes slavery and segregation following abolition. Chattel slavery[5] and the ongoing segregation and oppression that flowed from it are definitive for the experience of life for the entire country. The stolen labor of the enslaved substantially contributed the United States to be the political,

---

3. Holzman, *Yes We Can*, 37.
4. Gorod, "Supreme Court's New Term."
5. Chattel slavery refers to the enslavement of Africans and their descendants and their categorization as property in what came to be the United States.

industrial, technological, cultural, and financial power that is has become. Without slave labor, the US would not have the wealth and influence that it enjoys. Although slavery was most prominent in the southern part of the emerging country, the ideology of alleged white supremacy and so-called black inferiority combined with the economic benefit that the agricultural products provided the people and the textile industry of northern states made life somewhere between unconscionable to unbearable for African Americans.

The first enslaved Africans arrived in Jamestown, Virginia, aboard a Dutch ship in 1619. The purpose of enslaving the Africans in Virginia was to provide strong and cheap labor for the agricultural economy of the region. The entire economic and cultural base of the south was built on the exploitation of enslaved African people. Born exclusively on the grounds of race, the chattel slavery system employed in the US was brutal and dehumanizing. Slaves were not permitted to continue the cultural, linguistic and familial bonds from their places of origin. It was impossible, however, to obliterate all aspects of cultural forms and practices.[6]

Enslaved Africans had no rights. Slaveholders and members of the slavocracy were free to use and abuse slaves. The only limits imposed where for white people not to violate the property—meaning slaves—of others. Otherwise, enslaved Africans were vulnerable to the maltreatment of Europeans or white Americans. Slaves were subject to psychological, sexual, and physical violence, including family separation, rape, and death.[7] The sociological and financial impact of two centuries of legal slavery contributed to the economic vitality of the privileged classes in the United States and the ongoing fragility of African-American progeny.

The abolition of slavery that came with the end of the Civil War provided a brief hope of reprieve from the barbarity of racial hatred, but it was short lived. The ideology of white supremacy manifested itself following the end of slavery with the establishment of Black Codes. These were laws enacted by Southern states to restrict African-American freedom and force them to work under penalty of imprisonment. It was a way to intimidate and control the formerly enslaved. Black people without jobs, for example, could be charged with vagrancy. People convicted of vagrancy could be imprisoned and forced to work without pay. Local sheriffs could hire prisoners to private companies and plantation owners. For example,

---

6. Sociologist E. Franklin Frazier and anthropologist Melville J. Herskovits debated how accommodation (Frazier) or continuation (Herskovits) was present from African cultures into twentieth-century contexts. See Frazier, *Black Bourgeoisie*; Herskovits, *Negro Myth*.

7. See Goatley, *Were You There?*

Mississippi's law required blacks to have written evidence of employment for the coming year each January; if they left before the end of the contract, they would be forced to forfeit earlier wages and were subject to arrest. In South Carolina, a law prohibited blacks from holding any occupation other than farmer or servant unless they paid an annual tax of $10 to $100. This provision hit free blacks already living in Charleston and former slave artisans especially hard. In both states, blacks were given heavy penalties for vagrancy, including forced plantation labor in some cases.[8]

Black codes and vagrancy laws sought to establish another system of forced labor given the end of slavery in the south.

Although leasing prisoners eventually declined, robust new laws were established across the south designed to oppress and control blacks. The white elite designed systems to privilege poor whites above poor blacks to prevent their alliance for economic justice. "Segregation laws were proposed as part of a deliberate effort to drive a wedge between poor whites and African Americans. These discriminatory barriers were designed to encourage lower-class whites to retain a sense of superiority over blacks, making it far less likely that they would sustain interracial political alliances aimed at toppling the with elite."[9]

Implications for the Church

The Anglo-American church has too often been a co-conspirator in the marginalization and oppression of people of African heritage in the United States. Rather than being an agent of transformation and offering a prophetic vision of justice for all, the church has often been an enabler and partner of the oppressor. It has often blessed the perpetuation of racial injustice. The church has too often failed to adhere to the directive: "Do not be conformed to this world, but be transformed by the renewing of your minds, so that you may discern what the will of God—what is good and acceptable and perfect" (Rom 12:2, NRSV).

African-American Baptists have not been exempt from the pervasive presence of racial prejudice and racism—the exercise of power of white people that has imposed a worldview that people of African heritage are inferior to people of European heritage. Racism overtly desecrated black life in America historically, and continues to affect blatantly or subtly most

8. "Black Codes."
9. Alexander, *New Jim Crow*, 33.

aspects of life for black Americans today—economics, health, education, civic engagement, criminal justice, and the like. Black Baptists had to separate from the white Baptist churches to escape life denying racism and assert life affirming faith and practice.

Black Churches

The earliest experiences of black people in Baptist churches were in churches controlled by white people. There was no spirit of egalitarianism present. Black attendees, as well as those who were allowed to be "members," were not considered equal. The social caste system of chattel slavery and the privileging of white residents in the United States also existed in the church. This was true whether in parts of the country where slavery was practiced as well as in parts of the country where slavery was not practiced. The racism that established and enforced white privilege and black enslavement in the United States was very much present in churches in antebellum and postbellum contexts.

While some black believers participated in white dominated congregations, which resulted, generously speaking, in biracial churches, black believers also created private, clandestine gatherings were they engaged in self led and more authentic worship experiences. When blacks had their private gatherings as well as when they were able to have public congregations organized separately from white Christians, they exercised both religious and political agency.[10] In general, black Americans did not subscribe to a bifurcation of sacred and secular, of religious versus political. They were connected in a holistic or integrated way. One's theology informed ones public use of power to influence people, policies, and practices.

The separatism, or "come-outerism" of black Baptists in the United States is related to both religious and political consciousness in the context of enslavement, oppression, discrimination, marginalization, and in some cases attempts of annihilation. Black Baptists have separated from older traditions as well as from and within themselves because they had to make room to serve.

Racial prejudice made black Baptist organizations essential. Racism carried with it assumptions by white people in America that they were superior to black people and, consequently, that black people were not due rights, privileges, and opportunities to be free and flourishing. The ideology that separates people into racial groups and then proceeds to exploit and exclude threatened surviving and prevented thriving. If black people

10. Washington, *Frustrated Fellowship*, ix–xiv.

in America were going to avoid obliteration they were going to have to act decisively rather than to suffer the impositions of white people who forced their worldviews as universally normative. Exercising agency to achieve sustainability, security, and dignity was a theological mandate and a political priority.

James Melvin Washington has included a stunning quote from the 1891 Home Mission Board Report of the Southern Baptist Convention (SBC) *Proceedings* in his book *Frustrated Fellowship: The Black Baptist Quest for Social Power*:

> Nothing is plainer to any one who knows this race than its perfect willingness to accept a subordinate place, provided there be confidence that in that position of subordination it will receive justice and kindness. That is the condition it prefers above all others, and this is the condition in which it attains the highest development of every attribute of manhood. Whenever it shall understandingly and cheerfully accept this condition, the race problem is settled forever.[11]

Washington further cited a quotation from the subsequent year found in the 1892 SBC *Proceedings* where the Home Mission Board asserted that when black people were "brought to this country and sold as slaves, they were placed in the only relation to the white people in which it was possible for them to exist. The miasma emanating from the vices and corruptions of our civilization is death to any inferior race with which we come into contact, unless that race be subordinated to our control."[12]

The above sentiments that were memorialized in the official documents of the Southern Baptist Convention, whose 1845 origin is largely due to their affirmation that slaveholders could be missionaries, clearly expresses the reason that black Baptist had to come out from there. The embedded theology of these white Baptists, who were concentrated in the southern United States where the labor of black people was stolen to advance the economy and generate wealth for the slavocracy and for the country, is clear. Black people were believed to belong in a subordinate position to white people. This was equally true inside the church and outside of it. Not only was there an assumption of the rightful subordination of black people, there was the erroneous conclusion that this lopsided social contract was accepted by, and desired among, black people. White Baptists in the south held that the skewed relationship where white people had power and privilege while black people were secondary and enslaved left no room

11. Washington, *Frustrated Fellowship*, 179.
12. Washington, *Frustrated Fellowship*, 180.

for serving, learning, and growing. Even though there were white Baptists and white people in the country who fought for abolition and emancipation, the normative reality was that whites were not willing to accept black people as fellow citizens or sisters and brothers in Christ.

The clearly racist sentiments of many white Baptists were well known to black Baptist leaders. Elias Camp Morris, founding president of the National Baptist Convention, asserted in his 1900 annual meeting message, just five years after the organization's founding that,

> You will permit me here to repeat what I have said on former occasions: that the conditions in this country have forced the Negroes to be separate in their churches, associations, and conventions, from their white brethren and these smaller organizations have, by reason of the same conditions, been forced to form this national society and since we have this National Baptist convention, it is imperative that it have a high and noble object. . . . The National Baptist Convention, in this connection, stands for the complete development of the Negro as a man along all lines, beginning first with his religious life, and ending with the material, or business life.[13]

This sentiment was not limited to the nineteenth century. Joseph Harrison Jackson, President of the National Baptist Convention, USA, from 1953–1982 asserted in 1970 that,

> If all Negro Baptists joined with white Baptists of America in forming one big Baptist organization, we would still have some Negroes forming units that they might well call a black caucus, and these caucuses would not be for the purpose of urging Negroes to refine the talents that they have and harness the same in making the new body politic more spiritual and more dedicated to the cause of freedom and redemption. But there would be the drawing up of a list of demands and then protesting to the white majority for certain things the black minority felt they should have and receive.[14]

Whether the racially prejudiced white Baptist voices of the nineteenth century, or black Baptist leadership of the same era, or the leader of the largest black religious group in the country during the twentieth century, it was clear that remaining within white Baptist organizations was not a strategy for sustainability. Whether within individual congregations or collections of

---

13. Dixie, "How Firm a Foundation?," 327.
14. National Baptist Convention USA, *Minutes*, 286.

congregations, many black Baptists knew that they had to separate from the oppressors if they were ever to become free.

Black Associations

The earliest black Baptist churches affiliated with white associations. The first black Baptist associations developed between 1834 and 1841—three decades before the abolition of slavery. White Baptist associations organized for cooperation in domestic missions, mutual aid, and education. The earliest Black Baptist associations embraced these areas of concern but also had an additional distinctive priority. They all were committed to abolishing slavery.[15]

The Providence Association was organized in 1834 in Southeastern Ohio with six churches. It later changed its name to the Providence Antislavery (Colored) Baptist Association. The Union Baptist Antislavery Association was formed in 1840 formed by churches that withdrew (although a few simultaneously maintained ties with antislavery white churches) from the white association comprised of churches in Cincinnati, Columbus, Chillicothe, and Brush Creek Ohio. The Wood River Association, originally known as the Colored Baptist Association and Friends to Humanity (which reflected Baptist engagement with the abolitionist Quakers) was formed in 1839 when three black churches petitioned for membership in the white association with plans for them to then be authorized to organize their own association. An early priority was to provide missionary support to suffering black people who lived in deprivation across the Mississippi River. When a younger and better educated generation assumed leadership in the 1850s, the association asserted itself for the cause of abolition.

> These preachers were eager to harness Baptist energies to the antislavery cause. They had no difficulty in mingling politics and religion because they saw slavery as a moral issue that must be addressed rather than simply tolerated. When they began to take the reins of the Association, they managed to get their more cautious brethren to make public abolitionist statements. The statements became increasingly more radical as the national political climate reached a boiling point during 1859 and 1860.[16]

The Baptist Association for Colored People was formed in 1841 that involved churches in the present Southern Ontario to Detroit. Later called

---

15. Washington, *Frustrated Fellowship*, 27–38.
16. Washington, *Frustrated Fellowship*, 34.

the Amherstburg Association, James Melvin Washington reports that it "never lost sight of its abolitionist missionary concerns."[17] In 1849 it became the Canadian auxiliary of the Baptist abolitionist organization called the American Baptist Free Mission Society. Not wanting to be an auxiliary, however, a minority group withdrew in 1850 to become the Canadian Anti-Slavery Baptist Association. They reunited in 1857 and helped lead the formation of the Northwestern and Southern Baptist Convention in 1864.[18]

"As a result of the racial bitterness aggravated by Reconstruction politics, black Baptists could not even affirm church union with their most compatible protégés, the Free Missionists. By 1869," Washington asserts, "the die was cast. Ricard DeBaptiste, president of the black Consolidated Convention, confessed that 'in our organization we are separate, but we are one in the great principle of an anti-caste gospel for all the people on the earth.'"[19] The Consolidated American Baptist Missionary Convention was the first national united black Baptist body which formed through the merger of the American Baptist Missionary Convention and the Northwestern and Southern Baptist Convention largely because white Baptists were unable to affirm the social equality of black people, the belief that black Baptists in the south would be more accepting of black leadership, and black Baptists in the north felt inclined and obligated to evangelize and educate black people in the south.[20]

Growing Black Baptist Institutionalization —Some Case Studies

National Baptist Convention

Birthed in 1895, on the threshold of the first century when African Americans were not enslaved, the National Baptist Convention was envisioned to be an instrument that would contribute to the full development of African Americans. Injustice was the major historical context out of which the denomination was formed just three decades after the end of the American Civil War. The legacy of chattel slavery (which classified Africans and their descendants as property to be bought and sold, and used and abused at the will of slave owners or their designees) and the reality of Jim Crow laws (which made racial segregation and oppression legal) created the need for

17. Washington, *Frustrated Fellowship*, 37.
18. Washington, *Frustrated Fellowship*, 38.
19. Washington, *Frustrated Fellowship*, 83
20. Washington, *Frustrated Fellowship*, 84.

a network of churches to address challenges of poverty, illiteracy, and terrorism that subjugated black people. The NBC became a strategic response to help cultivate intellectual, material, and spiritual resources to strengthen black people domestically and globally.

Three organizations united to form the National Baptist Convention in 1895. They were the Baptist Foreign Mission Convention, formed in 1880 in Birmingham, Alabama to advance missions in Africa; the American National Baptist Convention, founded in 1886 in St. Louis, Missouri which aspired to organize all African-American Baptists in the United States; and the National Baptist Educational Convention, organized in 1893 in Washington, District of Columbia to establish educational policy that would produce educated leaders for the black Baptist church in the United States.

The Independent Strategy

A substantial cleavage in black Baptist communities from the latter part of the nineteenth century was around the strategies of separatists versus cooperationists. The separatists, who sometimes called themselves progressives, were advocates of black power. Cooperationist believed that engagement with, or perhaps the guardianship of, white people was essential given the economic and social predicament of black Americans following abolition of slavery.[21]

Black Baptist separatists called for working apart from white Baptists because they concluded that white Baptists *could not see black Baptists as equal partners in ministry and equal siblings in the family of God*. The history of race relations in the United States led them to conclude that racial cooperation for churches was not likely attainable in the late 1890s. Their experiences with and recollections of slavery, their encounters with discrimination following abolition, the brutalities of Jim Crow laws, and the terrorism of lynching and the like made possibilities for interracial collaboration difficult to imagine.

Those who advocated developing the new black Baptist denomination independent from white Baptists, however, proposed interracial collaboration along civil rights issues that included bringing lynch mobs to justice, integrating eating and lodging establishments, and eliminating Jim Crow segregation in public transportation. Those who asserted working separately also believed *that they owed to their posterity* the forming and maturing of a denomination that helped churches to develop capacities for missions,

---

21. Washington, *Frustrated Fellowship*, 176–77.

education, and achieving freedom in the United States for generations to come.

As the National Baptist Convention proceeded to exercise its independence from white Baptists, it developed its own publishing house to produce literature to advance its vision of Christian formation rather than depend upon white Baptist publishers to interpret doctrine and religious commitments. By 1915, however, another break in relationships materialized around the ownership and authority of the publishing board and the denomination. This was crucial because of a commitment to the intellectual resourcing of African-American Baptists and in creating a platform for black Baptist theologians and thought leaders to inform and educate their constituencies. The result was a split which resulted in the formation of the National Baptist Convention of America and the National Baptist Convention, USA, Inc.

Concerning Liberation

The hunger for freedom informed aspects of the theological framework of National Baptists which, although similar in many ways with white Baptists, developed a distinctive emphasis on liberation informed by the Exodus narrative of ancient Israel, the commitment of Jesus for good news for the poor, and freedom for the oppressed. The denomination sought to be a vehicle to promote the spiritual, social, and material progress of its people.

Black Baptists have been voices of conscience to the United States and the world. NBCUSA churches have produced prophetic leaders that have contributed to the liberation and progress of many people. They have been loyal dissenters to the Baptist world, and beyond, that often has been captured by the dominant culture's commitment to violence and consumption, and they have been advocates for justice on behalf of people victimized by power and greed. They have sought to embrace the vision of the Lordship of Christ, religious liberty, priesthood of all believers, and a world that is humane and habitable for all. Twentieth-century examples of prominent and transformational leaders out of the National Baptist tradition include: educator-missionary-activist Nannie Helen Burroughs (1879–1961), artist-activist Mahalia Jackson (1911–1972), pastor-politician-activist Adam Clayton Powell (1908–1972), pastor-educator-humanitarian-activist Samuel DeWitt Proctor (1914–2005), and pastor-activist Martin Luther King Jr. (1929–1968). Regrettably, however, the inability to form a vibrant denominational life has prevented African-American Baptists from providing institutional to resource its prophetic and transformational leaders.

The Progressive National Baptist Convention

The Progressive National Baptist Convention emerged in 1961 from tensions in the National Baptist Convention, USA primarily over the power of the organization's presidency. At the time, NBCUSA was the largest African-American organization in the country. Consequently, whoever was its president was one of the most prominent black leaders in the world. This influence extended beyond spiritual and ecclesial spheres. This influence extended to political, social, and economic realms of black life in America. As a powerful leader, the president also was positioned to be a chief negotiator and ambassador for black America with white structures of power.

Toward the end of the tenure of D. V. Jemison (1940–1953) the Convention was moving to establish tenure to impede efforts to establish long standing imperialistic presidencies. Previous Presidents enjoyed long tenures (E. C. Morris, twenty-seven years, 1895–1922; L. K. Williams, eighteen years, until his death in a plane crash, 1922–1940; D. V. Jemison, thirteen years, 1940–1953).

Following the contentious election of J. H. Jackson in 1953, his administration proceeded to lift the tenure of the presidency making way for, what Jackson's detractors would label as, the emergence of dynasties. Following subsequent reelections and his defeat of the prominent pastor and preacher Gardner Calvin Taylor, L. Venchael Booth proceeded to organize the Progressive National Baptist Convention. Booth contended that many of those who opposed the leadership of Jackson "have become so victimized by our fears until we have surrendered almost completely to dictatorship, mob rule, and high powered politics."[22]

While the issue of the tenure of the presidency of the National Baptist Convention is the key matter precipitating the formation of the Progressive Convention, the deeper issue has been about the role of democracy in a Baptist denomination. The leaders who were removed from places of influence in the National Baptist Convention because of their opposition to Jackson or their perceived threat to his hold on power were determined not to subject themselves to political manipulation and machinations in the church. Perhaps this commitment to democracy and its intrinsic relationship to freedom contributed to the PNBC's embrace of Martin Luther King Jr. and the Civil Rights Movement. While it is erroneous to assert that the issue of the unchecked power of an untenured president and the Civil Rights Movement together precipitated the birth of the PNBC, it is logical

---

22. Booth, *Call to Greatness*, 23.

that people committed to freedom in the church would concomitantly be devoted to freedom in the society.

Conclusion

African-American Baptist history and ecclesiology may work against solidarity and contribute significantly to its tendency toward separating strategically. Quinton Hosford Dixie points out that the Baptist polity of congregational autonomy works against institutional viability. This has contributed to the failure of the National Baptist Convention to become a coherent and cohesive community with capacity to be truly transformational for its constituency or the country.[23]

Baptists value congregational authority highly. This contributes to a congregation's energy for project and program support because they generally feel a sense of close partnership. Large scale support generally grows upward into associational, state, or national embrace. This does not exclude efforts at higher levels of organizational life to be proposed and pursued. But the ecclesiology of Baptists, and particularly black Baptists for our focus, makes it difficult for major initiatives to "come from the top" and be broadly successful. This focus on congregational authority also works against large scale institutional and organizational investment that can provide for robust infrastructure and cohesiveness.

Washington asserts that "In the case of the Black Baptist Movement, fusion has never really taken place. The solidarity needed to become an effective social and political force has been lacking because the various sociological consequences of more than 250 years of slavery have not been taken seriously by black Baptists themselves." Black Baptists could produce, and have produced, prophets but they have not been able to resource prophetic ministries with the institutional capital needed to translate vision into action.[24]

Beyond Washington's and Dixie's conclusions about challenges for institutional viability for African-American Baptists, I assert that *they tend to separate as a strategy for making room to serve*. Separation is an unintended, yet unavoidable, strategy for at least two reasons.

First, the institutions which frame national and congregational life for African-American Baptists, and all African-Americans, is infected with and informed by racial prejudice. Racism is in the US national and theological DNA. Consequently, African-American Baptists have never known a

---

23. Dixie, "How Firm a Foundation?," 328.
24. Washington, *Frustrated Fellowship*, 202–3.

national institution that contributed to their health and wholeness over a sustained period of time. This is true historically and presently. As a result, they have no vested interest in fighting for and working to sustain an institution when it underperforms or acts harmfully. They have little to nothing to lose, and everything to gain, by separating from institutions that are not serving their best interests.

Second, because African-American Baptists have not had good historical relationships with institutions, they have not benefitted from the leadership development that organizations afford constituents whom the bodies serve well. There are inadequate pathways to denominational leadership through service at various levels, with different programs, and in diverse roles. Consequently, African-American Baptist denominations appear most vibrant—and I emphasize *appear*—when they have charismatic leaders. This creates a problem, however, because charismatic leaders are not often as strong in their strategic and organizational capacities. The strategic and organizational strengths they may have seem to result in concentrating power close to themselves rather than distributing it throughout the organization. They do not operate with a pneumatological approach to power. This means that the charismatic leader is not facilitating the organization she or he leads to create opportunities for diverse leaders to operate in various capacities in different levels and several parts of the organization. As a result, gifted African-American leaders, with nowhere to contribute their abilities within, have to leave the denomination and form new organizations *in order to serve*.

Negotiating effectively the tension between congregational autonomy and voluntary association is a formidable challenge for collaboration among Baptists and Believers Churches in general. Sociological and psychological consequences emanating from institutional racism—whether intentional or unintended—amplify the likelihood of separations among African-American Baptists. It may be necessary if they are to make room to serve.

CHAPTER 8

Union Overtures by Maritime Baptists and Disciples of Christ, 1903–1908

Russell Prime

THIS PAPER IS A brief look at union efforts between Canadian Baptists and Canadian Disciples of Christ in the Maritime Provinces between 1903 and 1908. In the first decade of the twentieth century, union was in the air![1] Indeed, North America was on the threshold of an important trend towards unity of the deeply divided sectarian interests that separated Protestant North America.

Missionaries on the fields of both overseas areas and Western parts of this continent forged a co-operative spirit between themselves. It was not merely a matter of witnessing unity (important enough as this was), but it was a matter of economy—of realizing the importance of not duplicating another's work—and of perhaps common sense. Protestants were also coming together for other reasons. For instance, the Sunday School movement became popular across many denominations, and Sunday School conventions like the one held at Germain Street Baptist Church in Saint John from 14–16 October 1902,[2] had become common and institutionalized in the

---

1. Dr. Boggs at the Convention meeting for Maritime Baptists in 1907 at Wolfville. See the report on the Convention in the September 18, 1907 issue of *Maritime Baptist*.

2. *The Christian* (1902), 8. The Convention included the participation of the Mayor of Saint John and representatives of the Women's Christian Temperance Union and was the province's eighteenth such convention. *The Christian* was the monthly journal of the Home Mission Board of the Disciples of Christ in the Maritime Provinces, published by the Barnes's family in Saint John, New Brunswick, from 1883 to

late nineteenth century. Similar co-operation was experienced for a time in the North American and Maritime work of the Christian Endeavor youth movement.[3] This is not to say that there were still not hesitations and feelings of mistrust; these were to exist for a long time, but a new solidarity was developing as lay and clergy people met, talked, and shared with each other at conventions, prayer meetings, in the Evangelical Alliance groups, at tables of the developing YMCAs and YWCAs, during Temperance meetings, and in the Lord's Day Alliance.

Some Christians were not supportive of the emerging evangelical and "social gospel" movements,[4] and this theological suspicion would eventually win the day against this Modernist project. However, for many Canadian believers, sectarianism was lessening its negative grip, and there was a growing consensus that Protestant churches were needing to face their educational and missionary tasks together.[5]

This new spirit of unity first helped to fuel the desire to heal old wounds and separations within denominational groupings. In the United States, for instance, several of the denominations that had split during the Civil War began to make reparations. Canadian churches were also in a uniting mood. Presbyterians united in Canada largely by 1875, the Methodists by 1884, and the Ontario and Quebec Baptist conventions in 1888.[6] By the turn of the twentieth century, calls were being heard for wider union activity. Many anticipated the evangelization of the entire world in their time.[7]

1917; it merged to form *The Canadian Disciple* along with the Ontario paper in 1922. *The Christian* is preserved at the Pratt Library of Victoria University (Toronto) at the United Church of Canada Archives. A journal of the same name was published by William Wentworth Eaton in the 1830s and 1840s.

3. I note that R. Everett Stevenson (of the Halifax church) spoke at the Christian Endeavor Convention held at Cincinnati in 1901: *The Christian* (August 1901): 2. Stevenson was originally from Prince Edward Island and was active in the Home Mission work of the Disciples of Christ in Western Canada in the late 1800s and early decades of the 1900s. D. A. Morrison, a deacon at Douglas Avenue Christian Church in Saint John, served as the Maritime President for Christian Endeavor Union, beginning in 1901 for several years: *The Christian* (August 1901): 1 and *The Christian* (September 1901): 4. The Maritime C. E. Union would become the Convention of Young Peoples' Societies of the Maritime Provinces in 1903 in an attempt to continue strained linkages among existing denominations co-operating in C. E. work, the new Baptist Young Peoples' Union, and the Epworth League: *The Christian* (June 1903): 2.

4. Airhart, "Ordering a New Nation," 98–138.

5. This thesis is well-developed in Bower and Hayward, *Protestantism*.

6. Airhart, "Ordering a New Nation," 99.

7. Not all the interdenominational movements during this period resulted in unity movements. For instance, the Keswick and Christian Missionary and Alliance movements would lead to splits in the latter part of the nineteenth century that would

What kind of union? Organic union, federated union, co-operative union—Christians were contemplating all manners of church union. Union with whom? In this short paper, the discussion is about union between the Disciples of Christ and the United Baptist Convention of the Maritime Provinces. Other churches were also speaking about coming together. Indeed, many will be familiar with the union movement that took on steam in this time period that resulted in the formation of the United Church of Canada, primarily between Methodists in Canada and Bermuda and many Canadian Congregationalists and Presbyterians. Baptists and Disciples of Christ could not imagine at that time of joining a single church with paedobaptists; co-operation and fraternal relations were one thing—union was quite another.

Baptists

Baptists in Atlantic Canada grew out of several sources, and this history is well-known. For example, scholars such as George A. Rawlyk helped document some of the earliest beginnings: the Congregational New Light fervour in Nova Scotia (the greater Maritime Provinces) that awakened in the Planters under Henry Alline and others, particularly during the American Revolutionary War. Several New Lights became convinced of their need to be baptized by immersion and became Baptists in practice. The first co-operative association of Baptists in the Maritimes was formed in 1800 at Granville. They experienced significant growth in the nineteenth century and beyond. By 1906, most Regular and Free Baptist congregations had united into one convention in the Maritime Provinces.

Disciples of Christ

The Maritime roots of what would become the Disciples of Christ had their own distinct and independent origins but also share some Baptist beginnings. Recent research by Michael Christie and Roland McCormick sheds new light on these beginnings and challenges some of what was known

---

fan the growth of Pentecostalism in the first decade of the twentieth century. The Disciples of Christ would suffer their first split (a latten one from Civil War era) by 1906. The growth of the Plymouth Brethren and their dispensational theology also occurs during this period. The debate over the validity and implications of higher criticism would also grow (see Airhart, "Ordering a New Nation," 108–11). Even those in general support of union would discuss the "common" and "disputed" grounds surrounding issues, such as Baptism and the Lord's Supper. See, for example, Crawford, "Christian Union" 4; Motley, "Beginning at Jerusalem," 1.

before;[8] however, I did not have access to their book until after much of my paper was completed. In general, Baptist churches with roots in Scotland formed the nucleus of the Prince Edward Island Disciples or Christian churches; for example, the Cross Roads Christian Church (Lot 48) was holding services as early as 1810.[9] Haldane-trained Alexander Crawford emigrated from Scotland to Nova Scotia; he then moved to Prince Edward Island about 1812. Crawford is said to have baptized the first Christian adult believer on the Island. Many of the churches that Crawford had encouraged became associated with the Disciples of Christ under the influence of preacher and P.E.I. medical doctor John Knox. Baptist layman, John Stevenson, emigrated to the New Glasgow area of Prince Edward Island from Paisley, Scotland and founded a church there.[10]

In River John, Pictou County, Nova Scotia, James Murray of Banffshire, Scotland, another Baptist formed a small church there on 18 June 1815 (Waterloo Day).[11] Free Christian Baptist and Christian Connection movements had some influence on the growth of churches in Saint John, N.B., and Milton, Queens County, Nova Scotia in the 1830s. Leadership from this rather fluid Christian/Christian Connection/Free Baptist movement included William Wentworth Eaton and George Garrity in New Brunswick and William Ashley in the Liverpool area of Nova Scotia.[12]

Other churches in Nova Scotia (Hants County: Rawdon, West Gore, Newport, Shubenacadie, and Falmouth; Kings County: Cornwallis and Billtown; and Halifax) grew out of Regular Baptist bodies that had encountered and accepted the intellectual influences of Alexander Campbell and other American and British Disciples probably from *The Christian Gleaner* in the late 1830s. *The Christian Gleaner* was edited by Lewis Johnston, MD, and others who were part of Halifax's Granville Street Chapel (Baptist). This chapel (Burton's Church) was made of up several Black families, influential dissenters from St. Paul's Anglican, and others; out of it would come Cornwallis Street Baptist Church, other Halifax County African Baptist Churches, First Baptist Church of Halifax (at times, known as Third Baptist or Granville continued), and a Disciples of Christ Church (began as

---

8. See generally this excellent book by Christie and McCormick, *New Perspective*.

9. "The origins of this church begin with John R. Stewart, who came from Perthshire, Scotland. As early as 1810, he was holding worship services in his home. At this time, all of the adherents were of Scots ancestry and their faith was influenced by Baptist theology" (Canada's Historic Places, "Cross Roads Christian Church").

10. Butchart, *Disciples of Christ in Canada*, 286–87.

11. Butchart, *Disciples of Christ in Canada*, 337.

12. Butchart, *Disciples of Christ in Canada*, 353.

Disciple-influenced Second Baptist Church).¹³ John McDonald, the pastor of the Baptist Church in Rawdon was one of the first to make this transition along with several from his congregation.¹⁴ Eventually, those congregations that survived found each other through the efforts and journal of W. W. Eaton and other itinerant preachers. From the 1830s until the 1850s, the churches met in various meetings in Nova Scotia (Hants and Kings County churches) and Prince Edward Island to support field evangelists and to help and edify each other when they could.

During this early period, the churches are at times co-operative with the Baptist associations (especially in Halifax and Prince Edward Island) and at other times independent of them. George Garraty of the Oromocto area of the Saint John River Valley became an important figure in the Disciples' movement in the 1830s.¹⁵ It was said of Elder George Garraty, the long-time minister of the Saint John Duke Street congregation and extensive traveling evangelist, that he was named "the breaking-up plough" for his ability of "turning a Baptist church into a 'Christian' church at one visit." Garraty began in the Free Christian Baptist movement and was instrumental in organizing four lasting congregations in Nova Scotia nearly all of the New Brunswick churches. Garraty was known for his "merciless attacks on 'sectarianism'" and denominationalism.¹⁶ These attacks were principally against the Baptist organizations. To early Free Baptists such as Rev. Joshua Barnes of New Brunswick, the Disciples were trouble-makers extraordinaire. Much of the Baptist-Disciple controversy stems from the fact that many early leaders and church members of Disciples congregations come out of splits or takeovers of formerly Baptist supporters. Some of the theology of Disciples was also problematic, with a strong teaching on the place of baptism "for the remission of sins"—what some have called baptismal regeneration at its strongest. This teaching was not fully ascribed to by Alexander Campbell and other founders of the Christian movement; however, by the second generation of Disciples, many held views akin to that charge. It is no wonder that pamphlets like the one written by A. P. Williams, D.D. of

---

13. Five churches resulted from the turmoil of the Granville Street Chapel: "Granville Street, African Baptist, Hammond's Plains, Preston, and the Disciples of Christ—all reflected particular interests and social classes of the people involved" (Allwood, "First Baptist Church, Halifax," 119). See also Griffin-Allwood, "Disciple of Christ"; Shaw, "History of the Disciples of Christ," 20–26 (and a book by Shaw on the history of the North Street Christian Church [same subject]).

14. Butchart, *Disciples of Christ in Canada*, 347.

15. "Disciples of Christ, or Christians," 54. The two other ministers listed in the directory were W. W. Eaton in Saint John and J. B. Barnaby in West Isles.

16. Butchart, *Disciples of Christ in Canada*, 129.

the American Baptist Publication Society were circulated in the Maritimes in 1884. This pamphlet's title was "No Communion With Campbellites."

The Christian or Disciple movement in these provinces was wary of scriptural grounds for missionary societies, and it was not until 1855, that many of their representatives came together under American Disciple influence and formed the first Maritime co-operative society to encourage church growth and new congregations. The Milton church was instrumental in this effort. A Home Mission Board for New Brunswick and Nova Scotia was created by 1880 and operated in conjunction with the annual conventions. The churches desired to begin the publication of a journal at the Annual in Tiverton, Digby County, in 1883; this was the birth of *The Christian*, a major source of information for this paper. By 1903, there were approximately thirty-five active Disciples of Christ congregations in Maritime Canada.

It is important to note that the historic Disciples of Christ movement, sometimes called the Stone-Campbell Movement or the Restoration Movement, has encountered major splits at least two times since its maturity as a movment in Canada and the United States. Near the turn of the twentieth century, a largely *a cappella* group of churches became known as the Churches of Christ. From the 1950s to the 1970s, most of the congregations in the Maritime Provinces withdrew from the developing "Christian Church (Disciples of Christ)" denomination and simply called themselves Christian Churches or Churches of Christ, a non-denominational group of churches who partner with Maritime Christian College in Charlottetown and are sometimes loosely associated with the North American Christian Convention, Inc. in the United States. The South Lake Christian Church was the most recent church to withdraw from the Disciples' denominational structures in 1995; and, it is a congregation which shares a yoked pastorate with Kingsboro Baptist Church in East Point, P.E.I. All three streams of the movement are represented in the Maritime Provinces. At the time that this paper is published, there are approximately 39 congregations in Nova Scotia, New Brunswick, and Prince Edward Island, including five Churches of Christ (*a cappella*), twenty-nine Christian Churches/Churches of Christ, and five Disciples of Christ. There is also a Disciples of Christ congregation with some links to the Maritime Provinces in Lubec, Maine.[17]

17. In November 2016, there are 14 churches in Nova Scotia, 13 in New Brunswick, and 12 in P.E.I. of all three streams. The five *a cappella* congregations are in Kentville, Mill Village, and Halifax, N.S. and in Moncton and Saint John, N.B. The 29 Churches of Christ and Christian Churches are located in Charlottetown (three congregations), Cornwall, East Point, Greenmount, Montague, Murray Harbour, New Glasgow, O'Leary, and Summerside, P.E.I.; Back Bay, Burtt's Corner, Dieppe, Fredericton, Garnett Settlement, Leonardville, L'Etete, Lord's Cove, Nauwigewauk, St. George, and Saint John, N.B.; and, Dartmouth, Halifax, South Range, Southville, Tiverton, Westport, and

The Real Story Begins: Actual Overtures

Accordingly, for a time, there was little trust between the two groups in this region, and there is much evidence in the journals of both movements in the 1830s of controversy and distrust. However, by the turn of the twentieth century, things were changing. For example, we read of a pulpit exchange that involved the Baptist, Disciple, and Congregational churches in Milton, Nova Scotia in March of 1900.[18] And, on Monday morning, 18 November 1901, Rev. G. Nelson Stevenson, "the new pastor of the Coburg Street Christian Church" in Saint John, New Brunswick "was introduced and made a member of the [Baptist] Minister's Union," which included Alex White, the General Secretary of the Baptist Convention.[19] Dr. E. M. Kierstead of Acadia University brought an "eloquent address of a congratulatory nature" at the dedication of a new house of worship for Disciples at Port Williams, NS, on 12 April 1903.[20] And, in May of 1903, a newly formed Christian Ministerial Association in the Maritime Provinces and the State of Maine met for the first time in Saint John. It included clergy such as A. H. Foster of St. Matthew's Presbyterian and Rev. Dr. Gates of Germain Street Baptist Church. We read that Dr. Gates delivered "a most scholarly and exhaustive" paper on Galatians and that he echoed the prevailing thought of the period: "the Baptists, Free Baptists and Disciples should be one, and he saw no reason why Presbyterians, Methodists and Congregationalists should maintain separate organizations."[21]

In the December 1903 issue of *The Christian*, Editor E. C. Ford (then ministering on Long & Brier Islands in Southwestern Nova Scotia) and W. A. Barnes (office editor and publisher at Saint John, NB) note with keen interest that "an effort is being made to revive the question of union of the Baptist and Free Baptist churches of New Brunswick."[22] They recall that such an effort had been made "a number of years ago" but had failed. They suggest that there are strong people and good prospects of Regular and Free Baptist union this time around. Successful Baptist union, they suggest,

---

Weymouth, N.S. The five Disciples of Christ congregations are located in Charlottetown, P.E.I. and in Dartmouth, Milton, Summerville Centre, and West Gore, N.S.

18. *The Christian* (April 1900): 3.

19. *The Christian* (December 1901): 6. The same news article from the journal (a reprint from Saint John's *Daily Sun* of 19 November 1901) indicates that J.C.B. Appel, another Saint John Disciples of Christ minister, was already a member of the Association.

20. *The Christian* (May 1903): 1.

21. *The Christian* (June 1903): 2.

22. *The Christian* (December 1903): 4, on the editorial page.

might also open up dialogue with Disciples—if "our party feelings could be buried, and the spirit breathed in the prayer of our Lord for a united people, could fill all our hearts." They go on to write, "The obstacles to Christian union, especially among all immersionists, are matters of opinions, and certain interpretations of Scriptures. Already there is sufficient unity among these people, in all essentials of Christianity, to warrant a united effort in all Christian work."

Nova Scotia & New Brunswick

At the Disciples of Christ Annual Meeting for Nova Scotia and New Brunswick, in 1904 at Burtt's Corner (near Fredericton), NB, a Committee on Union was struck. It made distinctions between matters of faith and opinion and urged that union should be considered if accomplished with the Bible—the inspired Word of God—as the true basis for the unity move. They explained,

> To this end we plead for an unqualified return to primitive Christianity, both in faith and practice. We believe all churches and professing Christians should go back of all ecclesiasticisms, denominationalism, human creeds and party names to take their stand among the apostolic churches, and adopt their faith in purity and their approved practices without change. In other words, they should hold the same creed they held, wear the same names they wore, believe the same proposition and doctrine they believed, make the same good confession they made, practise the same baptism they practised, and, in short, do as they did in order to become Christians. . . . Nothing should be made a test of Christian fellowship and a bar to Christian union which Christ has not made a condition of salvation.[23]

It is not surprising that Archibald McLean was the speaker at the convention; he was raised in P.E.I., baptized by Donald Crawford, and trained at Bethany College in the US. He served as the President of the Foreign Christian Missionary Society and was a strong proponent of greater unity among faith families.

As a result of the report, a standing committee of three Disciples' ministers was appointed "to communicate with or receive communications

---

23. "Report of Committee on Union," 3. Committee members: J. C. B. Appel, H. Murray, and J. F. Floyd. Read and Adopted by the Annual Meeting at the Morning Session, Saturday, 20 August 1904 at Burtt's Corner, New Brunswick.

from various denominations regarding Christian union."[24] Similar motions were approved at the Disciples' annual meeting in Halifax on 17–20 August 1905, giving the Committee [on Church Union] the mandate "to hold negotiations with the Baptist Brethren with a view to Christian Union."[25] Up to this point, the Disciples had put themselves on record as favouring the union of God's people and had appointed a standing committee; yet, only informal discussions had taken place with various Baptist leaders. The Free and Regular Baptists had joined forces in New Brunswick in 1905, and agreement was reached for Baptist bodies in Nova Scotia to unite in 1906. The Disciples were the next logical subjects of union.

By chance or providence, both the United Baptists and the Disciples met in their annual conventions in Queen's County, NS, during the same week of 24–27 August 1906. The Disciples met at their church in Kempt near Caledonia and the headwaters of the Mersey River. The Baptists congregated downstream, near the mouth of the Mersey, at churches in Liverpool and Milton. The Disciples expanded their standing committee on Church Union to five members (four ministers and one elder/publisher),[26] sent greetings to the Baptists meeting in Liverpool by telephone, and asked if the Baptist Convention might consider appointed a standing committee to meet with the Disciples' committee at their next annual meeting, the place yet to be appointed (in Tiverton, Digby County, NS). *The Maritime Baptist* reported that the fraternal greetings were well-received and a recommendation was passed by the first (sixty-first) United Baptist Convention to appoint a committee of three to meet with the Disciples at their next annual gathering.

Cordial relations continued, and Archibald McLean and W. J. Wright (Corresponding Secretary of the American Christian Missionary Society (ACMS) and a leader in Home Missions in the Northwest) were invited to attend and address the next Baptist Convention at Wolfville in 1907. They were enthusiastically received.

Here are some of voices from the 1907 convention:[27]

"Union is in the air, not only here but in India." Dr. Boggs

---

24. *The Christian* (September 1904) 3. Committee consisted of J. Chas. B. Appel, J. F. Floyd, and E. C. Ford.

25. *The Christian* (September 1905): 2.

26. *The Christian* (September 1906): 1.

27. See the report on the Baptist Convention in *Maritime Baptist*, September 18, 1907.

> "Canada leads in the matter of church union. The great union of Methodists and Presbyterians is coming, and why should not the Disciples and Baptists unite." Dr. Archibald McLean, President of the Foreign Christian Missionary Society.[28]

> "We don't want Canada for the Anglicans, the Presbyterians, the Methodists, the Roman Catholics, or even for the Baptists [coming from a good Baptist], but for Christ." Rev. C. W. Corey[29]

The discussions of union did bring up the old heresy and debate on whether or not the Disciples taught baptismal regeneration. However, this did not seem to be the largest hurdle to closer co-operation. We read from *The Maritime Baptist* of 18 September 1907:

> Mr. Editor: Please allow space for an explanation respecting the failure of the U. B. Convention Committee to meet the Disciples in their Convention at Tiverton. I was not aware that it was intended for the committee of twelve to go or be represented at Tiverton owing, I suppose, to the fact that I was engaged with the Com. on nominations, when the Queen's Co. letter was read and referred, and absent from the committee on nominations when I was appointed chairman. The committee of twelve was struck, appointed by Convention, convened and dismissed without the Tiverton meeting being referred to as far as I remember. I very much regret the disappointment to our brethren the Disciples, and the loss of the opportunity for furthering a cause which I have long hoped to see realized. When a time mutually convenient can be arranged, the work assigned us will be taken up.
>
> Edwin Crowell, Chairman. Canning, NS, Sept. 12th 1907.

The committees did eventually meet and discuss matters at Port Williams. In August of 1908, both conventions approved the following resolution:[30]

> 1. That a fuller acquaintance be encouraged by the interchange of pulpits, and by the sending of fraternal delegates to the respective conventions.

---

28. Archibald McLean was a Disciples of Christ minister and administrator born in Prince Edward Island.
29. C. W. Corey was a minister representing Baptists in Western Canada.
30. *The Christian* (September 1908): 1.

2. That weak congregations be encouraged to co-operate in the sustaining of regular ministerial work, and that where necessary the Home Mission Boards unite in assisting these co-operating congregations.

3. That a Standing Committee on Union be appointed by both conventions with a view of bringing to pass this much-to-be-desired and organic union.

Edwin Crowell, Chairman.

J. C. B. Appel, Secretary.

More talks were held, but organic union did not come to pass. However, co-operation certainly continued in many parts of the Maritimes.

Prince Edward Island

Union discussions were not isolated to Nova Scotia and New Brunswick. Indeed, Baptists and Disciples in Prince Edward Island played a special role. Early in the first decade of the twentieth century, important island relationships were being rekindled. There were no Free Christian or Free Baptist churches on the Island to focus co-operative efforts on; instead, the Disciples and Baptists constituted the only two immersionist groups—both having been started by the common leadership of Christians influences by Baptist movements in Scotland such as Alexander Crawford and Donald Crawford. Dr. John Knox, a convert from Anglicanism was also an important builder of the Disciples movement in Prince Edward Island and Halifax. In 1904, the P.E.I. Annual Association of the Baptist Church meeting at East Point appointed a committee to attend the Annual Convention of Island Christian Churches "to confer with reference to a union of the two bodies." The Disciples of the Island met at Montague later in August and heartily endorsed the union movement and unanimously pledged themselves to doing all in their power to "speedily consummate such union."[31]

Exchanges of delegates and preachers continued on the Island over the next couple of years. The pastors and ministers of both associations worked closely in all parts of the province. In 1906, the Baptist, Episcopal, and Christian church buildings in Summerside were destroyed by fire. The Christian and Baptists churches made use of the Methodist Church as they decided whether to build a combined building or separate houses of worship. In the end, the Baptist congregation decided to rebuild its own building.

31. *The Christian* (August 1904): 3.

The most lasting relationships of these early union talks occurred in Prince Edward Island. Between 1907 and 1908 at least three Christian Churches co-operated in combined pastorates—at East Point, at Lot 48 near Charlottetown,[32] and in Montague. The yoked pastorate continued at Lot 48 until the 1960s, and co-operation is still ongoing at East Point where Baptist and Christian Church ministers alternate when possible.[33] The two churches making up the East Point work are Kingsboro United Baptist Church (formerly, East Point United Baptist Church) and South Lake Christian Church. South Lake co-operated with the more liberal restoration stream, the Christian Church (Disciples of Christ) in Canada until 1995. In that year, it became an independent Christian Church and began closer co-operation with other Island Restoration churches and Maritime Christian College in Charlottetown. Each church runs quite independently; however, some of the success in this co-operative pastorate has been the strong family and community connections in East Point.

Similar co-operative efforts between Scotch Village's Newport United Baptist Church, the Baptist Church in Cogmagun, and West Gore Church of Christ (Disciples) occurred between the 1940s and the 1980s. Cordial relations continue to exist in other villages in Nova Scotia at Tiverton and Westport in Digby County (with combined youth groups and vacation bible schools at various times) and at Milton near Liverpool on the South Shore.

Efforts at union were not isolated to the churches of the Maritime Provinces. For example, Free Christian Baptists and Disciples discussed union in the United States in 1905.[34] Individual congregations combined for a time in March of 1907 at Kenora, Ontario.[35] Another union happened at Vermillion, Alberta, and the two churches at Portage La Prairie, Manitoba came together as the Church of Christ (Baptist and Disciples) for a short while.[36] Regional talks took place in Boston in the same year,[37] and there were efforts focused on possible mission field co-operation in the Northwest and in Overseas areas. A joint committee was formed by Baptists and Disciples in Ontario and met in Toronto in 1906 and 1907.[38]

---

32. "By 1907, the Cross Roads Church was combined into one charge with Baptist churches in nearby Alexandra and Hazelbrook. This arrangement lasted until 1947" (Canada's Historic Places, "Cross Roads Christian Church").

33. See some of the Baptist and Disciple ministers that served during this period in Sinnott, *East Point United Baptist Church*.

34. *The Christian*, reprint from *Rel. Int.* (July 1905): 5.

35. *The Canadian Baptist* (27 June 1907).

36. *The Christian* (March 1908): 4–5.

37. *The Christian* (March 1908): 1.

38. *The Christian* (December 1906): 3.

Finally, I would like to suggest several reasons why organic union was not realized during this period. Indeed, there was a lingering mistrust from the past, especially around some doctrinal concerns with issues like "baptismal regeneration." And, then, there were the unfortunate circumstances where the Baptists missed meeting with Disciples at their convention in Tiverton in 1907. There were issues around what a united church would be called, and the Christian Churches or Disciples thought very highly of using "Church of Christ" and often pushed for it.[39] There was also the relatively small size of the Disciples, numbering around thirty-five congregations in the Maritime Provinces at the time, as compared to a much larger Baptist convention. And, while the leaders of the respective churches might have had interest in organic union, it is possible that there was significant resistance in local communities and congregations (although I have not seen evidence of this). Indeed, many communities had both churches present in them. In addition, most of the union efforts in Ontario, the West, and elsewhere failed in short order, and significant amounts of the energies of both communions were involved at the same time in creating national alliances, such as the Baptist Federation of Canada and the All-Canada Committee of the Churches of Christ (Disciples). There was also the rise of fundamentalist and liberal debates that may have weakened union efforts.

In the end, the union conversations did produce a lasting legacy. Besides the ongoing pastoral sharing at East Point, P.E.I. and shorter attempts elsewhere, the talks of 1907 and 1908 brought about greater co-operation rather than organic church union and led to significant relationships that would foster the work of Provincial Sunday School movements, Boys and Girls educational committees, Maritime Religious Education Council, Canadian Girls in Training (CGIT), Trail Rangers, summer camping, the Bible Society, Atlantic Ecumenical Council, and Canadian Council of Churches. Until recently, the two church bodies continued to share observers at their conventions and are recognizing their historic and perhaps future connections.

Nor would union efforts entirely end by 1908. Further discussions would take place in the 1950s and later in the century. Indeed, there was a strong legacy of co-operation which continued until the 1980s when some in the Baptist movement in Atlantic Canada began to shift to a more conservative outlook. Indeed, most of the Disciples of Christ congregations in the Maritime Provinces formally left the developing denomination structures of

---

39. *The Christian* (March 1907): 5–6. Here a reprint of a letter to the editor of the *Christian-Evangelist* (the Ontario Disciples of Christ paper) states "I candidly think that if the question of the name could be satisfactory settled, an organic union of the two bodies in Canada would soon be accomplished."

the more liberal parts of the Disciples of Christ from the 1960s to the 1970s. After this time, the remaining Disciples of Christ began to focus union efforts on the United Church of Canada and the Anglican Church. There is still hope by some, especially in the independent stream of the Restoration Movement, that one day some of the Christian Churches and Churches of Christ in the Maritime Provinces might join forces or work more closely together in some way with Canadian Baptists in Atlantic Canada.

I would like to end this paper with a quote by Australian Church of Christ minister, Murdoch Gunn, a student evangelist studying at Transylvania University in Lexington, Kentucky, who spent several months in Prince Edward Island in 1884 and 1885. He was visiting Tryon, P.E.I. in a much more sectarian time, where four churches dotted a small village. He makes this excellent plea for unity from there in November of 1884:

> Often and often, as I walked up and down the road in full view of these four churches did I think what a spectacle these four edifices must present to a reflective mind. Four different religious bodies having the same God and Father, the same Saviour, the same Heaven, the same Bible, the same Gospel to proclaim in order to save the same Human family, the same Holy Spirit to comfort and sanctify them. Yet each proclaiming a different system of religion, in some of its fundamental principles, each claiming to have the Truth, and each condemning those who differ therefrom: and oh, the prejudice, enough to make an angel weep. How many, oh, how many are driven into skepticism and infidelity by these divisions of the Lord's people.[40]

Summary

Disciples of Christ, Christian Churches/Churches of Christ, and Churches of Christ (*a cappella*) congregations in the Maritime Provinces separated out of the Baptist and associated movements in Atlantic Canada and New England in the early nineteenth century, and they were known in 1903 as Disciples of Christ or Christians. Baptists and Disciples of Christ congregations in Atlantic Canada nearly joined in organic union between 1903 and 1908; however, the circumstances of the union talks (a failure to meet at the appointed time), slight theological differences, and geographic concerns probably resulted in the failure of the overall effort in 1907. Local co-operation at the congregational level continued after the initial union

---

40. *The Christian* (November 1884): 2.

efforts ended, especially in a few areas of Nova Scotia and Prince Edward Island. Official talks and consultations at the convention level continued at various points throughout the twentieth century, with the joint sharing of pastoral ministry by Baptists and Christian Churches/Churches of Christ at East Point, P.E.I., being the most lasting legacy.

CHAPTER 9

Promiscuous Picnics

Newfoundland Pentecostalism as a
"Come-Outer" Tradition

Allison S. MacGregor

Pentecostalism has long been viewed as a separatist movement and such has not been a limited to a particular geographical location or demographic. The early pentecostals uniformly emphasized the Bible as the authoritative rule for both faith and practice and they strongly rejected creeds and liturgical practices. Their rejection of the Christian creeds was likely a contributing factor to their emphasis on practices, which led to tension within various pentecostal groups. Pentecostalism, as a revivalistic tradition with direct theological descent from the holiness movement, has always dealt with issues related to the taboos of both traditions.[1] They perceived themselves as "being in the world but not of the world." One might argue that their unwritten, yet oft spoken, motto was, "Come out from among them and be ye separate, saith the Lord" (2 Cor 6:17a, KJV).

In more recent years, urbanization, globalization, and affluence has led to the decline of many of these practices, yet these taboos are still points of contention in many pentecostal groups. Some of the obvious taboos in pentecostal groups are dancing, alcohol, tobacco, playing cards, and other forms of perceived "worldliness." Historically, attending the theatre was generally not acceptable within pentecostalism, yet since the middle of the twentieth century, most North American homes acquired a personal television, leaving little room to debate whether attending the theatre was sinful. Yet, a small minority of pentecostals still maintain this ideal. Also, a minority

---

1. Wilson, "Church Membership," 530.

of pentecostals in North America do not permit women to cut their hair, wear makeup, and impose certain standards of dress. Interesting to note is that the modern pentecostal movement has not been characterized by these traditional holiness taboos. Yet, historically, this was undoubtedly a defining factor in pentecostal ethos and identity. Newfoundland pentecostals are no exception. In fact, the Newfoundland pentecostals, in their devout expression of faith, took these cultural taboos to another extreme and also banned picnics, expressing such was a worldly gathering, worthy of condemnation. In the 1927 General Conference of the Pentecostal Assemblies of Newfoundland, an important decision was made. Minute twenty-seven reads, "Moved that this conference now in session of the Pentecostal Assemblies of NFLD place on record as standing against picnics."[2]

This paper will provide a brief introduction to both Methodism and Pentecostalism in the province of Newfoundland. It will demonstrate that Newfoundland Pentecostalism can be readily identified as a "come-outer" tradition, poignantly seen through key leaders who transferred directly from Methodism into Pentecostalism, bringing with them a unique sense of identity. Lastly, it will compare the lifespan of both movements and highlight questions related to the future of Pentecostalism in Newfoundland. The origin of the conversation must begin with a brief introduction to Methodism in Newfoundland.

Introduction to Methodism in Newfoundland

Laurence Coughlan,[3] formerly a Roman Catholic, was converted to Methodism at Drummersnave, today's Drumsna, Ireland in the early 1750s. He began serving as an itinerant Methodist preacher in Ireland and later England in approximately 1755.[4] After his ordination and presumed separation from the Wesleyan fold, Coughlan registered an independent meetinghouse—something he had been previously against—and was listed simply as a "Preacher of God's Word."[5] He was eventually contacted by those in Newfoundland who sought a minister for their newly erected church in Harbour Grace. It appears that a Congregationalist nonconformist in Con-

---

2. Pentecostal Assemblies of Newfoundland, "General Conference Minutes," s.v. "minute 27."

3. Other sources such as Winsor's *History of Methodism in Newfoundland* spell the name "Lawrence." More reputable sources such as Rollmann's "Origins of Methodism in Newfoundland" use the spelling I have maintained.

4. Scobie and Grant, *Contribution of Methodism*, 54.

5. Scobie and Grant, *Contribution of Methodism*, 57.

ception Bay took the initiative in introducing formal religious services there and thus may have also encouraged the construction of a church building in Harbour Grace.[6]

Shortly thereafter, Laurence Coughlan, along with his wife, Anne, and their daughter, Betsy, set sail for Newfoundland from Poole sometime in April 1766.[7] Naboth Winsor in *A History of Methodism in Newfoundland* described Coughlan's journey as a spiritual calling of sorts: "Under what auspices or impulse he was led to those rugged shores there are no contemporary records to tell, but read in the light of subsequent history we can ascribe his movements only to the guiding hand of God."[8] Regardless of his reasoning, he ended up in Conception Bay, which at that time was one of the most populous areas in Newfoundland.[9] The Church of England was the dominant religious affiliation of the people, to which approximately two-thirds of the population adhered. The remaining were Irish Catholics.[10] Yet at this point, as the colony was still in its infancy, society was still not well organized and most outport communities were still without resident clergy at all.

It was within this paradigm that Coughlan ministered. One can get a glimpse of the state of affairs in Newfoundland at that time by the words of Governor Palliser who observed that the inhabitants of the colony "live as mere savages without religion, without marrying or christening their children . . . who spend the Lord's Day in idleness and debauchery, every one living as he likes."[11] Thus, it was not surprising that in 1766 those inhabitants of Harbour Grace and Carbonear who did hold to Christian values, created a petition addressed to the Society for the Propagation of the Gospel that Laurence Coughlan should be appointed for ministry.

At its general meeting on 19 December 1766, the Society for the Propagation of the Gospel decided to appoint Coughlan "missionary at Harbour Grace and Carbonear with a salary of 50 £ annually" and advanced him half a year's salary.[12] According to correspondence with the Society in London, the missionary faithfully fulfilled his ministerial duties with great care and spurred the communities on to a higher moral life. He participated in the

---

6. Scobie and Grant, *Contribution of Methodism*, 57.
7. Scobie and Grant, *Contribution of Methodism*, 58.
8. Naboth Winsor, *History of Methodism in Newfoundland*, 24.
9. Scobie and Grant, *Contribution of Methodism*, 55.
10. Scobie and Grant, *Contribution of Methodism*, 55.
11. Public Record Office quoted in Parsons "Origin and Growth," 15.
12. General Meeting of the SPG quoted in Scobie and Grant, *Contribution of Methodism*, 59.

generally expected duties of a clergyman, including: marrying, burying, visiting and of course, preaching.[13] Although he was responsible to the Society for the Propagation of the Gospel—a society affiliated undeniably with the Church of England—he was clearly a Methodist in "discipline and doctrine."[14] In a letter to John Wesley written on 11 November, 1772, during his ministry in Harbour Grace, he said, "I am, and do confess myself to be a Methodist. The name I love, and hope I shall ever have. The plan which you first taught me, I have followed as to doctrine and discipline."[15]

While performing his duties as an Anglican clergyman, Coughlan also sought to preach religion, as it was known within Methodism, a "religion of the heart."[16] As was his Methodist tradition, he also organized those who were interested into small groups, for door-to-door evangelism. After little success with this methodology, a revival eventually took place within his church and in the gatherings of these small groups. Coughlan recounts the beginnings of this revival by saying, "Some prayed aloud in the Congregation; others praised aloud, and declared what God had done for their Souls: Nor was this only at their private Meetings, now and then, but also in the great Congregations."[17] Once the revival started, the force and frequency of the manifestations surprised even Coughlan and caused him to doubt their authenticity. After nearly every sermon the people worshipped with great "noise [and] rejoiced in loud Songs of Praise."[18]

Methodism, as it was introduced to Newfoundland through the person of Laurence Coughlan, was true to its revivalist nature. It provided the converted with a personal assurance of freedom from the punishment of sin. Once believers were free from this bondage they were able to truly experience God. The Movement conveyed the conviction of living a holy life, pleasing unto the Lord. These principles, though somewhat retained, had become watered down over the years as was demonstrated through the writings of some Methodist clergy.

---

13. Scobie and Grant, *Contribution of Methodism*, 61.

14. Winsor, *History of Methodism in Newfoundland*, 24. Methodists in Newfoundland were considered by some to be quite strict in their practices concerning Christian living. Coughlan was influential in establishing this Methodist disposition in the province's expression of the Methodist faith.

15. Laurence Caughlan quoted in Winsor, *History of Methodism in Newfoundland*, 24.

16. Scobie and Grant, *Contribution of Methodism*, 62.

17. Laurence Caughlan quoted in Scobie and Grant, *Contribution of Methodism*, 63.

18. Scobie and Grant, *Contribution of Methodism*, 63.

By the late nineteenth century, the Methodist Church had lost much of the zeal of its infancy in the province and was having membership difficulties. For example, Reverend R. W. Freeman reported that in Trinity, Bonavista Bay, Newfoundland:

> We have, by the help of God, endeavoured faithfully to do the work of a Methodist minister. Still we have not been permitted to share in the joy of the reaper. The entire number of those who professed faith in Christ at Cuchold's Cove[19] last spring, have returned to the world.[20]

This report was slightly different from that of Reverend A. Hill from Exploits. He wrote,

> In more than twenty places we have preached the Gospel on this mission and not without many tokens of the Master's presence and blessing. The great drawback seems to be the unsettled state of our people, their going to Labrador in the summer and into the Bay in the winter. This greatly interferes with the members meeting in class and consequently with their religious experience.[21]

It would seem that Reverend Hill was a little more hesitant to admit the fact that the Methodist Movement was in decline. Neither mission was experiencing a great deal of success, but Reverend Hill was apparently unwilling to accept the responsibility of possible failure on his part. In his opinion, the lifestyle of Newfoundlanders meant that he was unable to influence them because they were rarely in the community. While not making any suggestions, he makes it clear that the Mission needs to change its methods in order to effectively reach out to these nomadic fishers.[22] Calvin Hollett argues the same: "Intense seasonal production came into direct conflict with the doctrine of the Sabbath, with the result that a public stand refraining from breaking the Sabbath became part of the Methodist identity." At

---

19. There is some confusion with regard to the name "Cuchold's Cove." Some sources refer to a "Cuckold's Cove." It is unclear whether they are referring to the same community, but it seems so.

20. Methodist Church of Canada "Sixtieth Annual Report," lv. See also Dunton, "Origins and Growth," 65.

21. Methodist Church of Canada "Sixtieth Annual Report," lv.

22. Methodist Church of Canada "Sixtieth Annual Report," 66. Calvin Hollett argues the same: "Intense seasonal production came into direct conflict with the doctrine of the Sabbath, with the result that a public stand refraining from breaking the Sabbath became part of the Methodist identity" (Hollett, *Shouting, Embracing, and Dancing*, 110).

any rate, it was in this climate of decline that Pentecostalism was introduced to the island through the person of Alice Belle Garrigus.

Introduction to Newfoundland Pentecostalism

The Pentecostal faith came to Newfoundland in the early twentieth century through a single, American evangelist, Alice Belle Garrigus. Garrigus was born on 2 August 1858 in Rockville, Connecticut to Lewis and Julia Garrigus. According to Garrigus's birth certificate, her father was a sash and blind manufacturer.[23] Garrigus came from a well-respected family, yet her family life was severely damaged as a young child when she tragically lost her mother to illness; Garrigus was then sent to Rhode Island to live with her grandmother.[24] Despite this traumatic loss, Garrigus busied herself with her education and began teaching school at age fifteen. According to Burton K. Janes, a Newfoundland historian with particular interest in the early days of Newfoundland Pentecostalism and the life and ministry of Alice Belle Garrigus, she enjoyed being a teacher, but after a few terms of teaching, sensed a need for higher education.[25]

Alice, from an early age, demonstrated exceptional intellectual abilities. This has been displayed through both her academic pursuits and her influence in Newfoundland Pentecostalism. At a time when women were not expected to pursue academic interests, Alice enrolled in Mount Holyoke Female Seminary for the academic year of 1878–1879.[26] The founder of this institution, Mary Lyons, desired to see an institution designed solely for the educating of young women. She desired to offer female students a high academic standard, while remaining accessible to women of limited finances.[27] According to Kurt O. Berends, this institution marked the beginnings of a nation-wide movement dedicated to the higher education of females.[28] Under the guidance of Mary Lyons, Mount Holyoke Female Seminary gained recognition as a national trend-setter in educating women. The demanding curriculum included four years of math, science, Latin, English and Bible. In addition four years of Greek, German, or French was also recommended.

---

23. State of Connecticut, "Birth Certificate of Alice Belle Garrigus."
24. Janes, *Lady Who Came*, 11.
25. Janes, *Lady Who Came*, 21.
26. Garrigus's student records are available at the Mount Holyoke College Archives. See also Janes, *Lady Who Came*, 22.
27. Janes, *Lady Who Came*, 23.
28. Berends, "Cultivating For a Harvest," 37–49.

Although Alice never completed her education at Mount Holyoke, the training she received left her well equipped for her future work in ministry.[29]

After leaving the seminary, Garrigus resumed teaching, this time at a junior high school in Thomaston, Connecticut. At her boarding house, she became acquainted with a single female colleague, Gertrude Wheeler. Their friendship would last a lifetime and was the starting point for the spiritual pilgrimage of Alice Belle Garrigus. Kurt O. Berends wrote, "That journey would take her first within the sphere of the holiness movement and ultimately into Pentecostal circles."[30] Wheeler possessed a quality that Garrigus did not exhibit—a born again experience. It was through this friendship that Alice developed a hunger for God and was converted. Garrigus entered the holiness movement and later the Pentecostal movement.[31]

Around 1893, Garrigus gave up her teaching career to work full time in Beulah Mission Home, a home founded by her friend, Gertrude Wheeler, for destitute women and children. She took on the title of "Assistant Superintendant of Beulah Mission Home." However, after some time, she felt led to minister in another area of Bridgeport. In 1904, Garrigus travelled to Rumney, New Hampshire where she made contact with the First Fruit Harvesters Association (now the New England Fellowship of Evangelicals), an organization that sent missionaries to unreached areas of the world. "The organization looked for workers who, taking the Bible as their creed and allowing the Holy Spirit to lead them would conduct meetings from town to town. Garrigus, who stood for these principles, was a prime candidate."[32] She spent six years (1904–1910) as an itinerant preacher with the association.[33] In October 1908, Alice Belle Garrigus received her divine call to bring the full Gospel message to Newfoundland; Garrigus confesses to having to consult a map to find where on the globe it was.[34]

Alice Garrigus did indeed follow through with her calling. On Thursday, 1 December 1910, fifty-two-year-old Garrigus, accompanied by Mr. And Mrs. William D. Fowler, retired American evangelical ministers,

---

29. Berends, "Cultivating For a Harvest." Garrigus completed three years of the required four. She is considered a non-graduating member of the Class of 1882. See Mount Holyoke College Archives.

30. Berends, "Divided Harvest," 10.

31. Janes, *History of the Pentecostal Assemblies*, 3–4.

32. Janes, *History of the Pentecostal Assemblies*, 6.

33. Janes, *History of the Pentecostal Assemblies*, 6. Interestingly, Garrigus did not view these years as particularly successful. She recalls one meeting she conducted where no one was saved. Looking back at that night she wrote, "I suppose there is no such thing as failure when we do our best for God." See Garrigus, "Called Alone."

34. Garrigus, "Called Alone," 7

arrived in St. John's, Newfoundland, under the auspices of the First Fruit Harvesters Association.[35] While in prayer for the ministry to take place there, Garrigus was impressed to call the mission "Bethesda."[36] On Sunday, 16 April, 1911, the first service was held by Garrigus and the Fowlers at the Bethesda Mission. According to Burton K. Janes, Garrigus referred to herself as the "Evangelist in charge of Bethesda Mission" as late as 1918.[37] As maintained by James A. Hewett in the *Dictionary of Pentecostal and Charismatic Movements*, "Garrigus was a leader strong enough to control any fanatics yet sufficiently pliable to yield to the Spirit's work."[38]

It is this author's contention that in the formative years of the budding movement, those who joined this band of "Pentecostal" believers were still deciphering their doctrinal system. Even those in leadership of the growing group of Spirit-filled people were still working out their theological views. One must note that the early Pentecostal believers did not arrive at their theological views instantaneously. Rather, their doctrinal system developed gradually, drawing heavily from its parentage in the Methodist and holiness movements. Numerous doctrinal, practical, and moral tendencies were transferred directly from Methodism and the holiness movement into Pentecostalism in the province. As such, attention must be given to the impact of Methodism on Pentecostalism. Contributions to the development of what became Pentecostal theology and praxis in Newfoundland are found in the influence of several key figures in the development of the organization. It cannot be understated that several of the key leaders in the development of the early Pentecostal Movement in Newfoundland were transplanted from Methodism into the fledgling Pentecostal Movement, bringing with them elements of Methodist theology and praxis.

Robert English

Robert C. English was born in St. John's into the family of a respected business owner, William R. English, in the city. The English family had ten daughters and Robert English was their only son.[39] Naturally, his father hoped that English would carry on his trade as a jeweller and watchmaker at his successful business on Water Street, but the younger English had different plans and decided to pursue vocational ministry with the Method-

35. Garrigus, "Called Alone," 11.
36. Garrigus, "Called Alone," 12. For a reference to "Bethesda," see John 5:2–4.
37. Garrigus, "Called Alone," 14.
38. Burgess and Maas, *New International Dictionary*, 661.
39. Rollmann, "Indigenization and Cultural Participation."

ist Church instead.[40] English was educated as a child at the old Methodist College on Long's Hill.[41] The family was well established at Gower Street Methodist Church, also on Long's Hill, where English was Class Leader.[42] English married Jessie Moore in 1907 and they raised three children together: Violet, Gladys, and Jean.[43]

He met with his converts in his spacious home and later rented a larger hall. Sometime after the Demarest crusade, English received what Pentecostals describe as the baptism of the Holy Spirit in his own home.[44] Myrtle Eddy, one of the early Pentecostals who was present at this particular meeting, recalls seeing English, "with his head practically in the fireplace!"[45]

Within a short time, English and his band of believers joined forces with the Bethesda Mission. English shared ministry duties with Garrigus and after the incorporation of the denomination in 1925, English became the first Superintendent of the Bethesda Pentecostal Assemblies of Newfoundland.[46]

Jacob Noseworthy

One important figure who was implanted into the Bethesda Mission from Methodism was Jacob Noseworthy. Noseworthy was born in 1878 in St. John's. He was an engineer who worked with Green Shipyard in Chelsea,

---

40. English studied the family trade in Boston, MA. Thereafter, he returned to St. John's to work with his father. Where Pentecostals have been criticized for being uneducated and anti-intellectual, it should be noted that most of the figureheads in early Newfoundland Pentecostalism were more educated than the average citizen. Garrigus, unlike most women of her time, had post-secondary education. English, as well, had post-secondary education. This education was evident in some of his writings. For example, English wrote an essay entitled, "Is Divine Healing Part of the Atonement?" in the February 1929 edition of *Pentecostal Evangel*. See English, "Is Divine Healing," 1, 8.

41. The school was originally called Newfoundland Methodist College when it opened in 1860. It later became Holloway School and eventually Prince of Wales College.

42. Gower Street Methodist Church was founded in 1815 and became a major religious force in the city of St. John's for year. However, after the union of the Methodist, United, and some Presbyterian (Congregational) churches in 1925, the church was renamed Gower Street United Church. For a short history of the church, see Gower Street United Church, "Short History."

43. Janes, *History of the Pentecostal Assemblies*, 32.

44. The 1919 Victoria Booth-Clibborn Demarest crusade—along with the results for local religious groups—will be discussed in the next section.

45. Verge quoted in Janes, *History of the Pentecostal Assemblies*, 32.

46. Rollmann, "From Holiness to Pentecost."

Massachusetts for a period of time before transferring back to St. John's to work with Harvey Company.[47] Noseworthy's daughter, Jennie E. Greene, recalled her father as, "surely a devout Methodist."[48] She recalls how he attended church every Sunday morning, carrying with him a "envelope with such a small mite for the general offering and another small mite for the missionary offering, but he was faithful in so doing."[49] Noseworthy had been converted during the Demarest campaign in St. John's in 1919. Jennie recalls his conversion and what some Methodists know as "second blessing" or "sanctification":

> The Evening He went to the Alter for Salvation, He claimed not to feel any different, this bothered him. He prayed and read His Bible faithfully each day, still did not have the witness of his sins forgiven. It was two weeks later, on a Sunday Afternoon, He was singing, "Will your anchor hold," the first verse and chorus, then had started, "It is Safely moored," "twill the storm with-hold," the blessing fell, Praise God! It was then that He knew His sins had been forgiven, Mom got a large portion of that blessing, and, young and I was, believe me, I had a wonderful experience that afternoon, and the showers of blessing fell all over me, a Blessing I can not ever forget [sic].[50]

As was the case with many others belonging to more established denominations in Newfoundland, Noseworthy did not appreciate the Pentecostals. His daughter wanted to attend the Pentecostal mission with her

---

47. Green Shipyard was used by the Navy during WWII. The dry dock handled the huge influx of US, British, and Allied merchant and warships damaged during wartime. The property was sold after WWII and continued operating successfully for the next forty years as Munro Shipyard. After some failed business attempts by another developer in the 1980s, Fitzgerald Shipyard took over as a tenant and began to redevelop the dry dock in 1992. Since that time, numerous developments have taken place and Fitzgerald Shipyard is still fully operational. Fitzgerald Shipyard, "Facility/History." Harvey Company was founded by Alexander John Harvey. Harvey moved to St. John's in 1856 and opened an import/export business, as his father had done in Nova Scotia. The company became incorporated as A. Harvey and Company Limited in 1914. In 1889, the company also developed a transport service for transporting passengers and freight to coastal communities, known as the Newfoundland Coastal Steamship Company. Presently located on Water Street East in St. John's, the company is one of the few historic companies in the province and is quite diversified in its goods and services. See A. Harvey Group, "History."

48. Jennie E. Greene wrote a short biography of her father, Jacob Noseworthy, in 1983, addressed to the editor of *Good Tidings*, Burton K. Janes. Hereafter referred to as Greene, "Biography of Jacob Noseworthy."

49. Greene, "Biography of Jacob Noseworthy."

50. Greene, "Biography of Jacob Noseworthy."

friend, Myrtle Broomfield, but her father, "really did not like those people." His cousin, Minnie March, attended the Pentecostal mission and "he could never understand how a woman like her could belong to those people."[51]

However, quite some time after his conversion experience, he had a change of heart and decided to attend Bethesda Mission to hear Garrigus preach. Noseworthy and two friends attended the service and vowed they would never go again. Several weeks later, this happened again. They decided they did not appreciate this style of preaching. However, by the third visit, "the message was beginning to sink in deep" and the men unanimously decided, "This is really good Preaching [sic]."[52] Eventually, Noseworthy was baptized in water in Mundy's Pond. He became an important part of the Pentecostal fellowship and was one of the three individuals who signed the document forming the Pentecostal Assemblies of Newfoundland in 1925.[53]

Eugene Vaters

Another significant person in the transfer of values and beliefs from Methodism to Pentecostalism in Newfoundland was Eugene Vaters. Vaters was born on 10 October 1898 in Victoria, Newfoundland. His mother was a class leader in the Methodist church and Vaters recalls her praying diligently. His father had been quite limited in receiving formal education and, as such, he was determined to provide educational opportunities for his children. Vaters, like English, received his early education in the local Methodist school and recalled his conversion experience at age 11 in a cottage meeting.[54] While he was very young, this experience was life-changing and altered the course of his future. He recalled leaving the meeting and returning home saying, "there were times when it seemed my feet barely touched the ground. I felt so light and full of life."[55] Following graduation, seventeen-year-old Vaters became a teacher and taught at Rantem Station and Harbour Deep. He also conducted services in the Methodist church at this time. From 1916 to 1922 he became a circuit pastor, but was becoming increasingly uncomfortable with what he perceived as "modernism" creeping into the church. He described what he perceived as "compromise" and "infidelity" within the ranks of Methodism.[56] After his resignation, Vaters

51. Greene, "Biography of Jacob Noseworthy."
52. Greene, "Biography of Jacob Noseworthy."
53. Janes, "Personal letter to Mrs. Jennie Greene."
54. Janes, "Floods Upon the Dry Ground," 112.
55. Vaters, *Reminiscence*, 12.
56. Vaters, *Reminiscence*, 31.

studied at the Moody Bible Institute in Illinois. He later studied in the Rochester Bible Training School in New York, a Pentecostal institution, where he studied for one year. Eugene and Jennie Vaters came back to Newfoundland and began ministering in Victoria and many people came to faith in Christ. Eventually, Alice Garrigus made contact with Vaters by telephone and the two joined forces. Vaters became the second General Superintendent of the movement in 1927. Vaters, given that his early education, family life, and career were steeped in Methodism, naturally carried Methodist theology, praxis, and ethos with him into the budding Pentecostal Movement in Newfoundland. This leads to a discussion of the similarities between the two groups.

Similarities Between Pentecostalism and Methodism

The similarities between Newfoundland Pentecostalism in its infancy and its spiritual parent, Methodism, are obvious. The primary similarity was in its revivalistic nature with significant emphasis on emotional response. There was an emphasis on the ecstatic and the supernatural, albeit nuanced slightly differently in Pentecostalism. Calvin Hollett, a Newfoundland historian with particular interest in the history of Methodism in the province, described Methodism as a "populist movement energized by the religious dymanic of a quest for spiritual ecstasy."[57] One could quite easily describe Pentecostalism in the same manner. Further, the great emphasis and priority placed on personal holiness was also a point of convergence between the two movements. Both believed in a literal interpretation of Scripture and the importance of personal Bible study and prayer.

The early Newfoundland Pentecostals, in line with their Methodist roots, maintained the importance of a crisis experience in terms of personal salvation. They elevated the experience of Spirit baptism and speaking in tongues. Further, they held dearly to the idea of sanctification, although this emphasis diminished in later years.[58] They also upheld the practice of

---

57. Hollett, *Shouting, Embracing, and Dancing*, xv–xvi.

58. The author discusses the transition of Newfoundland Pentecostalism from five-fold to four-fold ministry in its infancy in an unpublished paper. Whereas Pentecostalism was true to its Methodism roots in its earliest beginnings, it maintained a distinct emphasis on sanctification as a distinct and separate experience from both salvation and Spirit-baptism. As Pentecostalism became more established, the idea of sanctification was replaced entirely with Spirit-baptism. For more information, see MacGregor, "Development."

believer's baptism by full immersion, in line with their Anabaptist lineage and association with other believer's churches.

Eugene Vaters recalls early water baptismal services in St. John's. He wrote, "It took courage to walk out into the sometimes ice-cold waters of Mundy's Pond before mocking crowds; but, believing baptism by immersion to be God's way, many have done so, and received a witness that they pleased God."[59] Their adherence to believer's baptism as well as other holiness practices was proof of their desire to remain true to what they perceived as being rooted in Scripture. However, at the same time, their desire to escape Methodism and other forms of "dead religion" was demonstrated in their separation from all other established churches and refusal to associate with even other Christian groups.[60] Newfoundland Pentecostalism "came out" from both Methodism and all forms of established religion, seeking what they perceived to be a biblical expression of faith.

To give a more intimate level of the Methodist connection, Robert C. English was said to have been quite strict in the way he raised his family, as was typical for a Methodist family. Methodism was known for its staunch rigidity and system of rules as it related to personal expectations of its adherents. Pentecostalism adopted this system fully. Some of these personal expectations would have been naturally transferred directly into the fledgling Pentecostal Movement, which, unfortunately led to a legalistic form of spirituality as opposed to one based on personal conviction and study of God's Word.

Alice Garrigus was concerned with physical appearance and maintaining an outward appearance in line with one's inward holiness. However, she was disturbed by secular culture that, in her estimation, lead young people to develop ungodly habits, such as immodest dress. She also discussed how women acted like men through their dress (i.e., wearing pants) and habits like smoking.[61]

The Pentecostals adopted this holiness standard as well. The Methodists were generally dressed modestly and promoted plain decorum. John Wesley is quoted in the *Pentecostal Evangel*, a Newfoundland Pentecostal publication, in 1928 saying, "Buy no velvets, no silks, no mere ornaments, though ever so much in fashion. Wear nothing, though you have it already, which is of a glaring colour, or which is in any kind gay, glistening, or showy; nothing made in the very height of fashion, nothing to attract the

---

59. Garrigus, "Pentecostal Assemblies in Newfoundland," 403. See also Vaters, "How Pentecost Found Newfoundland," 9.

60. This separation is still evident in many Pentecostal groups hesitancy to associate with Ecumenical Movements today.

61. Garrigus, "Signs of the Coming of the King," 5.

attention of bystanders."[62] Many of the idiosyncrasies of Pentecostalism in Newfoundland in its early years were not new; they were largely transferred from Methodism due to the transfer of key individuals. When certain Methodists found their own faith tradition leaning in tendency towards worldliness and institutionalization, these individuals with a particular longing for the "old time religion" found themselves "coming out from" the established church, in true separatist fashion.

The Impact of Methodism on Pentecostalism in Newfoundland

Newfoundland Methodism was not able to maintain the dynamic nature it had once been known by. When Methodism was beginning to slowly decline in Newfoundland, Pentecostalism was poised and ready for growth. In an interview between Pastor Carl Verge and Myrtle Broomfield Eddy, Eddy recalled her early memories of the budding Pentecostal mission on New Gower Street. Eddy indicated that in the early days of the Pentecostal Movement in St. John's, people from all over Conception Bay would come into the city on schooners, bringing in their loads of fish and doing their fall trading. Eddy indicated that everyone had heard of this "little old lady on New Gower Street" who was preaching the gospel. The stories of Spirit baptism, healing, anointed worship, and believers falling to the ground were enough to draw curious seekers to see for themselves what was happening at the New Gower Street mission.[63] Interestingly enough, Myrtle Broomfield Eddy shares of how this ecstatic worship was very similar to old time Methodism in Newfoundland. She shares that this experience was very much like what had previously been experienced in the Methodist class meetings.

> In those old-time class meetings they used to have the real times of refreshing from the Lord, but they don't . . . anymore. Some of them danced in the Spirit 'way back there. I remember in the old church back where I was born . . . Aunt Susie used to dance in the Spirit as much as I've ever seen in the Pentecostal ranks, but they didn't know about it, but they called it the 'glory fits' & people took them out of church and started to wipe their faces with cold rags & give them cold water to drink to bring them to, but it was just the anointing of the Lord & they didn't understand about it [sic].[64]

62. Wesley, "Self Indulgence," 8.
63. Verge, "Interview with Myrtle Broomfield Eddy."
64. Verge, "Interview with Myrtle Broomfield Eddy."

It would appear, both through these historical recollections of early Pentecostal converts, and through academic study of the historical evidence, that the early Pentecostal Movement in Newfoundland was, in some ways, replacing its holiness predecessor, Methodism.

Hans Rollmann, Professor of Religious Studies at Memorial University of Newfoundland, discusses some of the elements that led to the growth of Newfoundland Pentecostalism in outport communities:

> In Grates Cove, Trinity Bay, local Methodists experienced healing and the speaking in tongues. In North Harbour, Placentia Bay, Pentecostal tracts from the US-based Apostolic Faith led to an indigenous revival, as did a similar one in Clarke's Beach, Conception Bay. All of these places of revival were visited by Pastor English or other members of Bethesda, and an enduring relationship developed.[65]

Thus, it would appear that Pentecostalism, in some ways, thrived in the face of the demise of Methodism.[66]

By 1911, just one year after Alice Belle Garrigus arrived in Newfoundland and during the same year as the official establishment of Bethesda Mission in St. John's, the Newfoundland census records that there were 67,310 Methodists in the province.[67] However, students of religious history in Newfoundland may call this the end of an era for Methodism in the province. On Sunday afternoon, 16 April, 1911, the first service was held at the newly established Bethesda Mission. Garrigus reported "a congregation of about seventy-five, and in the evening more than a hundred were present."[68] This was the beginning of what could be described as dynamic and exponential growth for the fledgling Pentecostal movement in the province.[69]

---

65. Rollmann, "From Holiness to Pentecost."

66. It should be noted that this success was not limited to the Pentecostal denomination. The Salvation Army in Newfoundland also experienced great success in the years prior to the growth of Pentecostalism. Many of the early converts to The Salvation Army in Newfoundland came out of the Methodist Movement. Many of the same conclusions can be drawn between the growth of both denominations. For further reading on the growth of the Salvation Army and the influence of Methodism, see Moyles, *Blood and Fire in Canada*; Prowse, *History of Newfoundland*; Wiggins, *History of the Salvation Army*; Dunton, "Origins and Growth."

67. Internet Archive, "Census of Newfoundland and Labrador 1911."

68. Garrigus, "Extract from a Letter," 188.

69. The Pentecostal Movement did not extend outside of St. John's for the first ten years. Burton Janes discussed the impact of leadership on the growth of the Movement in its early years as well as the increased receptivity to religion after the First World War. See Janes, "Floods Upon the Dry Ground," 98ff.

Hans Rollmann argues that 1919 "represents an important date for evangelical Newfoundland and a turning point for the Pentecostal Movement."[70] It was at this time that Victoria Booth-Clibborn Demarest, along with her pianist husband, came to hold a series of evangelistic meetings in Newfoundland. Booth-Clibborn Demarest was the granddaughter of William and Catherine Booth, the founders of the Salvation Army. Eugene Vaters recalls her as, "God's instrument in the last great revival in the Methodist churches here."[71]

In the St. John's area, Booth-Clibborn Demarest held meetings at St. John's Gower Street Methodist Church that were revivalistic in nature and the impact of these meetings were far-reaching. Rollmann describes the renewal of religious fervour among St. John's evangelicals. Furthermore, he suggests that the resulting establishment of two new religious groups would generate a significant ripple in the existing disjointed holiness groups in the city.[72] Two of these existing groups led to the significant growth of Newfoundland Pentecostalism. The first was that led by Kenneth S. Barnes. Barnes was a Methodist and the proprietor of a local printing establishment who later opened Elim Pentecostal Mission on Bell Street in St. John's. He later became more Pentecostal in expression and joined his mission with Garrigus's Bethesda Mission.[73] The second of these significant groups was led by Robert C. English, as has already been mentioned.

In 1924, Pastor English, along with some gospel workers, travelled to Port de Grave to hold gospel meetings. According to Garrigus, this was known to be "such a hard field."[74] Many tried to dissuade English from this trip because "for twenty years there had been no moving of the Spirit in that place."[75] It is clear that in this particular location, individuals had been familiar with revivalistic experiences in the past. In fact, the Methodist message was first brought to Port de Grave in 1791 by Rev. William Black.[76] Yet,

70. Rollmann, "From Holiness to Pentecost."

71. Vaters, "Our Beginnings," 16.

72. Rollmann, "From Holiness to Pentecost."

73. Barnes had come into the holiness movement through the evangelistic ministry of Thomas Courtney. See Rollmann, "From Holiness to Pentecost."

74. Garrigus, "Newfoundland Stretching out Her Hands," 6.

75. Garrigus, "Newfoundland Stretching out Her Hands," 6.

76. William Black left for St. John's, NL, on August 2nd, 1791. His journal, which was printed in *The Arminian Magazine* in 1972, briefly outlines the details of his trip, including the locations in which services were held. He learned that there had once been "a great stir" in many of the communities, under the ministry of Coughlan, but there was not a resident minister and, as such, many had fallen away. There was only a small group of women meeting together on a consistent basis. On August 21st, 1791, Black preached to a crowd of 300 at Port de Grave in an outdoor meeting. See Black, "Journal of William Black."

time had eroded the impact of the revivalistic experience in that area. Garrigus reported, "However, they went and secured a hall seating about five hundred and it was filled with people who came to hear the "new religion" as they called it. More than forty were saved and some healed . . . this last year a church has been built and dedicated for the full Gospel."[77]

Garrigus described the nature of the early Pentecostal meetings in St. John's during the 1920s. She described revival among the young people, including praying, prophesying, singing, and deliverance.[78] This mirrors the ecstatic experience that typified Methodist meetings not a century earlier.[79]

It is not difficult to argue that Pentecostalism grew out of a sense of dissatisfaction within Methodism.[80] In 1925, the Methodist Church amalgamated with the United Church of Canada. While this came about as a practical and fiscal necessity, there was a certain degree of discontent around these circumstances. It is an unfortunate, yet noteworthy, detail that the growth of Pentecostalism coincides, at least loosely so, with the decline of Methodism.[81] One must question what factors contributed to this decline?

There would be little debate that the Pentecostal Movement in Newfoundland grew out of a reaction to organizational issues within Methodism. Many Methodists were dissatisfied with the amalgamation and there

---

77. Black, "Journal of William Black." It is interesting to note that in the 1935 Newfoundland Census, there were 340 less Methodists in Port de Grave than there were in the 1921 Census. During the same time, Pentecostalism was introduced in Port de Grave and grew to 385 self-identifying Pentecostal individuals. There was some obvious transfer between the two groups. See Internet Archive, "Census of Newfoundland and Labrador 1935."

78. Garrigus, "Marvelous Manifestation of God's Power," 3. This edition of the journal indicates a typing error in naming "Annie" as the author instead of "Alice."

79. Hollett, *Shouting, Embracing, and Dancing*. Hollett recounts many instances which demonstrate the highly ecstatic nature of Methodism in Newfoundland in its early years.

80. This theory could also be applied to the growth of the Salvation Army in Newfoundland. For the purpose of this discussion, however, attention shall focus on the Pentecostal Movement.

81. It must be noted that Pentecostals were not specifically listed in the Newfoundland Census Records until 1935. As such, it is difficult to get an exact comparison of the objective changes in membership in both religious bodies during this time frame. In the 1921 and 1925 census records, Pentecostals would have been included in the "other and not stated" religious category, whereas the statistics for Methodism were clearly defined. Further, in the 1935 census, Pentecostal numbers were recorded in a separate category, whereas Methodism would then have been included in the category with the United Church. As such, while various sources can contribute to a generalized interpretation of the historical trends and overall understanding of religious groups in Newfoundland history, it is virtually impossible to reduce these events to simplified figures with any amount of reasonable certainty.

was a sense that they had been abandoned. Some refused to take part in the process and immediately sought refuge within other religious bodies that still maintained the revivalistic flair that they felt was missing in Methodism. Others decided to stay within the newly formed United Church, but were opposed to the increasing sense of dull, cold religion without the emotional fervour that was known to characterize Methodism at its peak. Methodism had once been known for its emotional worship and the longing of its members for a supernatural experience; however, this was eventually replaced with a rationalistic approach that denied space for these types of experiences. Jennie Vaters in *The Independent Communion* discussed the worthless religion of "dead works" whereby people seek to "obtain the prize by works and a moral life."[82] Her perspective was that one could look perfect externally, yet be internally debased; the same was true for religious bodies. She wrote, "The churches, almost *en masse*, have left, or are leaving, the foundation truths upon which they have been raised. God is raising up a people in their stead; and, as usual, is giving that people a new impetus and fresh power."[83]

By 1929, the developing Pentecostal Movement in Newfoundland had taken a strong stance against the "old denominational churches." The early Pentecostals described this shift well and such a view is worth quoting at length. They believed that all established denominations,

> had their beginnings in a revival spirit. Strange as it may seem, as these movements cooled off in ardor and love toward God, and the new movements sprang into existence, red hot with love and devotion, members of the already established bodies forgot their beginnings, and rather than acknowledge their lukewarm condition and separation from vital relationship to God, they opposed and persecuted the new movements, taking refuge in the traditions of the past, instead of searching their hearts and seeking God for the fullness of His love for the present. On account of this opposition and persecution, the new movements were compelled to organize for protections, and when the revival ardor had cooled somewhat, it was found that another denomination had been born which differed but little from all the others which preceeded it [sic].[84]

82. Vaters, "Three-Fold Vision," 2.

83. Vaters, "Doctrinal," 3.

84. This was the sentiment of the primary Pentecostal body in the United States, the Assemblies of God, as it was becoming more established. The newly incorporated Pentecostal Assemblies of Newfoundland (later Pentecostal Assemblies of Newfoundland and Labrador) shared this article entitled "Who we are, and what we believe" in the

It would appear that Newfoundland Pentecostalism "came out" from the world, but they also, to a large degree, "came out" from the established denominations in St. John's, perhaps most notably, Methodism. What is perhaps most striking is that while these genuine believers left what they perceived as "dead religion" of the Methodist church, they did not gain much new by joining the new band of Pentecostal converts; rather, they recovered what Methodism had been in its revivalistic inception in the province. In a sense, the Pentecostals recaptured some of what Methodism had abandoned. Pentecostals perceived themselves as "coming out from" established religion, but a historical reading of the material indicates that they were perhaps less distinctive than they viewed themselves as being.

Questioning the Future of Newfoundland Pentecostalism

Pentecostalism in Newfoundland largely "came out from" the Methodist Movement in the province. Such can hardly be disputed. On the contrary, Methodism has scarcely been given enough credit by Pentecostals for their heritage in faith, doctrine, matters concerning personal praxis, as well as social issues. However, in attempting to study the rise of one denomination, nearly at the expense of another, one must deal with questions that arise related to the existing denomination at present. According to Hans Rollmann, Newfoundland Methodism "had grown into a respectable denomination in the nineteenth century. But in the beginning of the twentieth century suffered from premature aging."[85] By the time Pentecostalism was introduced in Newfoundland, Methodism was already weakening. "Especially the experiential religiosity and personal intimacy of the after-meetings and traditional classes had declined."[86] S. D. Chown, the Methodist General Superintendent of the Newfoundland General Conference, gave this warning in 1922, "The Class Meetings have been declining for the past twenty-five years. . . . This is of fundamental importance to the spiritual life of the Church and we urge that more attention be given to it."[87]

Rollmann mentions that Methodism in St. John's fared better than Methodism in the outport communities. In the city, followers could still

---

Nfld. Pentecostal Evangel in 1929, thus demonstrating their shared belief in the pitfalls associated with denominationalism. Interestingly, most Pentecostal groups to this day will not formally address themselves as 'denominations,' though by every definition they are such. Most still prefer to address themselves as movements. See Pentecostal Assemblies of Newfoundland, "Who We Are," 4.

85. Rollmann, "From Holiness to Pentecost."
86. Rollmann, "From Holiness to Pentecost."
87. Chown quoted in Rollmann, "From Holiness to Pentecost."

find satisfaction in the numerous holiness gatherings or in the revival services. However, in many outport communities where Methodism had been established, there was no resident minister; rather, clergy travelled to various communities on a rotating circuit. Having only one minister in charge of several congregations with significant geographical challenges separating them was far from ideal. The success of the Salvation Army in some of these communities is proof that demonstrated the religious need in these areas.

One could question whether Rollmann's assessment was too generalized, however, given that Pentecostalism experienced remarkable success in certain outport areas. For example, in 1922 Garrigus reported that there were "more people baptized in the Holy Ghost in Clark's Beach than in St. John's [sic]."[88] Further, she indicted that "practically the whole town is in the grip of the Spirit."[89] While Rollmann assesses Pentecostals through historical eyes, viewing their success as tied to the city of St. John's, the Pentecostals themselves, at least in 1922, connected their success to the outports, further indicating, "we are very dry at Bethesda."[90]

In any case, one may notice a difference between the lifespan of Pentecostalism and that of Methodism in Newfoundland in that Newfoundland Pentecostalism begun its decline much earlier than did Methodism. Where Methodism began its decline around the turn of the twentieth century, giving it approximately 150 years of success before its demise began to become evident. Newfoundland Pentecostalism, on the other hand, began to express concern for its organizational and spiritual well-being less than 100 years after its inception.[91]

For those within Newfoundland Pentecostalism, the downward trajectory is clearly observed, both through internal statistics and the messages

88. Garrigus, "Old Time Power," 7.
89. Garrigus, "Old Time Power."
90. Garrigus, "Old Time Power."
91. Beginning with the "State of the Fellowship Address" in 2008, concerns were expressed by leadership to the General Conference, outlining issues such as decline in attendance, church closures, pastoral drought, lack of discipleship, and fewer reports of adherents and members experiencing salvation, water baptism, and spirit baptism. These are the benchmarks by which the Pentecostal Assemblies of Newfoundland and Labrador has historically measured its success. One must note that there are external factors that have influenced these numbers, such as out-migration related to the cod moratorium in 1992, as well as an aging population. However, the internal factors are likely more significant. Along with the primary external factors, some key internal factors are noteworthy as well, namely, the collapse of the denominational school system in 1998 and the gradual discontinuation of Sunday School in most churches due to lack of enrollment and a declining volunteer base. There are many other factors that led to the decline, but these brief points are often referenced as it relates to the decline in PAONL membership.

conveyed by leadership at denominational conferences. What is less obvious is that it appears Pentecostalism is in lockstep with the history of Methodism. Pentecostalism took root in Newfoundland and its early followers first faced ridicule. However, as the denomination became established, it became recognized and respected. While Methodism began as a movement focused on a fiery evangelistic message, some of this focus was lost and "watered down" over time. Individuals who sensed dissatisfaction within Methodism found what they were looking for in early Newfoundland Pentecostalism. Once Methodism began its decline, it was only a short time before the denomination was absorbed into the United Church of Canada and virtually disappeared. The legacy of the Methodist Movement in Newfoundland is not at all reflective in the present day United Church; it has entirely dissolved.

Given that Newfoundland Pentecostals are beginning to observe their own decline and the denomination is cognizant of its own organizational lifespan, one must question will Pentecostals meet the same fate as their theological predecessors? One should hope not, as they still have much to offer. Garrigus, in speaking of what had grown in the Pentecostal Movement in her lifetime recalled,

> The wind that blows can never kill
> The tree God plants,
> It bloweth east, it bloweth west,
> The tender leaves have little rest,
> But any wind that blows is best.
> The tree God plants
> Strikes deeper roots, grows higher still,
> Spreads greater boughs: for God's good will
> Meets all its "wants."[92]

Garrigus goes on to explain that this poem "seems to express the experience of the little tree God planted in St. John's. Many chilling winds have blown upon it, many tests from within and without, still it lives and its boughs have spread throughout the land."[93] What is evident now that was possibly not evident at the time or was perhaps even intentionally ignored is that the seed from which this sturdy tree had grown was its spiritual parent: Methodism. Also becoming painfully clear is that trees have a lifespan, some longer than others. Where Methodism once occupied a prominent place in Newfoundland society, with a great impact on the local culture,

92. Garrigus, "Tree God Planted."
93. Garrigus, "Tree God Planted."

Pentecostalism grew in a similar fashion. However, Pentecostalism in Newfoundland is presently at a crossroads, whereby it understands its precarious place in terms of its lifecycle. To look only at the numbers may lead one to question whether this sturdy oak is nearing the end of its life. While there are undoubtedly an endless number of scenarios that one could envision as an image of the future, three potential paths that the Newfoundland Pentecostal Movement may take will be briefly suggested here.

The first potential future scenario is that Newfoundland Pentecostalism will meet the same fate as its predecessor—eventual collapse. Perhaps even suggesting such is sacrilegious. While no one would desire to see a religious group that has been a significant positive force, both locally and globally, dissolve and cease to exist, one must consider the logical possibility, given the historical trend for modern religious movements. The Methodist Movement met its fate by merging with two other religious groups out of necessity. In doing so, it essentially sealed its own fate and left its legacy only through its influence on the development of other denominations—namely, The Salvation Army and The Pentecostal Assemblies of Newfoundland and Labrador. While both groups should recognize with gratitude their theological heritage, there also exists a sense of melancholy in the recollection that the once thriving religious group now ceases to exist. One should hope that Pentecostalism in Newfoundland will not succumb to the same depressing fatality.

This leads to a second potential scenario. While the denomination will likely not merge with another, as the Newfoundland Methodists did, it could meet its end in the slow but steady decline, coupled with societal irrelevance. Traditional religious expressions of faith are declining all across Canada. If Newfoundland Pentecostalism follows the trend, it could eventually wither away into something so obscure that its impact will be essentially nonexistence. This scenario is perhaps less desirable than the first.

The third scenario that the Pentecostal Movement in Newfoundland will recognize its precarious place in its lifespan and re-launch itself through the intentional planting of new missions and ministries. According to Michael Wilkinson in *Canadian Pentecostals*, "Social process refers to recurring attitudinal and behavioural patterns that seem to reflect change in the short term but in the long term reflect cycles or recurring patterns. Transformation, on the other hand, is reflected in a broader context of change."[94] For Pentecostals, transformation is viewed a work of the Spirit (cf. Rom 12:2). While this is often expressed with personal sentiment, can Pentecostals adopt a view of corporate transformation as a work of the Spirit?

---

94. Wilkinson, *Canadian Pentecostals*, 8.

Rather than waiting and hoping a seed from its far-reaching boughs may hopefully take root, perhaps Pentecostals should intentionally plant seeds of new and unique missions and ministries, water them with its existing resources, and shelter them with its boughs until these small saplings are able to withstand the elements. This kind of planting may first require pruning of the existing tree; but pruning facilitates healthy growth. Perhaps the best legacy a religious movement can have is in replanting itself in new forms to meet the changing needs of society and to meet the needs of individuals longing for religious connection, yet who can't seem to find it in established churches.

Pentecostalism is and has always been a "come-outer" tradition. Yet, true to its separatist nature, perhaps other expressions of faith will "come out" from Pentecostalism, as Pentecostalism did from its spiritual mother, Methodism. "The wind that blows can never kill the tree God plants."[95]

---

95. Garrigus, "Tree God Planted."

Part III: The Principle Writ Large

CHAPTER 10

The Curse of Cults and the Scourge of Sects
Or a Come-Outing of New Religious Movements?

Eileen Barker

"What's in a name? That which we call a rose by any other name would smell as sweet."[1] Juliet, the Capulet, asked Romeo, the Montague.

But the star-crossed lovers were soon to discover that matters of life and death could depend on a name.

For centuries, even millennia, new forms of religiosity have been appearing throughout the globe. Some of these have quite clearly "come out of" a pre-existing religion; others would appear to have "popped up" out of nowhere—although on inspection it is usually possible to see at least one, but possibly many, pre-existing beliefs and practices that have been drawn on, re-examined and re-formed in some way or other. This chapter will look at a few of the thousands of religious innovations that can be found in contemporary society, particularly in the West, although, with increasing globalisation, many of these will have had their origins in the East. It will be argued that, despite the fact that generalizations are impossible (and to claim that there are some is almost bound to be wrong), there are certain points that can be made about such phenomena—whatever we might call them. But should we talk of the curse of cults and the scourge of sects? Or could we, less dramatically, talk about a coming out of new religious movements?

1. Shakespeare, *Romeo and Juliet*, 19.

Labels

Part of the answer to the question posed by the title lies in how the key concepts of cults, sects and new religious movements are defined. In a technical sense, sociologists of religion have distinguished between church, denomination, sect and cult, the first two being generally accepted by society, whereas sects and cults are in tension with the rest of society; and while the church and sect tend to have a self-conceived legitimacy and exclusiveness, the denomination and cult tend towards a more universal outlook, allowing for the possibility that there are "many ways."[2] There are quite a few problems with this model, but it has served a useful purpose in the past, particularly in pointing to the process known as denominationalisation, when sects in particular, but also cults, move from their position of tension with society to one in which they are more accommodating to and accommodated by society, and, at the same time, becoming more accepting and accepted.

It has, however, been pointed out, particularly by the British sociologist Bryan Wilson in his studies of nineteenth century sects,[3] that the process of denominationalisation does not always take place. For example, the Jehovah's Witnesses, the Plymouth Brethren Christian Church (popularly known as the Exclusive Brethren) and the Christadelphians have retained their sectarian characteristics through several generations. On the other hand, religions such as the Church of Jesus Christ of Latter-day Saints (commonly referred to as the Mormons) and the Seventh-day Adventists have denominationalized—at least in much of the West—although the Mormons could well be described as a church in Utah, a denomination in the rest of the United States,[4] but a sect in Russia and various other East European countries. One might, furthermore, point out that whilst the main Mormon church, by accepting the outlawing of polygamy around the end of the nineteenth century, took a significant step on the road towards denominationalisation, many of the schisms that broke away and continued to follow their founding fathers' embracing of polygamy, remained, and in most cases still remain, sectarian in character. And, as other contributors to this volume bear witness, a not entirely dissimilar pattern of breakaway groups, and yet further breakaways from these, have taken place since the Anabaptist

---

2. McGuire, *Religion*, 149–94; Wallis, *Road*, 13; Stark and Bainbridge, *Theory*, 328.

3. Wilson, *Religious Sects*.

4. The fact that Mitt Romney was able to secure a Republican nomination for the 2012 Presidential election could be taken as evidence that Mormonism had come to be accepted as an acceptable religion rather than a deviant sect by a sufficient proportion of the US population for it to be classified as a denomination.

movement first emerged in the sixteenth century. While "the Baptists" are now accepted as a denomination throughout most of the West, there are multiple branches that can still be regarded as sects in the technical sense, some of them featuring in the French list of *mouvements sectaires*.[5]

Christianity has certainly not been the only religion found in the history of the West, but it has been the predominant one, and most of the sects that have come to public attention in various periods, such as the European Middle Ages, England in the first half of the seventeenth century, or the Great Awakenings of North America, have been more or less rooted in some understanding of the Christian tradition. And while the typology of church, denomination, sect, and cult has served a useful purpose in the analysis of Christian religions in the West, it has been less helpful in describing and understanding processes for the other two Abrahamic faiths, and it is well-nigh useless when applied to Hinduism, Shinto, Taoism or most other Eastern religions.

Furthermore, while the typology has been employed in the technical sense by sociologists purely as a classificatory tool, with no evaluative judgement as to whether the sect was "better" or "worse" than the church, the terms cult and sect, as used today in popular parlance, are by no means impartial concepts. *The curse of cults and the scourge of sects* can make perfect sense as a headline in a tabloid newspaper where it is assumed that 'everyone knows' that cults and/or sects are dangerous pseudo-religions with satanic overtones, which brainwash and exploit their members, are involved in financial skulduggery and political intrigue, indulge in unnatural sexual practices, abuse their women and children, carry out numerous criminal activities and are likely to commit mass suicide.

It was because social scientists studying sects and cults did not want to start with a concept that took it for granted that the groups they were studying were "bad," that they preferred to use the term "new religious movement," commonly abbreviated to "NRM." It is not that these scholars wished to deny that some of the religions they study have engaged in what would be generally accepted as undesirable practices, but that they preferred to define their object of study in neutral terms, and then discover whether it did in fact abuse its women and children and/or indulge in diverse criminal activities. In other words, claiming a religion did or did not indulge in any such practices would depend on empirical investigation, rather than labelling. The object of study would have to be defined independently of any attributes that it might or might not exhibit.

---

5. See below. See also Guyard and Gest, *Les Sectes*. It is, incidentally, a linguistic curiosity that in France, *le culte* is a "good" religion, while *le secte* is the bad religion—or, more likely, doesn't deserve the classification of religion at all.

It should not be thought, however, that the concept of new religious movement has been free of any problems. The very fact that it was being used by social scientists in an attempt to combat the way in which the label "cult" bestowed a negative image on any movement to which it was applied led the movements' opponents to claim that the use of the concept of NRM was a way of denying that the movements did anything wrong. This added fuel to their argument that social scientists, sociologists of religion in particular, were "cult apologists."

Perhaps more seriously from a methodological point of view, have been the difficulties in agreeing how to define "new," "religious" and "movement." First, there is no generally agreed definition of religion, although some countries have tried to introduce legal definitions. These, however, have tended to be highly manipulable and generally unsatisfactory. Scholars have used a variety of definitions, that some have divided into functional definitions, which refer to what a religion *does* (such as providing a society with cohesion), as opposed to substantive definitions, which refer to what a religion *is* (such as belief in a supreme being).[6] Scholars studying the new religions have tended to opt for a rather wide definition along the lines of "a system of beliefs that address questions of ultimate concern, such as who am I? What is the meaning of life? Is there life after death? and/or Is there a God?"[7] Secondly, the concept of "movement" is used even more loosely. It can cover a group, a network, a community, a commune, a congregation, or various other ways in which those sharing similar beliefs and practices are bound together by those beliefs and practices.

Thirdly, whether or not a new religious movement is in fact new has given rise to further ambiguity. Sometimes NRMs are taken to refer to those which became visible after the Second World War; sometimes they include nineteenth-century sects such as Jehovah's Witnesses, the Salvation Army or the Plymouth Brethren; sometimes they refer to religions that are new to a particular society although they may have been around for centuries or even millennia elsewhere.

In my own work, I have found it most useful for purposes of research to classify NRMs as those religions that have a predominantly first-generation membership. That is, the members are more likely to have converted than to have been born into their religion. The advantage of this is that comparisons can be made with early Christianity, and all other religions at their inception. At the same time, one can observe differences that exist between first, second and subsequent generations. Another advantage is that it is relatively

---

6. McGuire, *Religion*.
7. Tillich, *Ultimate Concern*.

easy to decide what a "new" religion is without imputing the presence of contingent variables.[8] In other words, the NRM thus defined may or may not be involved in political intrigues, financial frauds, exploitation of its members—and so on. To repeat, whether it is or not needs to be discovered by investigation rather asserted by labelling.

Contextualization

If we want to go beyond merely defining new religions and discover more about them, it is important to recognize that they cannot be looked at in isolation. Even those religions that try to withdraw from the world—what Roy Wallis has called world-rejecting movements[9]—are likely to have at least some contact with the rest of the world, if only to gain new members.

New religions are part of a wider religious scene that includes both traditional religious and secular movements of various kinds. Some of these older religions will be fundamentalist, selecting what they consider to be universal and particular dogmas that should be accepted literally. These can embrace not only the Protestant fundamentals that were expounded at the end of the nineteenth century, but also contemporary atheists who exhibit extremist rejections of any kind of transcendental claim. At the other end of a continuum, there are the less bounded beliefs and practices one might find among mystics or some Eastern religions. It would, moreover, be a mistake to think that either the religious or the secular beliefs and practices to be found at any one time will display identical features at another time; there is a constant movement, with new religions both 'coming out of' and influencing more established religions.

Not only is it important to recognize that new religions are an integral part of the constantly shifting religious scene, it is also necessary to recognize that they will both affect and be affected by other sections of society. The relatives of converts may find that familial relationships undergo dramatic changes; government agencies, the law, the police, social workers, the medical profession, could all have to be taken into account by NRMs, just as they, in turn, could have to take the new religions into account. A significant

---

8. Even this is not without its difficulties. An actively proselytising movement such as the Mormons currently has more converts than members born into it, despite the fact that it has been around for several generations since it was founded by Joseph Smith in the 1820s. However, the fact that most of the Mormons in Utah are 'born-intos,' whereas in Eastern or African countries they are more likely to be converts, could go some way to explaining the different reception that they are likely to receive in such different places.

9. Wallis, *Elementary Forms*.

role may be played by the mass and social media, which are likely to present an image of a new religion that can have considerable consequences for how it is viewed by the rest of society, particularly when there is the prospect of a sensational story (see below).

Generalizations

One reason why the public has a tendency to generalize about new religious movements is that those movements which have hit the headlines can appear to share some kind of destructive characteristic that has led to very real tragedies. Among such early movements to come to public attention were the Manson Family, when the followers of Charles Manson brutally killed the pregnant Sharon Tate and others in California in 1967;[10] the Symbionese Liberation Army's 1974 kidnapping of Patty Hearst, resulting in the young newspaper heiress being photographed brandishing a gun in a bank raid;[11] and the mass suicides and murders in 1978 of over 900 members of the Peoples Temple in Jonestown, Guyana.[12] Later tragedies include the storming in 1993 by the FBI of the Branch Davidian compound in Waco, Texas, when seventy-six people died, including the children the state was purportedly saving from David Koresh and his movement;[13] and then, in 1997, there were the thirty-nine members of Heaven's Gate who killed themselves in order to board a spacecraft trailing the Comet Hale-Bopp which would, they believed, take them to a higher level of existence.[14]

Among the other new religions that became widely visible in the West around the 1970s was the Unification Church, popularly called the Moonies after its Korean founder, the Rev Sun Myung Moon (1920-2012), whom his followers believed to be the Messiah and who became well known for conducting mass weddings or Blessings with thousands of couples at one time.[15] Another movement, given the nickname of the Children of God by a reporter, which had been founded by David (Moses) Berg (1919-1984) as part of the Jesus movement, was to receive widespread publicity when, in the mid-1970s, Berg promoted what he called the Law of Love, which entailed the practice of "Flirty Fishing," with attractive young "Hookers for Jesus" demonstrating to potential converts and donors how much Jesus

---

10. Bugliosi, *Helter Skelter*; Wells, *Charles Manson*.
11. Grabner, *Patty's Got a Gun*.
12. Kilduff and Javers, *Suicide Cult*; Moore, *Understanding Jonestown*.
13. Ammerman, *Report*; Wright, *Armageddon*.
14. Balch, *From Self Initiation*; Perkins and Jackson, *Cosmic Suicide*.
15. Barker, *Making*; Bromley and Shupe, *Moonies*.

loved them by having sexual relations with them.[16] Although the practice was officially discontinued in the second half of the 1980s, the movement, which changed its name to The Family International, continued to be known as a sex cult and was the subject of a number of raids in various countries in order to rescue the children from the abuse that some had suffered as a result of the practice of free love within some (though not all) of the movement's communities.[17]

ISKCON (the International Society for Krishna Consciousness), popularly known as the Hare Krishna movement, started in the West when A. C. Bhaktivedanta Swami Prabhupada (1896–1977) sailed from India to bring his school of Vaishnavite Hinduism to the West. The devotees, drawn largely from the young hippies of that time, were soon to become a familiar sight on the streets, dancing and chanting their Hare Krishna mantra.[18] Like the Children of God, they were later to become known for the child abuse that had taken place in their gurukulas or boarding schools. This and a number of other scandals perpetrated by some of the "gurus" who took over after Prabhupada's death (including gun running, drug trafficking, sexual misdemeanours and murder) shocked many of the devotees and considerable effort was made to reorganize the movement and compensate those who had been abused.[19]

Bhagwan Shree Rajneesh (1931–1990), later known as Osho, started his movement in India, but later became popular in the West, building a large community known as Rajneeshpuram in Oregon where his Neo-sannyasins, sometimes known as the orange people, would gather from around the world to listen to their guru and partake in a variety of meditations and other practices. Osho was soon to give up his talks and his secretary, Ma Anand Sheela, took over the running of Rajneeshpuram with disastrous results, culminating in an attempt to gain a majority in local government positions by, among other things, sprinkling salmonella poison on salad bars in local restaurants. Sheela and Osho both escaped, Sheela eventually spending time in prison and Osho returning to die in India.[20]

---

16. Bainbridge, *Endtime Family*; Chancellor, *Life in the Family*; Williams, *Heaven's Harlots*.

17. As it turned out, none of the children who were removed during these raids was found to be have been abused and they were eventually returned to the movement. However, there are still numerous stories in circulation of sexual child abuse having occurred during the period.

18. Rochford, *Hare Krishna in America*.

19. Rochford, *Hare Krishna Transformed*.

20. Carter, *Charisma*; Fox, *Osho Rajneesh*; Milne, *Bhagwan*.

The Church of Scientology was founded as early as 1954 by L. Ron Hubbard (1911–1986), a prolific science fiction author, who had written a book, *Dianetics: The Modern Science of Mental Health*,[21] that offered people a way of overcoming obstructive blockages ("engrams") due to past experiences, including those they had experienced in previous lives. Those who became members of the Church were to practice the techniques of Dianetics as part of their religion and, after following some special courses, could become "clear," and, in some cases, move up 'the road to total freedom' becoming an ever-more efficient "operating Thetan."[22] Scientology has frequently been criticised for charging high fees for "auditing" and other courses and, by disillusioned apostates and journalists, for a number of nefarious activities,[23] but has been notably and staunchly supported by the actor Tom Cruise.

For years the Church tried to keep its theology secret, even from Scientologists who have not progressed sufficiently far along "the road to total freedom." However, former members have publicised most of their beliefs on the Internet and it is not difficult to discover that there are a number of aspects of the religion (such as other planets, space craft and extra-terrestrial persons) that can explain why it has been referred to as a UFO-religion.[24] There are several other religions, which although differing from Scientology quite radically, have been similarly categorised, and there are several more examples of NRMs that communicate with Beings on other planets. The Aetherius Society was founded by a London taxi driver who received a command in 1954 telling him "Prepare yourself! You are to become the voice of Interplanetary Parliament."[25] The Unarius Academy of Science was founded in 1954 by "cosmic visionaries Ernest L. and Ruth E. Norman."[26] An American woman, JZ Knight, channels Ramtha, a Lemurian warrior who fought the Atlanteans over 35,000 years ago.[27] The Raelians were founded when an extra-terrestrial purportedly appeared to a French racing-car driver and invited him to step into his space craft.[28]

But these movements represent only the tip of the iceberg. Following the Second World War, literally thousands of alternative religions and spiritual communities were 'coming out' and "popping up" throughout North

---

21. Hubbard, *Dianetics*.
22. Urban, *Church of Scientology*; Wallis, *Road to Total Freedom*.
23. Atack, *Piece of Blue Sky*; Miller, *Bare-Faced*; Wright, *Going Clear*.
24. Lewis, *Encyclopedia*; Partridge, *UFO Religions*.
25. King, *Cosmic Voice*; Wallis, *Aetherius Society*.
26. Norman, *Preparation*; Tumminia and Kirkpatrick, "Unarius."
27. MacLaine, *Out on a Limb*; Melton, *Finding Enlightenment*.
28. Palmer, *Aliens Adored*.

America,[29] Western Europe, Australasia, and, especially, Japan[30]—not to mention the new African religions that were mushrooming all over the continent.[31] In Britain alone there are well over 1000 religions currently active that have appeared since the middle of the twentieth century[32]—and, to repeat, the one fact that that can safely be said about them is that one cannot generalize about them. They differ according to their beliefs; their traditions; their rituals; their life-styles; their leadership and authority structures; their attitudes towards women, children and education; their finances; their propensity towards criminal behaviour, or anything else that one might think about—apart, perhaps, from being called a cult, a sect or a new religious movement.

It is, moreover, important to recognize that it would be foolhardy to generalize too much about a particular movement without awareness of the extent to which it can differ according to the place and time in which it exists. The Unification Church in California in the 1970s was significantly different from the Unification Church in Romania in the early 1990s, and this again differs from the movement in Korea in 2018.

Before leaving the subject of the danger of generalizing, one further point should be added. The characteristics of an NRM (or an older religion) differ according to the part or aspect of the movement to which reference is being made. The movement itself has certain characteristics (it is, for example, tightly or loosely organized), and it is rare for the characteristics of the leadership to be the same as those of the rank-and-file membership. If asked to describe Falun Gong one would give a different answer if one focussed on the movement as a social, political or economic entity from one that described the founder, Master Li Hongzhi, and this would, again, differ from a description of the characteristics of the practitioners. In other words, "he" has characteristics that are different from those of "it" or "them." And then a further investigation that any research would need to consider involves the dynamic relationships between these (and further) different aspects.

Potential Characteristics of New NRMs

Whilst insisting that one cannot generalize about new religions, it is still possible to suggest that there are certain characteristics or features which

29. Melton, *Encyclopedia*.
30. McFarland, *Rush Hour*.
31. Turner, *New Religious*.
32. Inform (Information Network Focus on Religious Movements) has over 5,000 religious organizations on its files. See Inform, "Home." See also Melton, *Encyclopedia*.

have been found to be frequently associated with *new* new religions, and which it might be useful to look for when trying to find out about a religious movement that consists predominantly of a first-generation membership.

First, by definition, the movement will have a large number of converts, and converts to a religion tend to be more enthusiastic, even fanatic, than those born into their religion. But it is also true that, while they may appear to themselves and others to be very certain about their new faith, they are also likely to be uncertain in a number of ways; they will not have fully absorbed the niceties of doctrine or how they are meant to behave; they still have taken-for-granted beliefs, values and attitudes that may not sit happily with the new world-view. In this sense they may be at their most vulnerable to deconversion, just because they have not yet become fully socialised into the movement. And, indeed, the turnover rate of converts is frequently greatest in the period soon after conversion.[33]

Next, NRMs rarely appeal to a normal distribution of the population. They are likely to be offering something that particular sections of society feel (or can easily be made to feel) they cannot get from traditional religions or the wider society. In the past, it has often been the politically, economically, or socially oppressed who have been attracted to religions offering them a better life—in this world or the next. The wave of new religions that became visible in the West around the 1970s, however, disproportionately attracted middle-class, well-educated, young whites. There were movements, such as the Rastafarians, that appealed largely to young, disadvantaged black males,[34] and others that appealed to different constituencies, but it would be difficult to find the membership of any first-generation NRM replicating the sociodemographic composition of the host society.

Thirdly, members of NRMs frequently accord their founder/leader a charismatic authority. That is, they believe that he (or, sometimes, she) has a special gift of "grace" or charisma, and this legitimises his or her right to determine a much wider span of the followers' lives than any "ordinary" leader, such as a prime minister or even a pope, would have, including such details as what they should wear, what they should eat, what kind of work they should do, where they should live, with whom they should live and/or have a relationship, and, perhaps, even whether they should live. This kind of authority (legitimised power) has been contrasted by the German sociologist Max Weber with traditional and legal-rational authority.[35] Because charismatic leaders are unconstrained by either tradition or bureaucratic

---

33. Wright, *Leaving Cults.*
34. Cashmore, *Rastafarian.*
35. Weber, *Theory of Social.*

rules, they are liable to be both unpredictable, being able to change direction at a moment's notice, and unaccountable to anyone—except, perhaps, God.

Fourthly, if the movement grows in number (though by no means all NRMs do) so that face-to-face interactions between the leader and his or her followers becomes difficult or undesirable, it is not uncommon for there to develop a hierarchical structure, with the one leader at the top, a second-level leadership just below, with a third-level leadership owing obedience to one of the second-level leaders—and so on down the chain of command to the "foot soldiers," who may find themselves prevented from enjoying much in the way of horizontal relationships. In some cases, this may involve various means of ensuring neither partnerships or close friendships are formed—at one extreme this may mean celibacy, at another extreme, frequent wife-swapping and/or institutionalised promiscuity. Again, it should be stressed that such arrangements are by no means always the case, but it certainly is not uncommon for authority structures and communication networks to be of a fairly clear top-down nature during the early years of an NRM, with everyone having a clearly defined place in the vertical hierarchy where those with whom they interact are either above or below them.

Fifthly, it is not uncommon for NRMs (especially, but by no means only, those of a "world-rejecting" type) to have a dichotomous world view. That is, rather than exploring grey areas, or holding qualified positions, there is a tendency for sharp distinctions to be drawn between, for example, "godly" and "satanic" for theological issues; "right" and "wrong" or "good" and "bad" for moral issues; and "before" and "after" for temporal periods, such as "before I joined this religion I was a miserable sinner," or "the world will undergo unimaginable changes when Jesus returns." And, perhaps most significantly for a sociologist, is the sharp distinction that can be drawn between "them" and "us." Membership is seen as the primary criterion for identity—you are either one of us, or one of them; we, the members of our religion, are good and godly compared to the rest of society which is bad and ungodly. The "them" and "us" boundary has frequently been reinforced through special terms, members of the NRM being referred to as part of a family—Father, Mother, brother, sister, "spiritual child"—whilst derogatory names might be given to non-members: "systemites" (for non-Children of God), "worldlies" (for non-Plymouth Brethren), "wogs" (for non-Scientologists). Such boundaries are likely to be particularly pertinent if the movement shares many of the characteristics of the host society. Thus a new religion claiming to be following "real" Christianity is quite likely to stress its distinction from, and superiority to, a Christian society more than it will feel the need to stress its differences from a Hindu society.

Reactions to New Religions

As has already been suggested, new religions cannot be viewed in isolation. A sixth characteristic commonly associated with NRMs (and other new, ideologically motivated groups) is that the wider society within which they exist has, throughout history, frequently tended to be suspicious and sometimes outright antagonistic towards them. Early Christians were fed to the lions; the mediaeval Cathars were burned at the stake,[36] as was Jan Hus in 1415.[37] More recently, Jehovah's Witnesses have been gassed in Auschwitz;[38] Bahá'í have been executed in Iran;[39] and members of the Ahmadiyya community are persecuted in Pakistan.[40] It is also the case, however, that there are hundreds, if not thousands, of new religions that coexist without any severe conflict in countries throughout the world. As one might expect, some countries are far more severe than other countries in their reactions to new religions.

No two people ever see exactly the same thing, even if they are both looking at what is, objectively, the same thing. Two witnesses to a road accident can come up with not only different but contradictory accounts of what happened, without either one consciously trying to alter the facts. Psychologists delight in demonstrating how we can have different "visions" of a picture—the rabbit that turns into a duck, or the old hag that can be seen as a beautiful young woman are among the many examples.[41] Furthermore, sometimes we look at what is, objectively, exactly the same thing and yet what we see has different connotations and implications—for one person the glass is half empty; for another, it is half full. The "real world out there" may suggest but it does not dictate the way we construct our images of it.[42]

What we perceive and how we react is not entirely random: we tend to select what we see according to different concerns, and this means that there are some systematic differences between different people's different versions of reality and the different images they construct of the reality "out

---

36. Lambert, *Cathars*; Martin, *Cathars*.
37. Fudge, *Trial*.
38. King, *Nazi State*; Liebster, *Crucible*.
39. Baha'i International Community, *Iran's Secret*.
40. Pakistan's Criminal Law (Amendment) Act (1986) includes the offence: "An Ahmadi, calling himself a Muslim, or preaching or propagating his faith, or outraging the religious feelings of Muslims, or posing himself as a Muslim" is subject to "three years imprisonment and fine," and the "use of derogatory remarks etc. in respect of the Holy Prophet" is punishable by "death and fine."
41. Gregory, *Seeing*.
42. Douglas, *Purity and Danger*.

there." Thus it is that the members of a new religion will have an interest in securing new converts and/or persuading other members of society that the movement not only has The Truth, but also that it is uniquely "good." The image they construct of their movement is likely to highlight its positive features whilst suppressing any skeletons lurking in cupboards.

On the other hand, from the early 1970s, there arose a number of groups that came to be known generically as the anti-cult movement (ACM). Initially these consisted of concerned relatives of the young adults who had "disappeared" into the "cults," but soon other opponents of the movements became involved.[43] The images that the ACM constructed of the NRMs were in several ways a mirror image of the religions themselves. The anti-cultists' interest was in warning others about the dangers of cults and, not infrequently, lobbying to have them controlled or banned altogether. Their images included all the "bad" features, generalizing these as applying to all the movements, and omitting any "good" or normal aspects in their depiction of the "cults." For the ACM it was "them," the cults, that were the baddies, while the rest of society ("us") were the goodies. The concept of brainwashing was popularised as a way of explaining the otherwise apparently inexplicable reason why anyone could be "recruited into" one of the movements (the term "conversion" was usually reserved for joining a "real religion"). The brainwashing thesis—that the members had been subjected to irresistible and irreversible techniques, rather than making a genuine choice—then came to be used as a reason for engaging in "deprogramming," a practice that involves illegally kidnapping "victims" and holding them against their will until they manage either to escape or to convince their captors that they have renounced their faith.[44]

Some anti-cultists have been concerned about a specific religion or group of religions; and there are, for example, several anti-Unificationist,[45] anti-Children of God,[46] and anti-Scientology campaigners,[47] as well as countless others who warn about the dangers of the cults in general, some being former members of one or other of the movements, a few being scholars and other professionals concerned about the harm the new religions can do[48]—usually to their own members, although anti-cultists rarely miss the

43. Bromley and Shupe, "Organized Opposition"; Shupe and Bromley, *New Vigilantes*.

44. Bromley and Richardson, *Brainwashing*; Patrick, *Let Our Children Go*.

45. Boettcher, *Gifts of Deceit*; Hassan, *Combatting*; Underwood and Underwood, *Hostage*; Yamamoto, *Puppet Master*.

46. Jones et al., *Not Without*; Kent and Hall, *Brainwashing*.

47. Atack, *Piece of Blue Sky*; Coleman, *Hacker*.

48. Patrick, *Let Our Children Go*; Ross, *Cults*; Singer and Lalich, *Cults*.

opportunity to remind others of horror stories such as the Peoples Temple or Aum Shinrikyo, the movement that released sarin gas in the Tokyo underground.[49]

Whilst the ACM concentrated primarily on the bad actions of the new religions, there were other groups that were more concerned about the religions' wrong beliefs. These, generically referred to as the counter-cult movement (CCM), have been more common throughout history, the Inquisition being one of the most effectively organized.[50] Since the 1970s the most vocal CCMs in the West have tended to consist of some evangelical Protestants and, as might be expected, it is the religions that they consider to be Christian heresies that receive most attention, with their construction of images of NRMs including those aspects of faith that differ from real Christianity, while all similarities are ignored. Many of these CCMs have concentrated on nineteenth-century religions such as the Jehovah's Witnesses and Mormons.[51] It might be added that there are a number of inter-faith groups that are careful to exclude not only what are considered Christian heresies, but will also deny membership to NRMs that draw on other traditions because the 'traditional' representatives of those traditions reject such new "heresies."

By no means all the traditional religions actively oppose new religions, but most are wary of engaging in formal dialogue. Several Orthodox Churches have been particularly active in opposing NRMs, partly because they, and their members, are depicted as 'foreign' on the assumption that to be a true Greek (or Russian), one must belong to the Greek (or Russian) Orthodox Church, even when converts have been born and raised in a Greek (or Russian) family in Greece (or Russia) and speak only Greek (or Russian).

In some countries, such as the USA, the UK, and Scandinavia, there is no requirement, or even possibility, to register as a religion *per se*.[52] In those countries where registration is possible or required, the criteria are frequently weighted against NRMs in so far as they stipulate that the religion must have a minimum number of members (in Slovakia, the number is 20,000)[53] and/or have been in the country for a given number of years

---

49. Lifton, *Destroying*.
50. Rawlings, *Spanish Inquisition*.
51. Enroth, *Lure*; Martin, *Kingdom*.
52. In the UK, religions can apply to register as a charity, which gives them a certain status and some tax privileges. However, simply being a religion is not sufficient reason to become a charity. It is also necessary to demonstrate that the religion is of "public benefit." See "Charitable purposes and public benefit."
53. At the time of writing, the Slovak National Party is attempting to amend

(state recognition as a religion cannot be granted to a movement that has not been in Lithuania for at least twenty-five years). The consequences of being registered vary. In Europe, it usually bestows the possibility of certain privileges; however there are countries in which registration can lead to restrictions and/or religions are not allowed to practice without formal recognition.

Several countries have set up formal enquiries into new religions and these have resulted in a number of influential Reports.[54] James Richardson and Massimo Introvigne (scholars who happen to be both sociologists of religion and lawyers) have drawn a distinction between what they call Type I and Type II Reports.[55] The former, of which the French and Belgian Reports are examples, are depicted as being responsible for the inflation of moral panics in so far as they refer to the movements as "cults" or "sects," distinguishing them from "religions," and explaining their presence with reference to brainwashing or mind control; apostates who leave are referred to as "victims" and the resources on which these Reports depended for their information were anti-cultists rather than scholars (let alone the movements themselves). Both the French (1995) and the Belgian (1997) Reports also included a list of sects, which have resulted in some members of movements on the lists having found themselves unable to get work, find accommodation or place their children in schools.[56] Interestingly, the lists included Amish, Quakers, some Baptists (as indicated above) and the Young Women's Christian Association (though not the YMCA). Type II Reports, on the other hand, which included the German Enquete Commission and a Report presented to the European Parliament, had drawn on information provided by scholars and displayed a far greater awareness of the complexity of the situation.

Nearly all Western countries are signatories of such international agreements as the 1948 General Assembly of the United Nations' Universal Declaration of Human Rights (UNDHR)[57] and the European Convention

---

this legislation and raise the required number of members to 50,000. See Grabner, "Slovakia."

54. Countries with Reports on NRMs include The Netherlands (Witteveen, *Onderzoek*); France (Vivien, *Les Sectes*; Guyard and Gest, *Les Sectes*); Belgium (Duquesne and Willems, *Enquete*); Germany (*Enquete Commission*); Sweden (Ingvardsson et al., *I God Tro*); Ontario, Canada (Hill, *Mind Development*); and the European Parliament (Berger, *Draft Report*).

55. Richardson and Introvigne, "Brainwashing."

56. Lheureux et al., *Report*.

57. UNDHR Article 18:
Everyone has the right to freedom of thought, conscience and religion; this

of Human Rights (ECHR),[58] and nearly all include a clause on freedom of religion and belief in their Constitutions (if they have one). However, although freedom to manifest one's religion is vouchsafed in principle, there are clear limitations as to just how far one's religious beliefs give one the right to do (as opposed to believe) anything the religion demands. Restrictions are spelled out in the second part of Article 9 of the ECHR and in Article 29 of the UNDHR.[59] Back in 1879, the United States Supreme Court ruled that although members of the Church of Jesus Christ of Latter-day Saints could hold whatever *opinions* they wished, Congress could legislate against *action*—in this case polygamy.[60] Since that time, numerous cases have come before the courts in attempts to adjudicate the extent to which religious freedom can trump the law of the land. In the United States, the "compelling

---

> right includes freedom to change his religion or belief, and freedom, either alone or in community with others and in public or private, to manifest his religion or belief in teaching, practice, worship and observance.
>
> UNDHR Article 19:
>
> Everyone has the right to freedom of opinion and expression; this right includes freedom to hold opinions without interference and to seek, receive and impart information and ideas through any media and regardless of frontiers.
>
> UNDHR Article 20:
>
> Everyone has the right to freedom of peaceful assembly and association.
>
> No one may be compelled to belong to an association.

58. ECHR Article 9.

> Everyone has the right to freedom of thought, conscience and religion; this right includes freedom to change his religion or belief, and freedom, either alone or in community with others and in public or private, to manifest his religion or belief, in worship, teaching, practice and observance.
>
> Freedom to manifest one's religion or beliefs shall be subject only to such limitations as are prescribed by law and are necessary in a democratic society in the interests of public safety, for the protection of public order, health or morals, or the protection of the rights and freedoms of others.

59. UNDHR Article 29:

> (1) Everyone has duties to the community in which alone the free and full development of his personality is possible.
>
> (2) In the exercise of his rights and freedoms, everyone shall be subject only to such limitations as are determined by law solely for the purpose of securing due recognition and respect for the rights and freedoms of others and of meeting the just requirements of morality, public order and the general welfare in a democratic society.
>
> (3) These rights and freedoms may in no case be exercised contrary to the purposes and principles of the United Nations.

60. *Reynolds v. United States*, 98 US (8 Otto.), 145 (1878).

state interest" test,[61] and the concept of "ministerial exception,"[62] have been evoked to decide whether to favour religious exemptions; in Canada the concept of "reasonable accommodation" is drawn upon to decide such matters.[63]

Although decisions vary, it would seem to be clear that NRMs present a challenge to the courts to a disproportionate degree in certain types of religious cases.[64] But perhaps even more to the point is the extent to which countries introduce special legislation addressing "the problem" of new religions. A crude distinction can be drawn between those societies that assume innocence until a crime is committed and whose laws apply to everyone, and those societies that try to protect their citizens by introducing laws that focus specifically on new religions in order to forestall their carrying out illegal or anti-social acts. In such countries, NRMs can feel that they are criminalised before committing any crime.

France provides an example of a country that tries to protect its citizens by introducing laws that target *les sectes*.[65] Furthermore, the Prime Minister's Office funds the *Mission interministérielle de vigilance et de lute contre les derives sectaires* (MIVILUDES), which stated in its 2004 annual report that:

By giving priority to the aspect of prevention, MIVILUDES respects its obligations:

- to inform the public about the risks, and in some cases the dangers, to which it is exposed by sectarian aberrations;

- to promote, while respecting the right of freedom of opinion, the coordination of preventive and repressive action by the authorities to deal with such behavior.[66]

Other countries that have laws specifically directed towards new religions include Russia and China. The now disgraced but then Minister of Public Security of the Chinese People's Republic, Zhou Yongkang, offered a clear exposition of the thinking behind the "prevent" position in a widely quoted speech when he stated:

---

61. Evans, *Religious Freedom*.
62. Slotte and Årsheim, "Ministerial."
63. Beaman, *Reasonable*.
64. Richardson, *Regulating*.
65. "LOI no 2001–504," 9337.
66. Langlais, *2004 Report*.

> We must make efforts to create a harmonious society and a good social environment for successfully holding the 17th Communist Party Congress and the Beijing Olympic Games. . . . We must strike hard at hostile forces at home and abroad, such as ethnic separatists, religious extremists, violent terrorists and 'heretical organizations' like the Falun Gong who carry out destabilizing activities.[67]

Countries such as the United States, Canada, the UK and Scandinavia have been more likely to adopt the "after" position; citizens are presumed innocent until they have been proved guilty in a court of law, and the law applies equally to all, whatever their religion.[68] Certainly, the actions of NRMs might lead to the introduction of new laws, but new laws are being introduced the whole time and they will apply to all, be they Methodist, Muslim, Mormon or "Moonie." However, the situation is always changing. Since "the troubles" in Northern Ireland, English law has banned some movements, but these, and a few Islamic new religions such as Al-Muhajiroun have been banned since the al-Qaeda attacks of 11 September 2001 because they "glorify" terrorist activity rather than because of their religion *per se*. More recently, the government has introduced the controversial "Prevent" programme, which has targeted several Islamic individuals and organizations.[69]

The Media

So far as non-governmental institutions are concerned, it is arguable that the mass media have been the most influential sector on account of their unprecedented capacity to reach a hitherto unreachable span and variety of people. It is, however, unlikely that the media's image of NRMs will be particularly sympathetic. A prime interest of the media is to get and keep their readers, listeners and viewers, and most potential audiences are likely to have an interest in reading, hearing, or watching stories that select the novel, sensational, exotic, and/or shocking, whilst omitting the ordinary, every-day features of a movement. It could be said that for much of the media, "bad news is good news." Furthermore, most journalists are given

---

67. Paulk, "Falun Gong."

68. It is true that England and Scotland and parts of Scandinavia have Established Churches, but individual Anglicans or members of a State Lutheran Church receive no special privileges on this account.

69. H. M. Government, *Revised Prevent*.

neither the space nor the time to go into qualifying details of the kind in which scholars are wont to indulge; what is wanted are pithy sound bites.

The scariness of the media depiction can be emphasised by depicting anything to do with rank and file members of NRMs in the passive voice, using concepts such as brainwashing rather than choice, recruitment rather than conversion, cult rather than religion. But particularly vivid are the images that stick in one's mind as they are shown over and over, even when they are accompanying a story that has nothing whatsoever to do with the NRM that is being discussed. Most people over forty will recognize a picture of the bodies of Jim Jones's followers after they had committed suicide or been murdered in the Guyana jungle in 1978; anyone over 25 and most younger audiences will be familiar with the picture of Al Qaida pilots flying into New York's twin towers on 9/11, and, even more recently, images of ISIS suicide bombers declaring their dedication to Allah. They are far less likely to remember, or to have even seen, pictures of NRMs doing charitable work in the black townships of South Africa or with refugees in war zones in the Middle East, or providing hot meals to the down-and-outs of Europe or America.

Change

The seventh and final characteristic one could look for in new religions is that they tend to change far more radically and far more rapidly than older, more established religions. Changes can be generated within the movements, or be the result of external factors; they can be specific to a particular movement, or more general and likely to affect the movements as a whole.[70]

Specific internal changes vary greatly, but will often involve some kind of revisionism of doctrines or practices that could originally have appeared to be central to a movement's *raison d'être*.[71] An obvious example occurs when a new religion has prophesied that some apocalyptic happening would occur on a particular date, the date arrives and nothing very special seems to have taken place—at least to the outsider. Sometimes this spells the death of the movement with disappointed and disillusioned members departing, but there are numerous ways in which NRMs have managed to survive such an apparent disconfirmation. One well-known study, entitled *When Prophecy Fails*, suggested that disconfirmation could actually lead to renewed activity and enthusiasms.[72] Sometimes, as with the Millerites when

70. Barker, "Not-So-New."
71. Barker, *Revisionism*.
72. Festinger et al., *When Prophecy*.

they faced apparent confirmation in 1843, the date was adjusted to a later one; but following the 'Great Disappointment of 1844, although William Miller was still convinced that Jesus' return was imminent, several of his followers gave up belief, while others moved to different Adventist groups, the largest number joining what was to become the Seventh-day Adventist Church which reinterpreted what Miller had assumed would be a happening on earth to the belief that in fact the prophecy had been fulfilled, but the happening (the "cleansing") had actually happened when Jesus had entered a sanctuary in Heaven.[73] The arrival of Jesus on earth was still awaited, but no longer was any definite date predicted.

The Jehovah's Witnesses is another well-known religion that has survived a number of disappointments, the most recent being 1975. However there is a limited number of times that a religion can continue to prophesy dates that are open to apparent confirmation, and eventually specifications a exact dates are abandoned, although there may remain an expectation that the endtime is indeed nigh. Some religions explain the absence of apocalyptic happenings by saying that these would have happened had the people of the world accepted God's revelations;[74] others say that they managed to prevent disaster through their actions.[75] Most, however, allow the disconfirmable prophecy to slip to the margins of their belief system, perhaps insisting that it was never really a central tenet of their theology.[76]

A different, less dramatic kind of revision occurred in Unificationists' understanding of the changes that were to be accomplished through their mass Blessings and, more importantly, the accompanying Holy Wine Ceremony. Nearly all the young converts with whom I talked in the 1970s and early '80s expected that their children, born without "fallen nature" (the Unification equivalent of original sin), would be very special—indeed the adjective "perfect" was frequently used. It was not too long, however, before the behaviour of these children, not least the "True Children," born of "True Parents" (the Reverend and Mrs Moon), resulted in a significantly modified understanding of the theology.

The Children of God, originally a "pure" Christian movement, underwent a radical change when the practice of "Flirty Fishing" was introduced in the 1980s; it underwent a further radical change when "FFing" was discontinued, due, among other reasons, to the introduction of sexually transmitted diseases into the communities. Further examples of changes in both

---

73. Bull and Lockhart, *Seeking*.
74. Barker, *Making of a Moonie*.
75. Prophet, *Prophet's Daughter*.
76. Melton, "Spiritualization."

beliefs and practices can be found among "Intentional Communities" which aspire to follow utopian lifestyles. Not infrequently these do not turn out to be as harmonious as had been expected; "back to the earth" communes can find that the community's lack of agricultural knowledge has led to disaster—or, alternatively, they became so successful that they set up small capitalist ventures that would seem, in some cases at least, to repudiate the simple communal life they had originally espoused.[77]

And, as already intimated, one consequence of change within an NRM is that it can give rise to schisms or splinter groups. This is particularly likely to occur after the death of a charismatic leader, as, for example, with ISKCON which has given rise to at least six different movements, and, following Moon's death in 2012, the Unification Church has spawned a number of factions led by his widow and some of his children, all claiming to represent the true teachings of Unificationism.[78] Alternatively, some movements disband altogether after the death of their leader, as was the case with the Source Family, a hippie Californian group that disintegrated following the death of Father Yod.[79]

One common motivation that can lead to breakaway groups is that an NRM is thought to have accommodated too far with the world and the schismatics decide that they will restore the original beliefs and/or practices—as they perceive these. But by no means all splits are on purely theological grounds. The over 400-sects spawned by Joseph Smith's original revelations and *The Book of Mormon* could just as easily be the result of personal vendettas and political or economic disagreements.[80] One interesting breakup occurred within The Independent Church (Hoton):

> The Bishop who had charge of the temporal things accused the President of visiting his pork barrel and the President accused the Bishop of visiting his wife. . . . These accusations resulted in a split between the two head officers and the organization fell apart.[81]

General internal changes are those that are likely to affect the majority, if not all NRMs, the most obvious of these being of a demographic nature. Charismatic leaders die—although there are NRMs which claim the leader and perhaps the followers have discovered the secret of eternal life on this

---

77. Miller, *American Communes*.
78. Vonck, *Life and Legacy*.
79. Aquarian, *Source*.
80. Bringhurst and Hamer, *Scattering*.
81. Shields, *Divergent Paths*, 22.

earth in their present physical forms. One example was Mabel Barltrop of the Panacea Society (the roots of which went back to the late eighteenth-century Southcottians), who taught that she and her followers would survive death. Unfortunately, Octavia, as Mrs Barltrop became known, did not return after her death and the last member of the Society died in 2012.[82] A still extant group, currently residing in Arizona and now known as People Unlimited, offers to share with its followers a method of achieving physical immortality.[83] Unfortunately the eldest of the three leaders died in 1914, and although his partners have continued running their lucrative movement, their message has undergone some subtle changes.[84]

Although there are exceptions (as when Elizabeth Clair Prophet succeeded her husband Mark as leader of the Church Universal and Triumphant),[85] charismatic founders are rarely replaced by another charismatic leader. It is far more common for authority to come to rely on tradition—which may be an "invented tradition"[86]—and/or some kind of bureaucratic structure.[87] As a result, the movement is likely to become increasingly predictable with the leadership being more accountable.

Not only do leaders die, but enthusiastic young converts will age and are likely to become more mature. If, as is usually (though not always) the case, children are born into the movement, then it becomes necessary to devote the scarce resources of time and money to their upbringing. As the children grow older, it is necessary to socialise them, and NRMs are usually keen to ensure that the second generation will follow in their footsteps. When (as happens not infrequently) the children rebel, the movement may impose harsh disciplinary measures to lick them into shape. As often as not, this has led to the children leaving as soon as they can. The movement may then accommodate to a lifestyle that encourages them to stay, using a carrot rather than a stick.[88] And then, as the remaining children grow even older, they may start to take on leadership positions, introducing new goals, values, understandings, and practices, which are often far more "denominational"—that is, the movement becomes more open and receptive towards

---

82. Shaw, *Octavia*.
83. Brown et al., *Together Forever*.
84. See People Unlimited, "Super Longevity Community."
85. Prophet, *Prophet's Daughter*.
86. Hobsbawm and Ranger, *Invention*; Cusack, *Invented Religions*.
87. Miller, *American Communes*.
88. Muster, *Child*; Palmer and Hardman, *Children*; van Eck Duymaer van Twist, *Perfect*.

the wider social environment, gradually eroding the more intransigent social (and other) boundaries that typified its early days.

By this time, it is likely that the NRM, no longer consisting predominantly of converts but having become one that consists largely of "born intos," will have undergone several radical changes, and no longer be exhibiting many of the characteristics of NRMs that were outlined above. Membership of their religion may no longer be the only or even primary focus of members' identification; rather than being part of a strong group, they may be part of a network (subject to what Douglas terms "grid," as opposed to "group," control),[89] with several friends and acquaintances who are not only unrelated to the movement, but also unrelated to each other. They may now live in a nuclear family rather than a centre, attend college, have an "outside" job, be in contact with grandparents and other non-member relatives; they may have children of their own and could be part of a Parent-Teacher group; they may even attend a traditional church, temple or mosque if they no longer live near one of the movement's centres.[90] The movement is, however, unlikely to be completely "normal." The images (be they accurate, exaggerated or false) that members of the general public have of the movements' early days are quite likely to survive the radical changes it has undergone—a potential problem made all the more cogent in the days of the Internet and social media.[91] Furthermore, the second generation will have been brought up in a new religion and undergone experiences that will have differed in a number of significant ways from those of their peers in the "outside world." And ageing converts may present a severe challenge to those NRMs that had not anticipated a need for pensions or insurance in old age.[92]

As always, however, it is important to recognize that there are exceptions; there will be religions that manage to keep many of their more sectarian characteristics throughout several generations. Examples include the Hutterites, the Amish, the Christadelphians, and the Jehovah's Witnesses. This is not to suggest such religions have not changed—they undoubtedly have. Indeed, it is possible to argue somewhat paradoxically that it is only by changing that they have been able to preserve their beliefs and practices.

Specific external changes are those that are brought about by one or more of the sectors of society focussing on one or more of the groups. The earlier section on social reactions to NRMs has already indicated some of the external influences on the movements, particularly those from

89. Douglas, *Natural Symbols.*
90. Barker, "Not-So-New."
91. Borowik, "Digital Revisionism."
92. Barker, "Ageing."

governments and the media, and there is no space here to elaborate further, except to stress that these influences have themselves been changing. At the individual level, it has been the relatives and friends of converts who were initially responsible for pushing NRMs towards change. On the one hand, if they preserved good relations with the convert they could temper some thoughtless enthusiasms and keep open the possibility of alternatives; on the other hand, if they were antagonistic and resorted to deprogramming, the repercussions could be serious, leading the movement to tighten its hold on its members, perhaps moving them to another country so the parents would no longer know where they were.[93] This reaction was fairly common during the 1970s and '80s, but with a general lessening of tensions, particularly when grandchildren came along, families became more likely to renew contact and have a more relaxed relationship.

Sometimes allegations by the movements' opponents have fed into legal cases that might be initiated either by or against an NRM and, especially in the 1970s and '80s, new religions found themselves involved in literally hundreds of lawsuits.[94] Many of these were connected with accusations of "brainwashing," deprogramming and conservatorship orders. These cases mobilised a number of scholars who appeared as expert witnesses testifying that a metaphor such as "brainwashing" had no scientific basis, and eventually the concept ceased to be admissible as evidence.[95]

The lawsuits were often financially crippling for both sides, even when they won. In 2002, several of the ISKCON temples filed for bankruptcy in order to avoid legal cases.[96] A notable case in 1996 resulted in a powerful anti-cult movement, the Cult Awareness Network (CAN), being bankrupted as the result of an action brought against it by a member of the Life Tabernacle Church, a small United Pentecostalist congregation in Washington State, who had been subjected to an attempted deprogramming facilitated by CAN.[97] Following the demise of CAN,[98] the largest American alternative,

93. Barker, "With Enemies"; Bromley, "Conservatorships."

94. Richardson and Bellanger, *Legal Cases*.

95. Anthony, "Religious Movements." Several scholars demonstrated statistically that a vast majority of people subjected to the so-called 'cult brainwashing techniques' were perfectly capable of resisting the movements' attempts to convert them, and the majority of those who did join (and first-cohort second-generation children brought up by the movement) were perfectly capable of leaving, thereby demonstrating the techniques were neither as irresistible nor as irreversible as their opponents claimed—and perhaps the movements would have liked. See Barker, *Making*; Bird and Reimer, "Participation"; Bromley and Richardson, *Brainwashing*; Wright, *Leaving Cults*.

96. Rochford, *Hare Krishna Transformed*.

97. Shupe and Darnell, *Agents*.

98. The Church of Scientology actually procured the Cult Awareness Network

the American Family Foundation (now the International Cultic Studies Association) became the main source of information and counselling but, unlike CAN, it advocated voluntary exit counselling and family reconciliation rather than deprogramming. It also underwent a number of changes, which contributed to the so-called "cult wars" between "strident anti-cultists" and "cult-apologist scholars" turning, in several instances, to a scene of mutual co-operation and respect.[99] This reconciliation has been less noticeable in Europe, however, and, as with the NRMs, when 'true believers' perceive too much accommodation, anti-cult schisms have occurred.

Some legal proceedings have resulted directly in religions having to undergo radical changes in their beliefs practices. One example was a case brought to the UK Family Court, which resulted in the Children of God having to renounce some of David Berg's teachings.[100] Another example was when the Plymouth Brethren Christian Community had to change its Trust Deeds in order to satisfy the Charity Commissioners' criterion of "public benefit" for charitable status.[101] South Korea provides an example of a minority religion being responsible for changing the law, rather than being changed by it. Although, as of 1 October 2016 there were 395 Jehovah's Witnesses in prison on grounds of conscientious objection (far more than in any other country),[102] the Witnesses have now won a case on appeal. Part of the three judges' opinion read:

> The State is self-contradictory, as it denies the need of alternative service but actually imposes alternative service upon the defendant after convicting him. There is no need to turn the defendant into a criminal before imposing this kind of service upon him. If alternative service is implemented, he would be given an opportunity to proudly contribute to the community in place of military duty.[103]

General external changes can occur in a society and affect NRMs despite not being directly focussed on them. An obvious example of such changes would be wars. General cultural and moral changes can also affect the religions—both their proselytising efforts and the reception they receive.

---

name and telephone number and became known as the 'New CAN' for a while, but is no longer noticeably active. Shupe and Darnell, *Agents of Discord*.

99. Barker, "From Cult War"; Giambalvo et al., "Changes."

100. Ward, "Judgement."

101. See "Preston Down Trust."

102. See Jehovah's Witnesses, "Jehovah's Witnesses Imprisoned."

103. Kim Uping-shik, Presiding Judge, Gwangju District Court, The Third Criminal Division, Judgement: Cho, Lak-hoon defendant. 18 October 2016.

A downturn in the economic situation can result in fewer potential converts taking a "gap year" to travel before continuing their education, thus being far from home and open to friendly approaches from enthusiastic recruiters. Changes in governments can have far-reaching consequences, one such change being the end of China's cultural revolution in 1976, after which a number of minority religions have been allowed to exist,[104] although pretty drastic punishment awaits movements such as Falun Gong or the Church of Almighty God which have found themselves on the official list of *xiejiao* (heretical organizations). Perhaps even more consequential was the fall of the Berlin Wall in 1989. Hundreds of NRMs found a great new opportunity to expand by offering their wares to a population that had lived for generations under an atheist regime and, whilst often thirsty for religious succour, were usually religiously illiterate and ready to accept whatever was on offer. Soon, however, the honeymoon was over as the traditional religions started attacking the foreigners as thieves who were stealing their flock: new freedoms were soon to turn to what were, at least in some respects, new restrictions.[105]

Another social change that indirectly focused attention *away* from many of the NRMs was the bombing of the Twin Towers on 11 September 2001. Almost overnight, Islamic terrorism became a far greater concern than "cults" or "sects." Islamophobia took pride of place in many sections of society that had previously been concerned with the new religions. This has become particularly noticeable in the media. There are, however, a number of other reasons why NRMs are not treated with the degree of suspicion to which they were subjected in the latter half of the twentieth century. One is that there have been a number of scandals involving old religious movements, thereby putting the practices of NRMs into some sort of perspective—an obvious example is the Roman Catholic Church's cover-up of thousands of cases of child abuse. Another factor is that many of the ideas and practices that the NRMs were offering potential recruits had become far more common place and attainable without joining a new religion. An example here would be the vegetarianism espoused by ISKCON which was condemned as unhealthy in the 1970s but is now promoted by hundreds of thousands as a healthy way of life.[106] Other examples of ideologies behind several new religions, such as ecological awareness and feminism, are now also culturally commonplace.

104. Yang, *Religion*.
105. Barker, "But Who's Going to Win?"
106. Dasa, "Changing Perception."

Perhaps the most noteworthy changes have been the result of technological innovations that have taken place over the past half-century, and perhaps most significant of these are the arrival and widespread use of the Internet and social media. When I published a general book about NRMs in 1989, there was not one mention of the World Wide Web or the Internet; in fact, incredible as it may now seem, the first time I saw the Internet was on a visit to an ISKCON farm in Sweden in the mid-1990s. It is difficult to exaggerate the difference that the electronic technology has made to NRMs. Obviously enough, it is responsible for a far more rapid and extensive dissemination of knowledge than was possible heretofore. Information, be it favourable or critical, accurate or false, can be (and is) transmitted throughout the world in a matter of nanoseconds.

NRM websites provide information about their beliefs, practices, history, up-coming events and contact details; they sell courses, literature, DVDs, crystals, mugs and T-shirts. Other websites provide negative information and create forums for former and/or current members to network and both learn from and support each other. The Internet can both promote and undermine the authority of leaders, who no longer have to rely on messages getting garbled through transmission by others, and their latest decisions can reach their followers almost instantaneously. But, at the same time, the existence of emails and forums enables members to exchange information at a horizontal level, thereby not only undermining the hierarchical authority structure, but also providing them with easy access to alternative information and ideas.[107]

Furthermore, the Internet provides a medium for a completely new type of NRM: the virtual or cyber religion—that is, a religion that exists primarily on the web with little or no physical contact between the followers. An example of these is Discordianism: a religion and subsequent philosophy whose members describe themselves as "a tribe of philosophers, theologians, magicians, scientists, artists, clowns, and similar maniacs who are intrigued with ERIS GODDESS OF CONFUSION and with Her Doings."[108] Another is the Universal Life Church Monastery, of which anyone can, without payment, become an ordained minister on line and thereby be eligible to conduct legal marriage ceremonies in parts of the USA and other countries.

Then there has been the appearance of a completely new genre of NRMs which have, variously, been called "invented," "imaginary," "fictive,"

---

107. Barker, "Crossing."
108. See "Principia Discordia."

"parody" or "hyper-real religions."[109] These are predominantly disseminated through the Internet, and are frequently associated with popular culture. Inspiration may be drawn from such sources as science fiction, films, books, comics, video games, or "ancient wisdoms." Examples include the Jedi Church, based on the *Star Wars* films; Matrixism or The Path of the One, inspired by the film trilogy *The Matrix*; the Otherkin; the Church of Moo; and the Church of Subgenius.[110] Such movements do not claim divine revelation as their origin but, quite explicitly, human imagination.

How seriously such NRMs are to be taken has been a question of contention, as when the 2001 census for England and Wales revealed that 390,000 individuals had reported their religion as Jedi Knight;[111] and, when the founder of the Jedi religion made an official complaint about discrimination by a superstore for telling him to take off his hood or leave the shop, he claimed, the religion dictated that he should wear his Jedi hood at all times in public places;[112] or when followers of the Flying Spaghetti Monster,[113] who refer to themselves as Pastafarians, argue for the right to wear their religious headgear—a colander—for their driving licence and other identity card photographs.[114]

Changes in "the cult scene"

Taking "the cult scene" as a whole, as has been suggested, the public focus on NRMs as dangerous cults and sects has been largely replaced by a fear of Islamic terrorism, but that does not mean that the new religions have disappeared. They have not, albeit the older new religions had undergone some dramatic changes, while a whole array of *new* new religions have been "coming out."

Looking at some of the religions that were well known in the 1970s, we find that ISKCON has changed from a movement consisting almost entirely of enthusiastic young white hippie devotees to a congregation of families of Asian origin who now provide most of the financial support and are regular attenders at Krishna temples and Hindu festivals. Neither they

109. Cusack, *Invented Religions*; Cusack and Kosnáč, *Fiction*; Cusack and Norman, *Handbook*; Possamai, *Religion*; *Handbook*.

110. See Jedi Church, "Home"; Matrixism, "Home"; Otherkin, "Welcome"; Church of Moo, " Occult"; Church of Subgenius, "Become an Ordained Minister Now."

111. Office for National Statistics, "390,000 Jedi There Are."

112. Carter, "Jedi."

113. See Henderson, *Gospel*; Church of the Flying Spaghetti Monster, "About."

114. See "Austrian driver allowed 'pastafarian' headgear."

nor the original Western converts are likely to live in the temples, nearly all now living in nuclear or extended families and engaged in "outside work."[115]

The Unification Church is no longer the united religion it once was. Reverend Moon's widow heads the largest faction, now called the Family Federation, with its headquarters in South Korea; the next largest group, known as the Global Peace Foundation, is led by Moon's oldest surviving son, Hyun Jin Moon, and is headquarted in Seattle, Washington State; the Sanctuary Church, led by Moon's youngest son, Hyung Jin Moon, is to be found in Pennsylvania; although the smallest of the family schisms, the Sanctuary Church has received some notoriety through its strong advocacy for the Second Amendment,[116] and the way in which it teaches members various martial arts and the use of guns, flourishing these during ceremonies such as their weddings. There are also a number of other Unificationist schisms in various places throughout the world. To an outsider at least, it can seem that the main preoccupation of these schismatic groups is to denounce the other groups and claim that they are the true inheritors of Moon's (financial and spiritual) legacy.[117]

The Children of God, later known as The Family International, has pretty well ceased to exist in a recognizable form. Nearly all its communities have been dissolved and the few remaining members have little more than a website to hold them together.[118] In other words, it has become a virtual community, with its members responsible for themselves, having to build new lives for themselves and often attending local Christian churches.[119] The legacy of Osho (as Bhagwan Rajneesh came to be known) lived on after the demise of Rajneeshpuram in the numerous books and recordings of his talks; the Osho International Meditation Resort continues in India at the Pune ashram where people from the around the world come to take part in meditation and a variety of courses—so long as they have a certificate to prove they are free of HIV/AIDS. There are also a number of places in other countries where Osho training is provided either by individual practitioners or in centres that offer an eclectic range of yoga, meditation and other courses.[120]

---

115. Rochford, *Hare Krishna Transformed*.

116. The Second Amendment to the United States Constitution protects the right of the people to keep and bear arms.

117. Vonck, *Life and Legacy*.

118. Family International, "Welcome."

119. Barker, "From the Children"; Borowik, "Digital Revisionism."

120. Osho, "Places to Meditate."

Courses continue to be provided by the Church of Scientology, which is one of the relatively few NRMs to have expanded their presence over the past half century despite, or possibly because of, the enormous amount of negative publicity it has received. The Scientologists themselves are likely to insist they have not changed but continue to follow Mr Hubbard's teachings and instructions, although scholars are more likely to point to a number of revisions that the Church has undergone.[121]

The New Age, with its expectation of a fundamental change in the world accompanying the arrival of the Age of Aquarius, has generally morphed into "the new spirituality" where it is up to each individual to change through one or more of various practices. Pagan movements (including Wicca, Druids, Heathens, Odinists and some Shamans) have continued to flourish.[122] This is partly because they have gained a certain degree of respectability (and are less likely than has been the case in the past to be confused with Satanists) thus resulting in several "solitary practitioners" having the courage to "come out" and declare their faith. Another growth area—at least in "coming out"—are a motley assortment of people involved in Western Esotericism.[123] There has also been an emergence of several new movements associated with traditional religions, such as the (Jewish-Buddhist) JuBus,[124] and various kinds of combinations of Christianity and Buddhism.[125] Whilst it has long been the practice of certain Amerindian tribes to use drugs such as peyote, and the Rastafarians have used ganja (marijuana or cannabis), the Brazilian religion Santo Daime, which uses the psychedelic drug ayahuasca in its ritual, has spread throughout North America and Europe in recent years.[126] Even more controversially, in 2015, the First Church of Cannabis became a registered church in Indiana.[127]

Meanwhile, there has been a noticeable growth in Mega-Churches, such as the Universal Church of the Kingdom of God which started as a Neo-Pentecostal church teaching a prosperity gospel,[128] and the charismatic The Embassy of the Blessed Kingdom of God for All Nations, founded by Sunday Adelaja, a Nigerian Pastor who, as an illustration of "reverse

---

121. Urban, "Church of Scientology."
122. Harvey, *Indigenous*; York, *Pagan Theology*.
123. Hanagraaf, *New Age Religion*; *Esotericism*.
124. "Why God Loves JuBus."
125. See, for example, Tan, "Can One Be Christian and Buddhist?"
126. Dawson, *Santa Daime*.
127. First Church of Cannabis, "Home."
128. Universal Church, "Jesus Cristo."

missionizing," preaches to a Ukrainian congregation of tens of thousands.[129] At the same time, there has been a proliferation of small "high control groups," which sometimes consist of little more than one or two families, one notorious example being the Westboro Baptist Church, which believes it to be God's will that it should conduct anti-gay demonstrations at American service-men's funerals.[130] Not far away, geographically, one can find an even smaller group of, at most, half a dozen believers in a small Kansas village where "Pope Michael" lives with his mother, Tickie.[131] Another "Pope" was "Pope Gregory XVII," who founded The Apostles of the Infinite Love in the Quebec countryside.[132]

Further relatively new developments include the spread of atheist and agnostic "religions." The Sunday Assembly is "a congregation for atheists and nonbelievers"; started in 2013 in London, which is now holding services in several other countries throughout the world.[133]

Finally, scores of movements emerged from an Islamic tradition have come to play a significant role amongst the minority religions in the public eye. Some of these, such as the Baha'i and the Ahmadiyya community, have settled their headquarters in the West due to persecution in their homelands; others are part of global networks, one of the most widespread of these being the Hizmet movement, inspired by the work of Fethullah Gülen, which has set up schools and other charitable organizations and businesses throughout the world,[134] but has been accused by President Erdoğan of Turkey of being responsible for the failed coup on 15 July 2016—an accusation vehemently denied by Gülen and the movement itself. Other Islamic movements accused of terrorist sympathy and/or activity include Hizb-ut-Tahrir,[135] and Mojahedin-e-Khalq (MEK),[136] and Tablighi Jamaat.[137]

Concluding Remarks

It has been argued that new religious movements have been "coming out" throughout the world and throughout history and that they cannot be

129. Christian Church, "Embassy of the Blessed Kingdom."
130. Westboro Baptist Church, "God Hates Fags."
131. Fairholm, "Pope Michael."
132. Côté, *Prophet*.
133. Sunday Assembly, "Celebrating Life Together."
134. Ebaugh, *Gülen*.
135. Maher, "Change."
136. Banisadr, *Masoud*.
137. Pieri, *Tablighi*.

viewed in isolation but have to be understood as part of the religious and social context in which they exist. Whilst emphasising that any generalization about NRMs is almost bound to be falsifiable, some characteristics that have frequently been associated with the religions were noted, one of these being that they have tended to be treated with suspicion, and another that they tend to change far more radically and rapidly than older, more established religions.

Nothing ever stays the same. We cannot tell what will happen to these religions in the future. All we can know is that a few will thrive, some will persist in some form or other, while yet others will disappear altogether. We also know that new NRMs are likely to continue to emerge in what will be ever-changing social settings. Some observers will view these newcomers as exemplifying the curse of cults and/or the scourge of sects; others will celebrate them as a come-outing of new religious movements.

CHAPTER 11

The Past and Future of the Believers Church Conferences

Teun van der Leer

An Autobiographical Pilrimage

By way of my own pilgrimage, in 2006 I encountered Donald Durnbaugh's *The Believers' Church*, a reprint in 2003 from the original in 1968. It fascinated me and I immediately started to use it in my class on Baptist and Anabaptist History. I soon discovered that in 1967 Durnbaugh had been one of the leading figures at the First Believers Church Conference (BCC) in Louisville and that these conferences had continued by then until 2004 in Harrisonburg. I began to gather the papers from these different conferences in books and journals. I was disappointed to discover in July 2008, that the sixteenth Believers Church Conference had been held in Winnipeg, Manitoba, just a month before. This was the more important for me since gradually I had developed the idea to write a PhD-proposal to look for the content and harvest of these conferences for the ecumenical debate on the church. When I read *The Church—Towards a Common Vision* in 2013, it struck me again how marginal the voice of our tradition was present in this debate. In November 2013, my PhD-proposal was accepted by the promotion commission of VU-University Amsterdam. I gave it the title "Looking Into The Other Direction," subtitle "A Believers Church Contribution to the Ecumenical Ecclesiological Debate." The title is a partial quotation from Karl Barth at the creation of the World Council of Churches (WCC) in 1948: "It is obvious that the last remnants of sovereign authority in the idea of a *corpus christianum* are disappearing; this suggests that we should now look in this other (Congregationalist) direction."[1] Barth was in fact referring to Friedrich Loofs who in 1901 wrote: "Who knows whether not, when finally the national churches from the old world collapse, the congregational churchform will have the future?"[2] At the end of the twentieth century, in 1998, fifty years after Barth and almost a hundred years after Loofs, Miroslav Volf states that "today's global developments seem to imply that Protestant Christendom of the future will exhibit largely a Free Christian form," and that we probably "are standing in the middle of a clear and irreversible "process of congregationalization" of all Christianity."[3] In that light I do hope that this research can serve the church as a whole, especially in its process "towards a common vision."[4]

In fact, I want to strengthen the voice of the so-called third type (E. Troelsch) or "force" (F. Littell), the Pentecostal voice as Leslie Newbigin called it,[5] the baptist voice with a small "b" as James McClendon called it.[6] It is not easy to define this third type, mentioned as it is under such diverse names as "Free Church," "Gathered" or "Gathering Church," "Pilgrim Church," and the Believers Church (BC).[7] What it shares is a vision for the gathering of conscious committed believers, separation of church and state, living under the rule of Christ in a "Congregational Way" and a deep desire to be a "New Testament Church" (restitution or primitivism). I choose to use the term Believers Church, since in it, several conferences have sought the *concept* of the Believers Church and in mapping its results, I would at least have a view of its own self-understanding, however diverse that remains.

Ideals and Ambitions at the Beginning

The first attempts to organize a Believers Church Conference were undertaken by two Dutchmen, Johannes Oosterbaan and Jannes Reiling, respectively the rector of the Dutch Mennonite Seminary and the rector of the Dutch Baptist Seminary. They tried to set up a so-called "Baptizer"

1. Barth, "Church," 76.
2. Barth quotes him in German written (larger) background paper For Amsterdam 1948: "Wer Weiss ob nicht dereinst, wenn einmal die Landeskirchen der alten Welt zusammenbrechen, die *kongregationalistische* Kirchenform auch bei uns ihre Zukunft hat?" and adds, "Das könnte nun wirklich ein prophetisches <Wer weiss?> gewesen sein," (Karl Barth, *Die Kirche*).
3. Volf, *After Our Likeness*, 13.
4. Church— *Towards a Common Vision*.
5. Newbigin, *Household of God*, 9.
6. McClendon Jr., *Ethics*, 17–44; *Doctrine*, 341–45.
7. I tried to describe it in van der Leer, "Which future Church(form)?," 40–51.

conference, preceding the conference of the European Baptist Federation in Amsterdam, to be held 12–16 August 1964. A press release announced that "the 'Baptizer' conference would be under the joint sponsorship of the Dutch Mennonite Theological Seminary in Amsterdam and the Dutch Baptist Theological Seminary in Den Dolder' and that participants will come from various denominations which practiced believer's baptism."[8] Among the proposed speakers for the conference were William R. Estep, John Howard Yoder, Dale Moody, and Johannes Schneider. The press release finished by saying that "the opening session was planned for 7 August, and the conference was to close on the evening of 11 August with a fellowship dinner," which shows that the plans were very concrete. But in the end the conference never took place, due to "insufficient interest."[9]

Oosterbaan and Reiling both participated in the World Council of Churches Faith & Order Commission and complained that the discussions there, as Yoder recalled, "seemed to be dominated by high-church assumptions."[10] This was less the result of "illegitimate manipulation by high-church theologians, than of the free churches not being themselves adequately articulate in the right times and places."[11] It made Oosterbaan aware of the fact that "whereas the churches of the major magisterial traditions have solid bases (both documents and institutions) from which to enter the ecumenical arena, the churches of the Radical Reformation traditions have neither a single language nor a concerted strategy."[12] Donald Durnbaugh observed that Oosterbaan "was struck by the fact that descendants of the Radical Reformation had no way of uniting their concerns or entering into the ecumenical dialogue with strength."[13]

---

8. European Baptist Press Service, *Newsletter*.

9. "A conference of "baptizer" theologians, chiefly from Europe, was planned for the summer of 1964 in Amsterdam, The Netherlands, but could not actually be held" (Garrett Jr., *Concept of the Believers' Church*, 6). Yoder writes that "Oosterbaan and Reiling proceeded to convene a conference of 'baptizer theologians' for Amsterdam in August 1964, but then had to cancel it" (Yoder, "Believers' Church Conferences," 8). It is Durnbaugh who mentions the reason: "It was cancelled because of insufficient interest" (Eller, "Origin and Development," xx).

10. Yoder, "Believers' Church Conferences," 7.

11. Yoder, "Believers' Church Conferences," 7, 8.

12. Yoder, "Introduction," 3.

13. Durnbaugh, "Origin and Development," xix, xx.

Our Concerns and Our Dilemmas

The initial Believers Church Conference at Louisville, Kentucky, had two overarching concerns: to develop a certain concept of the BC, to articulate clearer who we are or should be, and to participate more fully in the ecumenical debates of the era. Both concerns were difficult to meet, since the tradition is very diverse and there is no authoritative voice that can make decisions. In its published preface the Findings Committee of Louisville 1967 explained that the profusion of varied lists of the distinctive marks of the Believers Churches do not deny their identity, but point to the *character* of their identity. This congregational character, as it is called, affirmed the particular local togetherness of the congregation as the primordial form of the church and this centrality of the congregation dictates a specific Believers Church style of ecumenical relations.[14] As this also played a role in the continuation of the Believers Church Conferences (as a loose network, dependent on the inviting institutions)[15] there hasn't been a straight forward development towards a consensus or uniting voice. In that regard it may be more appropriate to speak of a concept or concepts while an ecumenical voice remains diverse. So Believers Church identity and what we have to bring are still not obvious.

At the same time representatives of Believers Churches know that even if we have some common vision on "who we are," we have to admit that this many times is in fact "who we would like to be." A "100 percent pure" Believers Church does not exist. There is always a difference between what Fernando Enns has called the "Believed Church" and the "Experienced Church."[16] From the very beginning there is this ambivalence between the passion for and belief in the strength of the concept of the BC and the awareness that in practice the "sect-type" and the "church-type" seem to be not so much fixed types over against each other, but are related in a dynamic tension, which asks for a constant theological and sociological reflection. Pannabecker writes about the sociological phenomenon of the sect passing

---

14. Again in Canada in 1978 this was confirmed: "BCC are not intended to become new ecumenical institutions. Nor create alternative ecumenical structures. . . . The theological focus of the conference is on the concept of the church (ecclesiology). What else could it be if the conference is designated as a study conference on the BC? . . . Evangelicals lack a common ecclesiological basis . . . paedobaptist church bodies control the ecumenical consensus" (Zeman and Klaassen, *Believers' Church in Canada*, 18–20).

15. See the overview of all seventeen conferences and their topics in the appendix.

16. Enns, "Believers Church Ecclesiology," 108. More on this in Enns, *Peace Church*, 1:1; "Tension between 'Believed,'" 1–9.

into the church as he perceives in the United States halfway through the twentieth century:

> The separatist church starts from scratch and it can do so because it rejects the old and sets new forms, calling out believers in a clear-cut voluntary decision to join a community of saints. The children of the saints . . . are not as free as their parents to start from nothing. Forms have been laid down; methods of expression have become current; the differences between being on the inside and on the outside are not as clear-cut. Consequently, training and tradition inevitably assume a larger portion in the picture. Thus successive generations build up a body of patterns from which it is not easy to deviate. The initial creative spark is no longer possible to the degree originally required. Thus one sees the sociological phenomenon of a sect passing into the 'church' type.[17]

Olof de Vries calls this the pendulum of the clock, going back and forth from institution to movement: most renewal movements start as an alternative to the institutional church, but become in the course of time an institute themselves, so when the pendulum is at its maximum, a renewal movement will again come into being as an alternative.[18] Maybe that is why John Howard Yoder could say that the Believers' Church-type is "a type *sui generis*, which . . . keeps arising again and again, in every country, taking on similar shapes, *mutatis mutandis*."[19]

So the "problem" is we cannot speak with one voice and if we could, there would be doubt whether we are speaking phenomenologically or just idealistically. Why not look for a more unified voice to articulate Believers Church identity and then try to embody what we think we should be as a continuous *"semper reformanda"* challenge for us as well as for our ecumenical partners?!

---

17. Pannabecker, "Anabaptist Conception of the Church," 36.

18. de Vries, *De dynamiek*.

19. Yoder, "Believers' Church Conferences," 12. Cf. "All of us share a common vertical identity which is essentially pneumatic. Unless He continues His gracious ministry of conviction and regeneration, a BC faces extinction in one generation" (Zeman and Klaassen, *Believers' Church in Canada*, 22), which Zeman also said in Louisville, 1967, "A BC is only one generation away from extinction. Unless God the Spirit continues His gracious ministry of regeneration, such a church is doomed to death" (Garrett Jr., *Concept of the Believers' Church*, 60).

A Way Forward

Max Weber's definition, "a community of personal believers of the reborn and only those,"[20] remains at the heart of Believers Church conviction, broader and more dynamic as defined by Prof. Donald Durnbaugh when he wrote, "The Believers' Church is the covenanted and disciplined community of those walking in the way of Jesus Christ."[21]

> The authors of the Findings Committee of Louisville 1967 wrote:
>
> We have found ourselves in agreement that the most visible manifestation of the Grace of God is His calling together a believing people. The congregation is therefore constituted by the divine call to which men and women respond freely in faith. The shorthand label BC therefore points first of all not to the doctrinal content of beliefs held, nor to the subjective believingness of the believer, but more to the constructive character of the commitment in defining the visible community.[22]

And then, quite sharp: "We therefore reject . . . any church practice . . . whereby Christian allegiance is affirmed, imposed, or taken for granted without the individual's consent or request. . . . We therefore reject any pattern of indiscriminate membership not conditioned upon commitment to discipleship."[23] So it is the faith act that comes first (*fides qua*, the faith *with* which we believe), before the faith content (*fides quae*, the faith *in* which we believe).[24] But before this becomes too individualistic, it is balanced by a second conviction, again in the words of the Findings Committee of Louisville 1967: "We have found ourselves in agreement that the particular local togetherness of the congregation is the primordial form of the church."[25]

For Yoder the centrality of the local congregation is *the* contribution of the Believers' Church Tradition to the ecumenical debate. It provides "an

---

20. Weber, *Protestant Ethic*, 136.

21. Durnbaugh, *Believers' Church*, 33.

22. Appendix I, "Report of the Findings Committee." Garrett, *Concept of the Believers' Church*, 315–16.

23. Appendix I, "Report of the Findings Committee." Garrett, *Concept of the Believers' Church*, 315–16.

24. "Certainly we affirm with full truth that the faith which is etched in the heart of everyone who believes . . . proceeds from a single doctrine, but it is one thing what we believe (ea quae creduntur), and another thing the faith with which we believe (fides qua creduntur)" (de Trinitate, XIII, 2, 5), (Gagliardi, "Look at the Catechism's Presentation").

25. Appendix I, "Report of the Findings Committee." Garrett, *Concept of the Believers' Church*.

alternative definition of 'the unity we seek.'"[26] "This new Christian community . . . is not only a vehicle or fruit of the gospel; it is the good news."[27] For Yoder, Christian fellowship was both the goal and the path. We reach this goal as we travel the path together—in real Christian fellowship. In Yoder's view, "there is no way to fellowship—fellowship is the way."[28] This is our unique contribution towards mainline as well as (evangelical) free churches. Belonging to Christ *is* belonging to the church as well, a concrete local church. This is where Christ is, according to His promise, "for where two or three are gathered in my name, I am there among them" (Matt 18:20, NRSV). It is the strong message of the First Letter of John, where he makes the church as concrete, visible and touchable, as the incarnation (1 John 1:1–3) and makes fellowship with God and with one another commutable (1 John 1:5–7).

The practice at the heart of each is baptism, in which the nature of the church is embodied by the personal commitment of the believer (*fides qua*) and the act of being baptized *into* the body (1 Cor 12:13; Acts 2:41). It is quite alarming that baptism still is a watershed in ecumenical relations, even with the growing consensus that believers baptism is the New Testament pattern.[29] Many times the Believers Church adherents are viewed as the hardliners in this regard, since they continue to re-baptize. Though we have to reflect seriously on our practice of re-baptism, the rebuke is quite one-sided. That might be one solution, that believers churches stop re-baptizing. But what about the equally important issue of ending the practice of infant baptism? This also would lead to an end of re-baptism. It was Karl Barth who once advocated for a moratorium on infant baptism and on re-baptism at the same time, thus hoping to solve the problem(s) within one generation. That might still be worth considering.

A Continuing Question

Are we as representatives of the Believers Church Tradition in time to create a more robust and unified voice, or has the momentum already dissipated? It is almost fifty years now since the first conference and more than sixty

---

26. Garrett, *Concept of the Believers' Church*, 283.
27. Garrett, *Concept of the Believers' Church*, 274.
28. Yoder, *Real Christian Fellowship*, 15.
29. For example, in the important Lima-report, *Baptism, Eucharist, and Ministry*: "While the possibility that infant baptism was also practised in the apostolic age cannot be excluded, baptism upon personal profession of faith is the most clearly attested pattern in the New Testament documents."

years since the ideas were initially discussed.[30] Is the concept of the Believers' Churches and its contribution to the wider church family something that is in the hearts and minds of pastors and congregations, or is it just a scholarly interest and then even with mainly Euro-North American fifty-plus male scholars? Are we too late, since presently, the emphasis is upon church planting, fresh expressions, and new ways of "being" church, all very contextual and flexible? And—on top of that—hasn't the way people belong or do not belong changed drastically? At a symposium on "Baptist Identity and Ecclesial Transformation" in April 2013, at VU-University in Amsterdam, Miranda Klaver said:

> Since the 1960s, profound changes took place in the Dutch context, observed in the changing social structures of society often described as the networked society. With regard to religion, forces of secularization had a profound impact on the decline of church membership. Contrary to what was expected by sociologists, this has not led to the irrelevance of religion per se. Rather, being religious no longer implies membership of a religious institution as in the past. The need for belonging and community is now based on personal choice rather than tradition. Furthermore, how one chooses to be engaged in or committed to a particular community has changed as well. In a highly mobile and individualized society, long-term commitments to one community are often not possible and exclusive commitments to one community are not self-evident either.[31]

Parallel to this boils up something else: the way one does theology, from "lived faith" to "learned faith," since religious identity is foremost observed and constituted in religious and everyday practices. That is a very different methodological course than to start with proposing a construct on historical and/or systematic grounds, the norm in Believers Church conferences over the years.

The challenge seems to be to find a way to keep doing constructive revision work on our ecclesiology. This is all the more relevant when we realize that pietism, revivalism and evangelicalism speak loudly to the hearts of believers churches. In some regards this is good, but when it comes to

---

30. I refer to the three articles in *Mennonite Quarterly Review* 25.1 (1951): Waltner, "Anabaptist Conception of the Church," 5–16; Kreider, "Anabaptist Conception of the Church," 17–33; S. F. Pannabecker, "Anabaptist Conception of the Church," 34–46; and to the General Conference Mennonite Church at Mennonite Biblical Seminary in Chicago, 1955, on the "Believers' Church" (Mennonite Church, *Proceedings of the Study Conference*).

31. Klaver, "We are the World?," 425–26.

ecclesiology it is very weak, even an oxymoron,[32] or an escape by a superficial call on "the invisible church." What and where is the "invisible church"? Even if it exists, it cannot be located, let alone joined. Once there was a church that practised open communion and invited people to stand and tell their name and the church they belonged to, when they wanted to partake in the Lord's Supper. A candidate stood up and said, "I am so and so and I am a member of the invisible church," to which a pastor immediately responded: "If that is the case my friend, then I propose that you go to that church to partake."

Some radicalism may be appropriate here. The church is not optional: it belongs to the Gospel, it might even be the Gospel (Yoder). Moreover, this Gospel is "beyond the good feeling," it is about following Christ and carrying the cross, sometimes the cross of community! However, belonging itself is now of increasing importance. There is a growing tendency towards "belonging before believing."[33] While people are very entrepreneurial when it comes to new forms of church, and many times have no "catholic" approach with a real beating heart for the unity of the broader church and to be part of that tradition, they *are* looking for new ways of belonging, for more than a loose network, even in some cases for monastic forms and communities. As Miranda Klaver has observed, "the story of the church through all ages reveals how the gospel in essence is a power for community formation,"[34] so let's keep communicating that, maybe not in the same style, but in a way that new generations can profit from. In his published sermon on Matthew 28:16–20, Johannes Verkuyl, professor for Missiology at VU-University 1965–1978, said: "When Jesus promises: And lo, I am with you always (in Dutch more literally translated as: every day),[35] then it is our responsibility to ask ourselves: and what day is it today?"[36] What are we called to as a church in this particular time and in this particular situation? What is "das Gebot der Stunde," the command for the hour? Let us take up that challenge as the present generation of Believers Churches!

---

32. Hindmarsh, "Is Evangelical Ecclesiology an Oxymoron?," 15–38.
33. Murray, *Church After Christendom*, 9–38.
34. Klaver, "We are the World?," 420.
35. The Greek text uses *tas hèmeras*.
36. Verkuyl, *Preken en preekschetsen*, 13.

Appendix

17th Believers' Church Conference
Findings Summary

THE SEPARATIONIST (OR "COME-OUTER") tendency has been a significant theme in the Believers' Church tradition, both historically and in our churches today, first noted in modern times by Franklin H. Littell. All Believers' Church groups began as renewal movements within a larger tradition that eventually led to a clear break. But even as we celebrate the distinctive theological, ethical and ecclesial convictions that birthed our churches—sometimes at great cost to early members—we also recognized that those same convictions can disguise on-going weaknesses and internal separations. For example:

- The quest for holiness and purity of ideals has often resulted in separation, division, and lack of clarity about the locus of authority.
- A commitment to the primacy of the local congregation has led to a weak theology of the church in its broader expressions and an overly negative view of ecumenism.
- A focus on religious voluntarism and response to religious liberty can easily become confused with modern individualism and autonomy.
- The perfectionist and sectarian impulses in the Believers' Church tradition can foster a tendency to self-sufficiency that can be narrow, schismatic, and even idolatrous.

We recognized a variety of inter-related sources behind the separationist tendency within the Believers' Church tradition, including: conflict within the broader social, economic, political and cultural context; new theological insights/understandings . . . and competing hermeneutical views that gave rise to them; differing understandings of church polity; competing visions of reform and renewal; personality conflicts among leaders ("*prima donna-ism*"); and racial/ethnic tensions.

On-going challenges among Believers' Churches include: a more robust understanding of the nature of the church beyond the local congregation; greater attention to the nature of power and competing claims of authority; and a clearer theology of church unity.

Overview of Conferences and Themes

#	Year and place	Theme
1	1967, Louisville, Kentucky, USA	The Concept of the Believers' Church
2	1970, Chicago, Illinois, USA	Is There a Christian Style of Life in Our Age?
3	1972, Laurelville, Ohio, USA	Believers Church Conference for Laity
4	1975, Malibu, California, USA	Restitution, Dissent, and Renewal: Concept of the Believers' Church
5	1978 Winnipeg, Manitoba, Canada	The Believers' Church in Canada
6	1980, Bluffton, Ohio, USA	Is There a Believers' Church Christology?
7	1984, Anderson, Indiana, USA	Believers' Baptism and the Meaning of Church Membership: Concepts and Practices in an Ecumenical Context
8	1987, Oak Brook, Illinois, USA	The Ministry of All Believers
9	1989, Fort Worth, Texas, USA	Balthasar Hubmaier and His Thought
10	1992, Goshen, Indiana, USA	The Rule of Christ: Church Discipline and the Authority of the Church
11	1994, Ashland, Ohio, USA	The Meaning and Practice of the Lord's Supper in the BCT
12	1996, Hamilton, Ontario, Canada	The Believers Church: A Voluntary Church

#	Year and place	Theme
13	1999, Bluffton, Ohio, USA	Apocalypticism and Millennialism: Shaping a Believers Church Eschatology for the Twenty-First Century
14	2002, Notre Dame, Indiana, USA	Legacy of Yoder
15	2004, Harrisonburg, Virginia, USA	God, Democracy, and US Power
16	2008, Winnipeg, Manitoba, Canada	Congregationalism, Denominationalism, and the Body of Christ
17	2016, Wolfville, Nova Scotia, Canada	The Tendency Towards Separation. Come-outers Among the Believers Churches: Historical Realities and Ecclesial Concerns in the Continuing Dissenter Tradition

Bibliography

Preface

Durnbaugh, Donald F. *The Believers' Church: The History and Character of Radical Protestantism*. Scottdale, PA: Herald, 1968.

Chapter 1

Atwood, Craig D. "Separatism, Ecumenism, and Pacifism: The Bohemian and Moravian Brethren in the Confessional Age." In *Confessionalism and Pietism: Religious Reform in Early Modern Europe*, edited by Frederik A. van Lieburg, 71–90. Mainz: Philipp von Zabern, 2006.

———. *The Theology of the Czech Brethren from Hus to Comenius*. University Park, PA: Pennsylvania State University Press, 2009.

Audisio, Gabriel. *Preachers by Night: The Waldensian Barbes (Fifteenth to Sixteenth Centuries)*. Leiden: Brill, 2007.

———. *The Waldensian Dissent: Persecution and Survival, c. 1170–c. 1570*. Cambridge: Cambridge University Press, 1999.

Bahlcke, Joachim, and Werner Korthaase, eds. *Daniel Ernst Jablonski: Religion, Wissenschaft und Politik um 1700*. Wiesbaden: Harrassowitz, 2008.

Balázs, Mihály. "Antitrinitarianism." In *A Companion to the Reformation in Central Europe*, edited by Howard Louthan and Graeme Murdock, 171–94. Leiden: Brill, 2015.

Brock, Peter. "Faustus Socinus Against War: From the First Chapter of the Third Part of His Reply to Jacobus Palaeologus (1581)." *Mennonite Quarterly Review* 70 (1996) 419–30.

———. "Gregorius Paulus Against the Sword: a Polish Anabaptist on Nonresistance." *Mennonite Quarterly Review* 65 (1991) 427–36.

———. "Marcin Czechowic in Defense of Nonresistance, 1575." *Conrad Grebel Review* 9 (1991) 251–57.

———. "Marcin Czechowic on the Via Crucis, Self-Defense, and Government (1575)." *Mennonite Quarterly Review* 67 (1993) 451–68.

———. "A Polish Antitrinitarian Against Nonresistance: Krowicki's Letter of 1573." *Mennonite Quarterly Review* 72 (1998) 441–48.

———. *The Political and Social Doctrines of the Unity of Czech Brethren in the Fifteenth and Early Sixteenth Centuries*. Gravenhage: Mouton, 1957.

Cameron, Euan. *The Reformation of the Heretics: The Waldenses of the Alps, 1480–1580*. Oxford: Clarendon, 1984.

———. *Waldenses. Rejections of Holy Church in Medieval Europe*. Oxford: Blackwell, 2000.

Coggins, James R. *John Smyth's Congregation: English Separatism, Mennonite Influence, and the Elect Nation*. Waterloo, ON: Herald Press, 1991.

Daugirdas, Kęstutis. *Die Anfänge des Sozinianismus. Genese und Eindringen des historisch-ethischen Religionsmodells in den universitären Diskurs der Evangelischen in Europa*. Göttingen: Vandenhoeck & Ruprecht, 2016.

David, Zdeněk V. *Finding the Middle Way: The Utraquists' Liberal Challenge to Rome and Luther*. Washington, DC: Woodrow Wilson Center, 2003.

Dingel, Irene. "Luther's Authority in the Late Reformation and Protestant Orthodoxy." In *The Oxford Handbook of Martin Luther's Theology*, edited by Robert Kolb, et al., 525–39. 2nd ed. Oxford: Oxford University Press, 2016.

The Evangelical Church in Germany. *Justification and Freedom: Celebrating 500 Years of the Reformation in 2017*. Translated by Stephen Buckwalter. Gütersloh: Gütersloher, 2015. https://www.ekd.de/english/download/justification_and_freedom.pdf.

Fock, Otto. *Der Socinianismus nach seiner Stellung in der Gesammtentwicklung des christlichen Geistes, nach seinem historischen Verlauf und nach seinem Lehrbegriff*. Kiel: Schröder, 1847.

Fudge, Thomas A. *Jan Hus: Religious Reform and Social Revolution in Bohemia*. London: Tauris, 2010.

Goll, Jaroslav. *Der Verkehr der Brüder mit den Waldensern. Wahl und Weihe der ersten Priester*. Vol. 1 of *Quellen und Untersuchungen zur Geschichte der Böhmischen Brüder*. Prague: Otto, 1878.

Goris, Wouter, et al., eds. *Gewalt sei ferne den Dingen! Contemporary Perspectives on the Works of John Amos Comenius*. Wiesbaden: Springer, 2016.

Gregory, Brad S. "Anabaptist Martyrdom: Imperatives, Experience, and Memorialization." In *A Companion to Anabaptism and Spiritualism, 1521–1700*, edited by John D. Roth and James M. Stayer, 467–506. Leiden: Brill, 2007.

———. *Salvation at Stake. Christian Martyrdom in Early Modern Europe*. Cambridge, MA: Harvard University Press, 1999.

Haberkern, Phillip N. *Patron Saint and Prophet: Jan Hus in the Bohemian and German Reformations*. New York: Oxford University Press, 2016.

Hamilton, Alastair, et al., eds. *From Martyr to Muppy: A Historical Introduction to Cultural Assimilation Processes of a Religious Minority in the Netherlands: the Mennonites*. Amsterdam: Amsterdam University Press, 1994.

Holeton, David R. *La communion des tout-petits enfants: Étude du mouvement eucharistique en Bohême vers la fin du Moyen-Âge*. Rome: Edizioni Liturgiche, 1989.

Höhne, Wolfgang. *Luthers Anschauungen über die Kontinuität der Kirche*. Berlin: Lutherisches Verlagshaus, 1963.

Hutterian Brethren. *The Chronicle of the Hutterian Brethren*. Rifton: Plough, 1987.

Just, Jiří. "Kralitzer Bibel." In *Religiöse Erinnerungsorte in Ostmitteleuropa. Konstitution und Konkurrenz im nationen-und epochenübergreifenden Zugriff*, edited by Joachim Bahlcke, et al., 360–71. Berlin: Akademie, 2013.

Just, Jiří, and Martin Rothkegel, eds. "Confessio Bohemica. 1575/1609." In *Reformierte Bekenntnisschriften, Bd. 3/1: 1570–1599*, edited by Andreas Mühling and Peter Opitz, 47–176. Neukirchen-Vluyn: Neukirchener, 2012.

Köpstein, Horst Köpstein. "Über den deutschen Hussiten Friedrich Reiser." *Zeitschrift für Geschichtswissenschaft* 7 (1959) 1068–82.

Krmíčková, Helena. *K počátkům Kalicha v Čechách: studie a texty* (On the Beginnings of the Chalice in Bohemia: Studies and Texts). Brno: Masaryk University, 1997.

———. "Utraquism in 1414." In *The Bohemian Reformation and Religious Practice IV*, edited by Zdenek V. David and David R. Holeton, 99–106. Prague: Academy of Sciences, 2002.

Kurze, Dietrich. "Märkische Waldenser und Böhmische Brüder. Zur brandenburgischen Ketzergeschichte und ihrer Nachwirkung im 15. und 16. Jahrhundert." In *Festschrift für Walter Schlesinger*, edited by Helmut Beumann, 456–502. Vol. 2. Köln: De Gruyter, 1974.

Lange, Albert de. "La fin tragique de Vaudois au Nord des Alpes à la lumière du destin de Friedrich Reiser." *Revue d'histoire et de philosophie religieuses* 88 (2008) 3–19.

Lange, Albert de, and Kathrin Utz Tremp, eds. *Friedrich Reiser und die 'waldensisch-hussitische Internationale' im 15. Jahrhundert*. Heidelberg: Regionalkultur, 2006.

McGoldrick, James Edward. *Baptist Successionism: A Crucial Question in Baptist History*. Metuchen, NJ: ATLA, 1994.

Molnar, Amedeo, and Romolo Cegna, eds. *Confessio Taboritarum*. Roma: Istituto Storico, 1983.

Müller, Joseph Theodor. *Geschichte der Böhmischen Brüder*. 3 vols. Herrnhut: Missionsbuchhandlung, 1922–1931.

Mulsow, Martin, and Jan Rohls, eds. *Socinianism and Arminianism: Antitrinitarians, Calvinists, and Cultural Exchange in Seventeenth-Century Europe*. Leiden: Brill, 2005.

Packull, Werner O. *Hutterite Beginnings: Communitarian Experiments during the Reformation*. Baltimore: John Hopkins University Press, 1995.

Pirnát, Antal, ed. *De falsa et vera unius Dei Patris, Filii et Spiritus Sancti cognitione libri duo (Alba Iulia 1568)*. Facsimile ed. Budapest: Akadémiai Kiadó, 1988.

Podmore, Colin. "The Bishops and the Brethren: Anglican Attitudes to the Moravians in the Mid-Eighteenth Century." *The Journal of Ecclesiastical History* 41 (1990) 622–46.

Pohlig, Matthias. *Zwischen Gelehrsamkeit und konfessioneller Identitätsstiftung. Lutherische Kirchen- und Universalgeschichtsschreibung 1546–1617*. Tübingen: Mohr Siebeck, 2007.

Priarolo, Mariangela, ed. *Fausto Sozzini e la filosofia in Europa*. Siena: Fondazione Monte dei Paschi, 2006.

Říčan, Rudolf. *The History of the Unity of the Brethren: A Protestant Hussite Church in Bohemia and Moravia*. Bethlehem: Moravian Church in America, 1992.

Roth, John D. "How to Commemorate a Division? Reflections on the 500th Anniversary of the Lutheran Reformation and its Relevance for the Global Anabaptist-Mennonite Church Today." *Mennonite Quarterly Review* 91 (2017) 24–35.

Roth, John D., and James M. Stayer, eds. *A Companion to Anabaptism and Spiritualism, 1521–1700*. Leiden: Brill, 2007.
Rothkegel, Martin. "Reformation, Nonkonformismus, Freiheit. Freikirchliche Anmerkungen zum allzu deutschen Lutherjubiläum 2017." *Zeitschrift für Theologie und Gemeinde* 21 (2016) 157–73.
———. "The Living Word: Uses of the Holy Scriptures among Sixteenth-Century Anabaptists in Moravia." *Mennonite Quarterly Review* 89 (2015) 357–403.
Salatowsky, Sascha. *Die Philosophie der Sozinianer: Transformationen zwischen Renaissance-Aristotelismus und Frühaufklärung*. Stuttgart-Bad Cannstatt: Frommann-Holzboog, 2015.
Schäufele, Wolf-Friedrich. *»Defecit Ecclesia«: Studien zur Verfallsidee in der Kirchengeschichtsanschauung des Mittelalters*. Mainz: Friedrich von Zabern, 2006.
Schlachta, Astrid von. *From the Tyrol to North America: The Hutterite Story Through the Centuries*. Kitchener, ON: Pandora Press, 2008.
———. *Hutterische Konfession und Tradition (1578–1619): Etabliertes Leben zwischen Ordnung und Ambivalenz*. Mainz: Philipp von Zabern, 2003.
Schmidt-Biggemann, Wilhelm. "Flacius Illyricus' 'Catalogus testium veritatis' als kontroverstheologische Polemik." In *Reformer als Ketzer. Heterodoxe Bewegungen von Vorreformatoren*, edited by Günter Frank and Friedrich Niewöhner, 263–91. Stuttgart-Bad Canstatt: Frommann-Holzboog, 2004.
Segl, Peter. *Ketzer in Österreich. Untersuchungen über Häresie und Inquisition im Herzogtum Österreich im 13. und beginnenden 14. Jahrhundert*. Paderborn: Schöningh, 1984.
Šmahel, František, and Ota Pavlíček, eds. *A Companion to Jan Hus*. Leiden: Brill, 2015.
Strübind, Andrea. "Erbe und Ärgernis. Was gibt es für Kirchen aus täuferischen und nonkonformistischen Traditionen anlässlich des Reformationsjubiläums 2017 zu feiern?" In *Luther und die Reformation aus freikirchlicher Sicht*, edited by Volker Spangenberg, 71–88. Göttingen: V&R Unipress, 2013.
Szczucki, Lech, ed. *Faustus Socinus and his Heritage*. Kraków: PAN, 2005.
Tazbir, Janusz. "Die Stellung der polnischen Antitrinitarier zu Luther und der lutherischen Tradition." In *Martin Luther: Leben, Werk, Wirken*, edited by Günter Vogler, et al., 438–50. Berlin: Akademie, 1983.
Vio, Tommaso de (Cajetan), "Num fides ad fructuosam absolutionem saeramentalem necessaria sit (Augsburg, 26.9.1518)." In *Opuscula omnia Thomae De Vio Caietani [...] in tres distincta tomos*, Lyon: Junta, 1562, fol. 111ra (Digital Library of the Catholic Reformation).
Visser, Piet. "Mennonites and Doopsgezinden in the Netherlands, 1535–1700." In *A Companion to Anabaptism and Spiritualism, 1521–1700*, edited by John D. Roth and James M. Stayer, 299–346. Leiden: Brill, 2007.
Volf, Miroslav. *After Our Likeness: The Church as an Image of the Triune God*. Grand Rapids, MI: Eerdmans, 1998.
Wendebourg, Dorothea. "Kirche." In *Luther-Handbuch*, edited by Alfred Beutel, 403–14. Tübingen: Mohr Siebeck, 2005.
White, B. R. *The English Separatist Tradition: From the Marian Martyrs to the Pilgrim Fathers*. Oxford: Oxford University Press, 1971.
Williams, George H., ed. *The Polish Brethren: Documentation of the History & Thought of Unitarianism in the Polish-Lithuanian Commonwealth and in the Diaspora, 1601–1685*. 2 vols. Missoula: Scholars, 1980.

———. *The Radical Reformation*. 3rd ed. Kirksville: Truman State University Press, 2000.
Zeman, Jarold K. "Restitution and Dissent in the Late Medieval Renewal Movements: The Waldensians, the Hussites and the Bohemian Brethren." *Journal of the American Academy of Religion* 44 (1976) 7–27.
Zijlstra, Samme. *Om de ware gemeente en de oude gronden. Geschiedenis van de dopersen in de Niederlanden 1531–1675*. Hilversum: Verloren, 2000.
Zijpp, Nanne van der. "Drekwagen, de." In *The Mennonite Encyclopedia: A Comprehensive Reference Work on the Anabaptist-Mennonite Movement*, edited by Harold S. Bender and Cornelius Krahn, 99. Vol. 2. Hillsboro, KS: Mennonite Brethren, 1956.

Chapter 2

Avant, Albert A., Jr. *The Social Teachings of the Progressive National Baptist Convention, Inc., Since 1961: A Critical Analysis of the Least, the Lost, and the Left-out*. New York: Routledge, 2004.
Baker, Robert A. *Relations Between Northern and Southern Baptists*. Fort Worth, TX: Seminary Hill, 1948.
Barclay, Wade Crawford. *Early American Methodism in Two Volumes: Part One*. New York: The Board of Missions and Church Extension of the Methodist Church, 1949.
Baxter, Norman A. *History of the Freewill Baptists: A Study in New England Separatism*. Rochester, NY: American Baptist Historical Society, 1957.
Benedict, David. *A General History of the Baptist Denomination in America and Other Parts of the World*. New York: Lewis Colby, 1848.
———. *Fifty Years Among the Baptists*. 1860. Reprint, Glen Rose, TX: Newman and Collings, 1913.
Billington, Ray Allen. *Westward Expansion: A History of the American Frontier*. 3rd ed. New York: MacMillan, 1967.
Brackney, William H. *Baptists in North America: An Historical Perspective*. Oxford: Blackwell, 2006.
———. *A Genetic History of Baptist Thought, with Special Reference to Baptists in Britain and North America*. Macon, GA: Mercer University Press, 2004.
———, ed. *Historical Dictionary of the Baptists*. 2nd ed. Lanham, MD: Scarecrow, 2009.
———. "Hypocrites, Jews, or Nobodies: Seventh Day Men in Seventeenth-Century England." In *Sabbat und Sabbatobservanze in der Frühen Neuzeit*, edited by Anselm Schubert, 201–25. Schriften des Vereins für Reformationsgeschichte, Band 217. Gütersloh: Gütersloh Verlaghaus, 2016.
———. "Leonard Busher." In *Bibliotheca Dissidentium*, Tome XXX. Baden-Baden & Bouxwiller: Éditions Valentin Koerner, 2016.
Brackney, William H., with Charles K. Hartman. *Swansea, Massachusetts*. Baptists in Early North America 1. Macon, GA: Mercer University Press, 2013.
The Confession of Faith of those Churches which are Commonly (though falsly) Called Anabaptists. London: Matthew Simmons in Aldersgate-street, 1644.
Durnbaugh, Donald. *The Believers' Church: The History and Character of Radical Protestantism*. Kitchener, ON: Herald Press, 1968.

Durso, Pamela R. *A Short History of the Cooperative Baptist Fellowship Movement*. Brentwood, TN: Baptist History and Heritage Society, 2006.
Estep, William R. *The Anabaptist Story*. 3rd ed. Nashville, TN: Broadman, 1996.
Fitts, Leroy. *A History of Black Baptists*. Nashville, TN: Broadman, 1985.
Gillette, A.D., ed. *Minutes of the Philadelphia Baptist Association 1707–1807*. Philadelphia, PA: American Baptist Publication Society, 1851.
Goen, C. C. *Revivalism and Separatism in New England 1740–1800: Strict Congregationalists and Separate Baptists in the Great Awakening*. New Haven, CT: Yale University Press, 1962.
Hassell, Cushing Biggs. *History of the Church of God, from the Creation to AD 1885; Including Especially the History of the Kehukee Primitive Baptist Association*. Middletown, NY: Gilbert Beebe's Sons, 1886.
Hayden, Roger. *English Baptist History and Heritage*. Didcot: Baptist Union of Great Britain, 2005.
Littell, Franklin H. *The Anabaptist Vision of the Church*. New York: MacMillan, 1965.
McBeth, H. Leon. *The Baptist Heritage: Four Centuries of Baptist Witness*. Nashville, TN: Broadman, 1987.
Olson, Adolf. *A Centenary History As Related to the Baptist General Conference of America*. Chicago, IL: Baptist Conference, 1952.
Pratt, J. Kristian. *The Father of Modern Landmarkism: The Life of Ben M. Bogard*. Macon, GA: Mercer University Press, 2013.
Raboteau, Albert J. *Slave Religion: The "Invisible Institution" in the Antebellum South*. New York: Oxford University Press, 2004.
Renfree, Harry A. *Heritage and Horizon: The Baptist Story in Canada*. Mississauga, ON: Canadian Baptist Federation, 1988.
Shurden, Walter B. *Associationalism among Baptists in America 1707–1814*. New York: Arno Press, 1980.
Smyth, John. "To the Lovers of the Truth." In *The Differences of the Churches of the Seperation: Contayning, A Description of the Leitovrgie and Ministerie of the Visible Church*. Amsterdam: n.p., 1608.
Sobel, Mechal. *Trabelin' On: The Slave Journey to an Afro-Baptist Faith*. Princeton, NJ: Princeton University Press, 1979.
Torbet, Robert G. "The Story of a People—the Baptists." Philadelphia, PA: Printed for the American Baptist Churches by the American Baptist Convention, 1957.
Washington, James Melvin. *Frustrated Fellowship: The Black Baptist Quest for Social Power*. Macon, GA: Mercer University Press, 1986.
Weaver, C. Douglas. *In Search of the New Testament Church: The Baptist Story*. Macon, GA: Mercer University Press, 2008.
White, B. R. *The English Separatist Tradition*. Oxford: Oxford University Press, 1971.
Woyke, Frank H. *Heritage and Ministry of the North American Baptist Conference*. Oakbrook Terrace, IL: North American Baptist Conference, 1979.

Chapter 3

Braght, Thieleman J. van. *The bloody theatre or Martyr's mirror of the defenceless Christians who baptized only upon confession of faith, and who suffered and died for the testimony of Jesus, their Savior, from the time of Christ to the year AD 1600*. 28th ed. Scottsdale, PA: Herald, 2007.

Denck, Hans. "Concerning True Love (1527)." In *Early Anabaptist Spirituality: Selected Writings*, edited by Daniel Liechty, 119. New York: Paulist, 1994.

Glock, Paul. "Letter to Loenhard Lanzenstiel (1563)." In *Sources of South German/Austrian Anabaptism*, edited by Walter Klaassen, et al., 325–28. Classics of the Radical Reformation 10. Kitchener, ON: Pandora; Herald, 2001.

Godwin, Colin. *Baptizing, Gathering, and Sending: Anabaptist Mission in the Sixteenth-Century Context*. Kitchener, ON: Pandora, 2012.

Goertz, Hans Jürgen. *The Anabaptists*. Christianity and Society in the Modern World. New York: Routledge, 1996.

Hubmaier, Balthasar. "On the Christian Baptism of Believers (1525)." In *Balthasar Hubmaier, Theologian of Anabaptism*, edited by H. Wayne Pipkin and John Howard Yoder, 95–149. Classics of the Radical Reformation 5. Scottdale, PA; Kitchener, ON: Herald, 1989.

Hut, Hans. "On the Mystery of Baptism. Baptism as Symbol and as Essence, the Beginning of a True Christian Life. John 5 (1526)." In *Early Anabaptist Spirituality: Selected Writings*, edited by Daniel Liechty, 64–81. New York: Paulist, 1994.

Hutter, Jacob. "Letter 5 (1535)." In *Brotherly Faithfulness: Epistles from a Time of Persecution.*, 95–98. Anabaptist Texts in Translation. Rifton, NY: Plough, 2006.

———. "Letter 8 (1535)." In *Brotherly Faithfulness: Epistles from a Time of Persecution*, 151. Anabaptist Texts in Translation. Rifton, NY: Plough, 2006.

Klaassen, Walter. *Living at the End of the Ages: Apocalyptic Expectation in the Radical Reformation*. Lanham, MD: University Press of America, 1992.

Littell, Franklin H. *The Origins of Sectarian Protestantism: A Study of the Anabaptist View of the Church*. Rev. ed. New York: Macmillan, 1964.

McClendon, James Wm. *Systematic Theology: Ethics*. 2nd ed. Nashville, TN: Abingdon, 2002.

Murray, Stuart. *The Naked Anabaptist: The Bare Essentials of a Radical Faith*. North American ed. Scottdale, PA: Herald, 2010.

Nadler, Hans. "Declaration of the Needle Merchant Hans at Erlangen and the Refutation of the Articles of the Needle Merchant Hans (1529)." In *Sources of South German/Austrian Anabaptism*, edited by Walter Klaassen, et al., 139–54. Classics of the Radical Reformation 10. Kitchener, ON: Herald, 2001.

Philips, Dirk. "Concerning the New Birth and the New Creature: Brief Admonition and Teaching From the Holy Bible (1556)." In *The Writings of Dirk Philips 1504-1568*, translated and edited by Cornelius J. Dyck, et al. 200–18. Scottdale, PA: Herald, 1992.

———. "Concerning Spiritual Restitution (1559)." In *The Writings of Dirk Philips 1504-1568*, translated and edited by Cornelius J. Dyck, et al., 218–46. Scottdale, PA: Herald, 1992.

———. "The Enchiridion (Handbook) (1564)." In *The Writings of Dirk Philips, 1504-1568*, edited by Cornelius J. Dyck, et al., 51–440. Classics of the Radical Reformation 6. Scottdale, PA: Herald, 1992.

Riedemann, Peter. *Peter Riedemann's Hutterite Confession of Faith (1565)*. Translated by John J. Friesen. Classics of the Radical Reformation 9. Waterloo, ON: Herald, 1999.

Schlaffer, Hans. "Instruction on Beginning a True Christian Life (1527)." In *Early Anabaptist Spirituality: Selected Writings*, edited by Daniel Liechty, 99–109. New York: Paulist, 1994.

Simons, Menno. "Foundation of Christian Doctrine (1539)." In *The Complete Writings of Menno Simons, c. 1496–1561*, edited by J. C. Wenger and Harold Stauffer Bender, 103–227. Scottdale, PA; Kitchener, ON: Herald, 1986.

———. "A Meditation on the Twenty-fifth Psalm (1537)." In *Early Anabaptist Spirituality: Selected Writings*, edited by Daniel Liechty, 248–72. New York: Paulist, 1994.

Snyder, C. Arnold. *Anabaptist History and Theology: An Introduction*. Kitchener, ON: Pandora, 1995.

———. *From Anabaptist Seed: The Historical Core of Anabaptist-related Identity*. Kitchener, ON: Pandora, 1999.

Snyder, C. Arnold, et al. *Biblical Concordance of the Swiss Brethren, 1540*. Anabaptist Texts in Translation. Kitchener, ON; Waterloo, ON: Herald, 2001.

Stayer, James M. *Anabaptists and the Sword*. Lawrence, KS: Coronado, 1972.

———. *The German Peasants' War and Anabaptist Community of Goods*. McGill-Queen's Studies in the History of Religion 6. Montreal, QC: McGill-Queen's University Press, 1991.

Warren, Rick. "The Anabaptists and the Great Commission: The Effect of the Radical Reformers in Church Planting." In *The Anabaptists and Contemporary Baptists: Restoring New Testament Christianity: Essays in Honor of Paige Patterson*, edited by Malcolm B. Yarnell, 83–100. Nashville, TN: Broadman & Holman, 2013.

Williams, George Huntston. "Sectarian Ecumenicity: Reflections on a Little Noticed Aspect of the Radical Reformation." *Review & Expositor* 64.2 (1967) 141–60.

Yoder, John Howard. *The Schleitheim Confession*. Scottdale, PA: Herald, 1977.

Chapter 4

Bergeson, Ronald Scott. "The Plea for Christian Unity: Enthymeme and Metaphor in the Rhetoric of the Restoration Movement, 1800–1830." PhD diss., University of Oregon, 1978.

Campbell, Alexander. "Any Christians Among Protestant Parties." *Millennial Harbinger* (September 1837) 411–14.

———. *The Christian System*. 1839. Reprint, Nashville, TN: Gospel Advocate, 1980.

———. "Christian Union—No. I." *Christian Baptist* 2 (4 July 1825) 234–39.

———. "Elder William F. Broddus, of Lexington, and the Union Meeting." *Millennial Harbinger* (June 1841) 265.

———. "The Foundation of Hope and of Christian Union." *Christian Baptist* 1 (5 April 1824) 220.

———. *Memoirs of Elder Thomas Campbell*. Cincinnati: H. S. Bosworth, 1861.

———. "A Restoration of the Ancient Order of Things." *Christian Baptist* 2 (April 4, 1825) 173.

———. "Union of Christians—No. I." *Millennial Harbinger* (May 1839) 212.

Campbell, Thomas. "Christian Union." *Millennial Harbinger* (April 1839) 164.

———. *Declaration and Address of the Christian Association of Washington*. Reprint, Coraopolois, PA: Record, 1908.

Christian Church (Disciples of Christ) in the United States and Canada. "Stone Campbell Dialogue." Christian Unity and Interfaith Ministry, 1999–2016. http://councilonchristianunity.org/stone-campbell-dialogue.

Conkin, Paul K. *Cane Ridge: America's Pentecost*. Madison, WI: University of Wisconsin Press, 1990.
DeGroot, Alfred T. *The Restoration Principle*. St. Louis, MO: Bethany, 1960.
Department of Commerce and Labor, Bureau of the Census. *Religious Bodies: 1906, Part 1, Summary and General Tables*. Washington, DC: US Government Printing Office, 1910.
Foster, Douglas A. "The 1906 Census of Religious Bodies and Division in the Stone-Campbell Movement: A Closer Look." *Discipliana* 66 (2006) 83–93.
Garrison, Winfred E. *Christian Unity and Disciples of Christ*. St. Louis, MO: Bethany, 1955.
Garrison, Winfred E., and Alfred T. DeGroot. *The Disciples of Christ: A History*. St. Louis, MO: Bethany, 1948.
Haggard, Rice. *An Address to the Different Religious Societies on the Sacred Import of the Christian Name*. 1804. Reprint, Nashville, TN: Disciples of Christ Historical Society, 1954.
Holloway, Gary, and Douglas A. Foster. *Renewing God's People: A Concise History of Churches of Christ*. Abilene, TX: ACU Press, 2006.
Kershner, Frederick D. *The Christian Union Overture*. St.Louis, MO: Bethany, 1923.
L. "A Plea for Union." *Millennial Harbinger* 41 (September 1870) 524, 526.
L., J. "Remarks on L.'s 'Plea for Union.'" *Millennial Harbinger* 41 (October 1870) 569.
Lester, Hiram J. "The Form and Function of the Declaration and Address." In *The Quest for Christian Unity, Peace, and Purity in Thomas Campbell's Declaration and Address: Text and Studies*, edited by Thomas H. Olbricht and Hans Rollmann. Lanham, MD: Scarecrow, 2000.
MacClenny, W. E. *The Life of Rev. James O'Kelly and the Early History of the Christian Church in the South*. Raleigh, NC: Edwards & Broughton Co., 1910.
Marshall, Robert, et al. *Apology of the Springfield Presbytery*. In *Autobiography of Barton W. Stone*, edited by John Rogers, 147–91. 1814. Reprint, Nashville, TN: M. & J. Nowell, 1847. https://www.yumpu.com/en/document/view/17065696/apology-of-the-springfield-presbytery-bellsouthpwpnet.
McAllister, Lester G. *Thomas Campbell: Man of the Book*. St. Louis, MO: Bethany, 1954.
Morrill, Milo T. *A History of the Christian Denomination in America, 1794–1911*. Dayton, OH: Christian Publishing Association, 1912.
Osborn, Ronald E. *Experiment in Liberty: The Ideal of Freedom in the Experience of Disciples of Christ*. St. Louis, MO: Bethany, 1978.
Richardson, Robert. *Memoirs of Alexander Campbell*. 2 vols. 1868–1870. Reprint, Indianapolis, IN: Religious Book Service, 1980.
Rouse, Ruth. "Voluntary Movements and the Changing Ecumenical Climate." In *A History of the Ecumenical Movement 1517–1948*, edited by Ruth Rouse and Stephen Charles Neill, 309–49. Philadelphia, PA: Westminster, 1968.
Scott, Walter. "Union." *The Evangelist* 9 (1841) 141.
Stone, Barton W. *The Biography of Eld. Barton Warren Stone, Written by Himself; With Additions and Reflections by Elder John Rogers*. Cincinnati, OH: J. A. & U. P. James, 1847.
———. "Christian Union." *Christian Messenger* 3 (1828) 37–38.
———. "The Convention." *Christian Messenger* 12 (1842) 195.
———. "Friendly Hints." *Christian Messenger* 13 (1844) 281–287.
———. "Remarks." *Christian Messenger* 9 (1835) 180.

———. "Reply to the Above Letter." *Christian Messenger* 12 (1841) 20.

———. "The Union of Christians. Lecture IV." *Christian Messenger* 11 (1841) 334.

Stone, Barton W., and John T. Johnson. "Editors' Address." *Christian Messenger* 7 (1833) 1.

Stone, Barton W., et al. *Last Will and Testament of Springfield Presbytery*. 1804. Reprint, St. Louis, MO: Mission Messenger, 1975.

Thompson, David M. "The Irish Background to Thomas Campbell's Declaration and Address." *Discipliana* 46 (1986) 23.

Toulouse, Mark G., ed. *Walter Scott: Nineteenth-Century Evangelical*. St. Louis, MO: Chalice, 1999.

West, William Garrett, et al. *Footnotes to Disciple History* 3. Nashville, TN: Disciples of Christ Historical Society, 1955.

Williams, D. Newell, et al., eds. *The Stone-Campbell Movement: A Global History*. St. Louis, MO: Chalice, 2013.

Williams, John Augustus. *Life of Elder John Smith*. Cincinnati, OH: R. W. Carroll, 1870.

Yoder, Don Herbert. "Christian Unity in Nineteenth-Century America." In *The History of the Ecumenical Movement 1517–1948*, edited by Ruth Rouse and Stephen Charles Neill. Philadelphia, PA: Westminster, 1968.

Chapter 5

Anderson, Cory. "Retracing the Blurred Boundaries of Twentieth-Century 'Amish-Mennonite' Identity." *Mennonite Quarterly Review* 85 (2011) 361–412.

Beachy, Leroy. *Unser Leit: The Story of the Amish*. Millersburg, OH: Goodly Heritage, 2011.

Biesecker-Mast, Susan. "A Genealogy of the *Confession of Faith* in a Mennonite Perspective." *Mennonite Quarterly Review* 81 (2007) 371–98.

Bullinger, Heinrich. *Von dem unverschampten farfel*. Zurich: n.p., 1531.

Cate, S. Blaupot ten. *Geschiedenis der Doopsgezinden in Holland, Zeeland, Utrecht en Gelderland* I. Amsterdam: P. N. van Kampen, 1847.

Center for the Study of Global Christianity at Gordon-Conwell Theological Seminary. "Status of Global Mission, 2014, in the Context of AD 1800–2025." January 2014. http://www.gordonconwell.edu/resources/documents/StatusOfGlobalMission.pdf.

Deleuze, Gilles, and Felix Guattari. *A Thousand Plateaus: Capitalism and Schizophrenia*, Translated by Brian Massumi. Minneapolis, MN: University of Minnesota Press, 1987.

Evana Network. "Home." http://www.evananetwork.org.

Franck, Sebastian. *Chronica, Zeitbuch vund Geschichsbibell*. Ulm: J. Varnier, 1536.

Goshen College. "Global Anabaptist Profile." Goshen, IN: Institute for the Study of Global Anabaptism, 2017. www.goshen.edu/isga/gap/.

Grant, Michael C. "The Trembling Giant." *Discover Magazine*, October 1, 1993. http://discovermagazine.com/1993/oct/thetremblinggian285.

Grimsrud, Ted. "The Logic of the Mennonite Church USA 'Teaching Position' on Homosexuality." *Brethren Life and Thought* 55.1–2 (2010) 10–23.

Grimsrud, Ted, and Mark Thiessen Nation. *Reasoning Together: A Conversation on Homosexuality*. Scottdale, PA: Herald, 2008.

Hartmann, Andrew. *A War for the Soul of America: A History of the Culture Wars*. Chicago: University of Chicago Press, 2015.

Hunter, James Davison. *Culture Wars: The Struggle To Define America*. New York: Basic, 1992.

Johns, Loren L. "Homosexuality and the Mennonite Church." In *Encyclopedia of Homosexuality and Religion*, edited by Jeffrey S. Siker, 149–55. Westport, CT: Greenwood, 2006.

Jenkins, Philip. *The Next Christendom: The Coming of Global Christianity*. Oxford: Oxford University Press, 2004.

Kniss, Fred. *Disquiet in the Land: Cultural Conflict in American Mennonite Communities*. New Brunswick, NJ: Rutgers University Press, 1997.

Kraus, Norman, ed. *To Continue the Dialogue: Biblical Interpretation and Homosexuality*. Telford, PA: Cascadia, 2001.

Kraybill, Donald B. *Concise Encyclopedia of Amish, Brethren, Hutterites, and Mennonites*. Baltimore, MD: Johns Hopkins University Press, 2010.

Kraybill, Donald B., and C. Nelson Hostetter. *Anabaptist World USA*. Scottdale, PA: Herald, 2001.

Kreider, Alan. *The Patient Ferment of the Early Church: The Improbable Rise of Christianity in the Roman Empire*. Grand Rapids, MI: Baker Academic, 2016.

Kreider, Luke Beck. "Mennonite Ethics and the Ways of the World: Rethinking Culture for Renewed Witness." *Mennonite Quarterly Review* 86 (2012) 465–92.

Lapp, John, and Ed Van Straten, "Mennonite World Conference 1925–2000: From Euro-American Conference to Worldwide Communion." *Mennonite Quarterly Review* 76 (2003) 8–45.

Meihuizen, H. W. "Spiritualistic Tendencies and Movements Among the Dutch Mennonites of the Sixteenth and Seventeenth Centuries." *Mennonite Quarterly Review* 27 (1953) 288–91.

Mennonite Church USA. "Forbearance in the midst of differences." July 2015. http://mennoniteusa.org/wp-content/uploads/2015/05/ForbearanceResolution.pdf.

———. "On the Status of the Membership Guidelines." July 2015. http://mennoniteusa.org/wp-content/uploads/2015/05/ResolutiononStatusofMembershipGuidelines_Final.pdf.

Mennonite Church and General Conference Mennonite Church. *Human Sexuality in the Christian Life: A Working Document for Study and Dialogue*. Newton, KS: Faith and Life, 1985.

Mennonite Church Canada and Mennonite Church USA. *A Shared Understanding of Church Leadership: Polity Manual for Mennonite Church Canada and Mennonite Church USA*. Harrisonburg, VA: MennoMedia, 2014.

Mennonite Historical Library. "Global Anabaptist Wiki." https://anabaptistwiki.org.

Mennonite World Conference. "Global Anabaptist Mennonite Shelf of Literature." 2018. www.mwc-cmm.org/article/global-anabaptist-mennonite-shelf-literature.

———. "Global Mennonite History Series." 2015. http://www.mwc-cmm.org/article/global-mennonite-history-series.

———. "Interchurch Dialogue." 2017. https://www.mwc-cmm.org/article/interchurch-dialogue.

———. "Renewal 2027." 2017. www.mwc-cmm.org/renewal2027.

———. "Shared Convictions." 2006. www.mwc-cmm.org/article/shared-convictions.

———. "World Directory." https://www.mwc-cmm.org/article/world-directory.

Moore, Charles E., and Timothy Keiderling, eds. *Bearing Witness: Stories of Martyrdom and Costly Discipleship*. Walden, NY: Plough, 2016.
Noll, Mark. *The New Shape of World Christianity: How American Experience Reflects Global Faith*. Downers Grover, IL: InterVarsity Academic, 2009.
Roth, John D. "The Complex Legacy of the Martyrs Mirror among Mennonites in North America." *Mennonite Quarterly Review* 87 (2013) 277–316.
Sanneh, Lamin. *Encountering The West: Christianity and the Global Cultural Process: The African Dimension*. Maryknoll, NY: Orbis, 1993.
Shenk, Wilbert R. "Mission and Service and the Globalization of North American Mennonites." *Mennonite Quarterly Review* 70 (1996) 7–22.
Stories Project. "Bearing Witness." https://martyrstories.org.
Stutzman, Ervin. "Frequently Asked Questions regarding the two resolutions on polity and practice." Mennonite Church USA, June 18, 2015. http://mennoniteusa.org/menno-snapshots/frequently-asked-questions-regarding-the-two-resolutions-on-polity-and-practice.
Swartley, Willard M. *Homosexuality: Biblical Interpretation and Moral Discernment*. Scottdale, PA: Herald, 2003.
Tshmika, Pakisa, and Tim Lind. *Sharing Gifts in the Global Family of Faith: One Church's Experiment*. Intercourse, PA: Good Books, 2003.

Chapter 6

Adcock, Rachel. *Baptist Women's Writings in Revolutionary Culture, 1640–1680*. Farnham, UK: Ashgate, 2015.
"The Assembly or Second London Confession, 1677 and 1688." In *Baptist Confessions of Faith*, edited by William L. Lumpkin, 235–95. Rev. ed. Valley Forge, PA: Judson, 1969.
Baptist Magazine 2 (1810) 348–49, 388.
Baptist World Alliance. "The Word of God in the Life of the Church: A Report of International Conversations between the Catholic Church and the Baptist World Alliance, 2006–2010." *American Baptist Quarterly* 31 (2012) 40.
Briggs, John H. Y. "She Preachers, Widows, and Other Women." *Baptist Quarterly* 31.7 (July 1986) 339.
Broom, J.R. *A Bruised Reed, The Life and Times of Anne Steele*. Trowbridge, UK: Cromwell, 2007.
Burrage, Champlin, ed. "A Trve and Short Declaration, both of the Gathering and Ioining Together of Certain Persons [with John More, Dr. Theodore Naudin, and Dr. Peter Chamberlen]: and also of the lamentable breach and division which fell amongst them." *Transactions of the Baptist Historical Society* 2.3 (1911) 145–46.
Crawford, Patricia. *Women and Religion in England 1500–1720*. Abingdon: Routledge, 1993.
Curriers Hall (Cripplegate). *Church Book 1689–1723*. London: Angus Library, n.p.
"A Declaration of Faith of English People remaining at Amsterdam, 1611." In *Baptist Confessions of Faith*, edited by William L. Lumpkin, 114–23. Rev. ed. Valley Forge, PA: Judson, 1969.
Durnbaugh, Donald F. *The Believers' Church: The History and Character of Radical Protestantism*. Scottdale, PA: Herald, 1968.

Edwards, Thomas. *Gangraena or a fresh and further discovery of the Errors, Heresies, Blasphemies and dangerous Proceedings of the Sectaries of this time.* London: T.R. & E.M., 1646.

Fiddes, Paul S. *Tracks and Traces: Baptist Identity in Church and Theology.* Carlisle: Paternoster, 2003.

———. "'Walking Together': The Place of a Covenant Theology in Baptist Life Yesterday and Today." In *Pilgrim Pathways: Essays in Honour of B.R. White*, edited by William H. Brackney and Paul S. Fiddes, 47–74 Macon, GA: Mercer University Press, 1999.

Fiddes, Paul S., et al., eds. *Bound to Love: The Covenant Basis of Baptist Life and Mission.* London: Baptist Union 1985.

Freeman, Curtis W. *A Company of Women Preachers: Baptist prophetesses in Seventeenth-Century England, A Reader.* Waco, TX: Baylor University Press, 2010.

———. "Visionary Women Among Early Baptists." *Baptist Quarterly* 43 (2010) 260–83.

Hayden, Roger, ed. *The Records of a Church of Christ in Bristol 1640–1687.* Bristol, UK: Bristol Record Society, 1974.

Keach, Benjamin. "The Solemn Covenant of the Church at its Constitution." In *The Glory of a True Church and its Discipline display'd.* London: n.p., 1697.

Kreitzer, Larry J. *William Kiffen and His World (Part 1).* Oxford: Regent's Park College, 2010.

———. *William Kiffen and His World (Part 2).* Oxford: Regent's Park College, 2012.

———. *William Kiffen and His World (Part 5).* Oxford: Regent's Park College, 2016.

"Mary Elyett." *Baptist Magazine* 3 (1811) 73.

Morgan, Edmund S. *Visible Saints: The History of a Puritan Idea.* New York: New York University Press, 1963.

"Mrs. Esther Horsey." *Baptist Magazine* 2 (1810) 347.

Ottoway, Susannah R. *The Decline of Life: Old Age in Eighteenth-Century England.* Cambridge: Cambridge University Press, 2004.

Parr, Susanna. *Susanna's Apologie against the Elders.* Oxford: Henry Hall, 1659.

Payne, Ernest A. *The Fellowship of Believers.* London: Kingsgate, 1944.

Riso, Mary. *The Narrative of the Good Death: The Evangelical Deathbed in Victorian England.* London: Routledge, 2016.

Rosman, Doreen M. *Evangelicals and Culture.* London: Croom Helm, 1984.

"Sarah Miell." *Baptist Magazine* 18 (1826) 136.

Smith, Karen E. "Baptists at Home." In *Challenge and Change: English Baptist Life in the Eighteenth Century*, edited by Stephen Copson and Peter J. Morden, 101–22. Didcot, UK: Baptist Historical Society, 2017.

———. "British Women and the Baptist World Alliance: Honoured Partners and Fellow Workers?" *Baptist Quarterly* 41.1 (2005) 25–46.

———. "Forgotten Sisters: The Contributions of Some Notable but Un-noted British Baptist Women." In *Recycling the Past or Researching History?*, edited by Philip E. Thompson and Anthony R. Cross, 163–83. Studies in Baptist History and Thought 11. Milton Keynes, UK: Paternoster, 2005.

———. "Preparation as a Discipline of Devotion in Eighteenth-Century England: A Lost Facet of Baptist Identity?" In *Baptist Identities*, edited by Ian M. Randall, et al., 22–44. Studies in Baptist History and Thought 19. Milton Keynes, UK: Paternoster, 2006.

———. "The Role of Women in Early Baptist Missions." *Review and Expositor* 89.1 (1992) 35–48.

Stannard, David E. *The Puritan Way of Death, A Study in Religion, Culture and Social Change.* Oxford: Oxford University Press, 1977.

Sutton, Katherine. *A Christian Woman's Experiences of the Glorious Working of God's Free Grace.* 1663. Reprint, Ann Arbor, MI: Text Creation Partnership, 2009. http://name.umdl.umich.edu/A62005.0001.001.

Trapnel, Anna. "Letter to the Church at Allhallows." In *A Legacy for Saints.* 1654. Reprint, Ann Arbor, MI: University of Michigan Library, 2011. http://name.umdl.umich.edu/A94794.0001.001.

Underhill, E. B., ed. *Records of the Churches of Christ, gathered at Fenstanton, Warboys and Hexham, 1644–1720.* London: Hanserd Knollys Society, 1954.

Wakefield, Gordon. *Puritan Devotion.* London: Epworth, 1957.

Walker, Austin. "Benjamin Keach (1640–1704) Tailor Turned Preacher." In *Pulpit and People Studies in Eighteenth-Century Baptist Life and Thought,* edited by John H.Y. Briggs, 25–42. Milton Keynes, UK: Paternoster, 2009.

Watts, Michael R. *The Dissenters.* Oxford: Oxford University Press, 1978.

Wilson, Linda. *Constrained by Zeal: Female Spirituality amongst Nonconformists.* Carlisle, UK: Paternoster, 2000.

Wrigley, E. A., and R.S. Schofield. *The Population History of England 1546–1871: A Reconstruction.* Cambridge Studies in Population, Economy, and Society in Past Times. Cambridge: Cambridge University Press, 1989.

Chapter 7

Alexander, Michelle. *The New Jim Crow: Mass Incarceration in the Age of Colorblindness.* New York: New Press, 2010.

Banaji, Mahzarin, and Anthony Greenwald. **Blindspot: Hidden Biases of Good People. New York: Delacorte, 2013.**

"Black Codes." *History,* June 1, 2010. http://www.history.com/topics/black-history/black-codes.

Booth, William D. *A Call to Greatness: The Story of the Founding of the Progressive National Baptist Convention.* Lawrenceville, VA: Brunswick, 2001.

Dixie, Quinton Hosford. "How Firm a Foundation?: The Institutional origins of the National Baptist Convention, USA, Inc." In *Church, Identity, and Change: Theology and Denominational Structures in Unsettled Times,* edited by David A Roozen and James R. Nieman, 327–335. Grand Rapids, MI: Eerdmans, 2005.

Frazier, E. Franklin. *Black Bourgeoisie.* New York: Free Press, 1957.

Goatley, David Emmanuel. *Were You There?: Godforsakenness in Slave Religion.* Maryknoll, NY: Orbis, 1996.

Gorod, Brianne. "Supreme Court's New Term: Racial Prejudice in the Justice, Electoral Systems." *The Hill,* October 3, 2016. http://thehill.com/blogs/congress-blog/judicial/298911-supreme-courts-new-term-racial-prejudice-in-the-justice.

Guo, Jeff. "Why Black Workers Who Do Everything Right Still Get Left Behind." *Washington Post,* October 3, 2016. https://www.washingtonpost.com/news/wonk/wp/2016/10/03/why-black-workers-who-do-everything-right-still-get-left-behind.

Herskovits, Melville J. *The Negro Myth*. New York: Harper Brothers, 1941.
Holzman, Michael. *Yes We Can, The Schott 50 State Report on Public Education and Black Males*. Cambridge: Schott Foundation for Public Education, 2010.
National Baptist Convention USA. *Minutes 1970*. Nashville, TN: Sunday School Publishing Board, 1970.
Washington, James Melvin. *Frustrated Fellowship: The Black Baptist Quest for Social Power*. Macon, GA: Mercer University Press, 2004.

Chapter 8

Airhart, Phillis D. "Ordering A New Nation and Reordering Protestantism, 1867–1914." In *The Canadian Protestant Experience, 1760–1990*, edited by George A. Rawlyk, 98–138. Burlington, ON: Welch, 1990.
Allwood, Philip G. A. "First Baptist Church, Halifax: Its Origin and Early Years." MA thesis, Acadia University, 1978.
Bower, William Clayton, and Percy Roy Hayward. *Protestantism Faces Its Educational Task Together*. Appleton, WI: CC Nelson, 1949.
Butchart, Reuben. *The Disciples of Christ in Canada Since 1830*. Toronto, ONT: Churches of Christ [Disciples], 1949.
Canada's Historic Places. "Cross Roads Christian Church." November 10, 2008. http://www.historicplaces.ca/en/rep-reg/place-lieu.aspx?id=10552.
Christie, Michael, and Roland McCormick. *A New Perspective: The Origins of New Brunswick's Free Baptists*. Sheet Harbour, NS: M. Christie, 2011.
Crawford, Donald. "Christian Union . . . " *The Christian* 17.8 (1900) 4.
"Disciples of Christ, or Christians." In *The New-Brunswick Almanac & Register for the Year of our Lord 1851*, edited by Fredericton Athenaeum, 54. Saint John, NB: Henry Chubb, 1850.
Griffin-Allwood, Philip G. A. "Disciple of Christ roots among the Regular Baptists." Unpublished Essay, Acadia Divinity College, 1978.
Motley, W. R. "Beginning at Jerusalem." *The Christian* 20.4 (1903) 1.
"Report of Committee on Union." *The Christian* 21.11 (1904) 3.
Shaw, Robert E. "History of the Disciples of Christ in Halifax, Nova Scotia." In *The Collections of the Nova Scotia Historical Society* 34, 20–26. Halifax, NS: Nova Scotia Historical Society, 1968.
Sinnott, Frank, ed. *East Point United Baptist Church: Historical Record, 1933–1972*. East Point, PEI: Island Offset, 1972.

Chapter 9

Berends, Kurt O. "Cultivating For a Harvest: The Early Life of Alice Belle Garrigus." *Pneuma* 17.1 (1995) 37–49.
———. "A Divided Harvest: Alice Belle Garrigus, Joel Adams Wright, and Early New England Pentecostalism." MA thesis, Wheaton College, 1993.
Black, William. "The Journal of William Black, in His Visit to Newfoundland." *The Arminian Magazine* 15 (1792).

Dunton, Jefferson D. "The Origins and Growth of the Salvation Army in Newfoundland: 1885–1901." MA thesis, Memorial University of Newfoundland, 1996.

English, R. C. "Is Divine Healing Part of the Atonement?" *Pentecostal Evangel* 2.6 (February 1928) 1–8.

Fitzgerald Shipyard. "Facility/History." http://fitzgeraldshipyard.com/index.php?option=com_content&view=article&id=2&Itemid=2.

Garrigus, Alice Belle. "Extract from a Letter of Sister Garrigus." *Word and Work* 23.6 (1911) 188–89.

———. "Newfoundland Stretching out her Hands to God." *Full Gospel Missionary Herald* 11.1 (1927).

———. "The Old Time Power." *Full Gospel Missionary Herald* 6.7 (1922) 7.

———. "Signs of the Coming of the King." *The Pentecostal Herald* 1.2 (1928) 1–8.

———. "A Marvelous Manifestation of God's Power: The Supernatural Overwhelms the Natural." *Full Gospel Missionary Herald* 11.1 (1925).

Gower Street United Church. "A Short History." http://www.gowerunited.ca/tp40/page.asp?ID=137443.

Greene, Jennie E. "Biography of Jacob Noseworthy." n.p., 1983.

Hewett, J. A. "Garrigus, Alice Belle." In *The New International Dictionary of Pentecostal and Charismatic Movements*, edited by Stanley M. Burgess and Eduard van der Mass, 661. Grand Rapids, MI: Zondervan, 2002–2003.

Hollett, Calvin. *Shouting, Embracing, and Dancing with Ecstasy: The Growth of Methodism in Newfoundland: 1774–1874*. Montreal, QC: McGill-Queen's University Press, 2010.

Janes, Burton K. "Floods Upon the Dry Ground: A History of the Pentecostal Assemblies of Newfoundland 1910–1939." MA thesis, Memorial University of Newfoundland, 1991.

———. *History of the Pentecostal Assemblies of Newfoundland*. St. John's, NL: Pentecostal Assemblies of Newfoundland, 1996.

———. *The Lady Who Came*. St. John's, NL: Good Tidings, 1982.

———. Personal Letter to Mrs. Jennie Greene. August 28, 1991.

MacGregor, Allison S. *The Development of Early Newfoundland Pentecostal Christology*. Unpublished essay, 2011.

Methodist Church of Canada. "Sixtieth Annual Report of the Missionary Society of the Methodist Church of Canada, 1883–1884." Toronto: Methodist Church of Canada, 1885.

Mount Holyoke College. "Alumnae Biographical File (RG 27.1)." South Hadley, MA: Mount Holyoke College Archives and Special Collections, n.p.

Moyles, R. Gordon. *The Blood and Fire in Canada: A History of the Salvation Army in the Dominion 1882–1976*. Toronto, ON: Peter Martin, 1977.

Parsons, Jacob. "The Origin and Growth of Newfoundland Methodism: 1765–1855." MA thesis, Memorial of Newfoundland, 1964.

Pentecostal Assemblies of Newfoundland and Labrador. "General Conference Minutes of the Pentecostal Assemblies of Newfoundland, Minute 27, October 17–24, 1927." Archives of the Pentecostal Assemblies of Newfoundland, St. John's, NL.

———. "State of the Fellowship Address." St. John's, NL: PAONL, 2008.

Prowse, D. W. *A History of Newfoundland from the English, Colonial, and Foreign Records*. London, UK: Macmillian, 1895.

Rollmann, Hans. *The Origins of Methodism in Newfoundland* in *The Contribution of Methodism to Atlantic* Canada. Montreal & Kingston: McGill-Queen's University Press, 1992.
Scobie, Charles H. H., and John Webster Grant, eds. *The Contribution of Methodism to Atlantic Canada*. Montreal & Kingston: McGill-Queen's University Press, 1992.
Smallwood, J. R., ed. *The Book of Newfoundland*. Vol. 2. St. John's, NL: Newfoundland, 1937.
State of Connecticut, Bureau of Vital Statistics. "Birth Certificate of Alice Belle Garrigus. Born 2 August 1858." Mount Holyoke College Archives and Special Collections, South Hadley, MA, Alunmae Biographical File, RG 27.1.
Statistics Canada. "Newfoundland Census, 1911." https://archive.org/stream/19119819 11fnfldv451914eng#page/n7/mode/2up.
Vaters, Eugene. "Doctrinal." *The Independent Communion* 1.4/5 (1924) 3.
———. "How Pentecost Found Newfoundland." *The Testimony* 24.24 (1943).
———. "Our Beginnings." *Good Tidings* 22.3 (1966) 16.
———. *Reminiscence*. St. John's, NL: Good Tidings, 1983.
Vaters, Jennie. "A Three-Fold Vision." *The Independent Communion* 1.2 (1924) 2.
Verge, Carl. "Interview with Myrtle Bloomfield Eddy." In *History of the Pentecostal Assemblies of Newfoundland,* edited by Burton K. Janes, 32. St. John's, NL: The Pentecostal Assemblies of Newfoundland, 1996.
Wesley, John. "Self Indulgence." *Pentecostal Evangel* 2.2 (1928) 8.
"Who we are, and what we believe." *Nfld. Pentecostal Evangel* 3.2 (April 1929) 4–5.
Wiggins, Arch R. *The History of the Salvation Army*. New York: Salvation Army, 1964.
Wilkinson, Michael, ed. *Canadian Pentecostals: Transition and Transformation*. Montreal, QC: McGill-Queen's University Press, 2009.
Wilson, D. J. "Church Membership." In *The New International Dictionary of Pentecostal and Charismatic Movements*, edited by Stanley M. Burgess and Eduard van der Mass, 529–530. Grand Rapids, MI: Zondervan, 2002-3.
Winsor, Naboth. *A History of Methodism in Newfoundland: 1765–1925*. Vol. 1. Gander, NL: BSC, 1982.

Chapter 10

Ammerman, Nancy T. "Report to the Justice and Treasury Department Regarding Law Enforcement Interaction with the Branch Davidians in Waco, Texas." In *Recommendations of Experts for Improvements in Federal Law Enforcement after Waco*, edited by US Department of Justice, 1–10. Washington, DC: Department of Justice, 1993.
Anthony, Dick. "Religious Movements and Brainwashing Litigation: Evaluating Key Testimony." In *In Gods We Trust: New Patterns of Religious Pluralism in America*, edited by Thomas Robbins, 295–344. 2nd ed. New Brunswick, NJ: Transaction, 1990.
Aquarian, Isis, with Electricity Aquarian. *The Source: The Untold Story of Father Yod, Ya Ho Wa 13 and the Source Family*. Los Angeles: Process, 2007.
Atack, Jon. *A Piece of Blue Sky: Scientology, Dianetics, and L. Ron Hubbard Exposed*. New York: Lyle Smart, 1990.

"Austrian driver allowed 'pastafarian' headgear photo." *BBC News*, July 14, 2011. https://www.bbc.com/news/world-europe-14135523.

Baha'i International Community. *Iran's Secret Blueprint for the Destruction of a Religious Community: An Examination of the Persecution of the Baha'is of Iran*. New York: Bahai International Community, 1999.

Bainbridge, William Sims. *The Endtime Family: Children of God*. Albany, NY: SUNY Press, 2002.

Balch, Robert W. "From Self-Initiation to Heaven's Gate: Charisma and Conversion in Two New Age Cults." In *Sects, Cults, & Spiritual Communities: A Sociological Analysis*, edited by William W. Zellner and Marc Petrowsky, 1–26. Westport: Praeger, 1998.

Banisadr, Masoud. *Masoud: Memoirs of an Iranian Rebel*. London: Saqi, 2004.

Barker, Eileen. "Ageing in New Religions: The Varieties of Later Experiences." *Diskus: The Journal of the British Association for the Study of Religions* 12 (2011) 1–23. http://diskus.basr.ac.uk/index.php/DISKUS/article/view/21/20.

———. "But Who's Going to Win? National and Minority Religions in Post-Communist Society." In *New Religious Phenomena in Central and Eastern Europe*, edited by Irena Borowik and Grzegorz Babinski, 25–62. Kraków: Nomos, 1997.

———. "The Changing Scene: What Might Happen and What Might Be Less Likely to Happen?" In *New and Minority Religions: Projecting the Future*, edited by Eugene V. Gallagher, 7–19. Farnham: Routledge, 2017.

———. "Crossing the Boundary: New Challenges to Authority and Control as a Consequence of Access to the Internet." In *Religion and Cyberspace*, edited by Morten Thomsen Højsgaard and Margit Warburg, 67–85. London: Routledge, 2005.

———. "From the Children of God to the Family International: A Story of Radical Christianity and Deradicalising Transformation." In *The Handbook of Contemporary Christianity: Movements, Institutions & Allegiance*, edited by Stephen Hunt, 402–21. Leiden: Brill, 2016.

———. "From Cult War to Constructive Cooperation—Well, Sometimes." In *'Cult Wars' in Historical Perspective: New and Minority Religions*, edited by Eugene Gallagher, 9–22. Abingdon, Oxon: Routledge, 2017.

———. *The Making of a Moonie: Brainwashing or Choice?* Oxford: Blackwell, 1984.

———. *New Religious Movements: A Practical Introduction*. London: HMSO, 1989

———. "The Not-So-New Religious Movements: Changes in 'the Cult Scene' over the Past Forty Years." *Temenos* 50.2 (2014) 235–56.

———, ed. *Revisionism and Diversification in New Religious Movements*. Farnham: Ashgate, 2013.

———. "With Enemies Like That . . . Some Functions of Deprogramming as an Aid to Sectarian Membership." In *The Brainwashing/Deprogramming Debate: Sociological, Psychological, Legal, and Historical Perspectives*, edited by David G. Bromley and James T. Richardson, 329–44. New York: Edwin Mellen, 1983.

Beaman, Lori G., ed. *Reasonable Accommodation: Managing Religious Diversity*. Vancouver: UBC Press, 2012.

Berger, Maria. *Draft Report on Cults in the European Union*. Strasbourg: European Parliament Committee on Civil Liberties and Internal Affairs, 1997.

Bird, Frederick, and William Reimer. "Participation Rates in New Religious Movements and Parareligious Movements." In *Of Gods and Men: New Religious Movements in the West*, edited by Eileen Barker, 215–38. Macon, GA: Mercer University Press, 1983.

Boettcher, Robert. *Gifts of Deceit: Sun Myung Moon, Tongsun Park, and the Korean Scandal.* New York: Holt, Rinehart, and Winston, 1980.
Borowik, Claire. "Digital Revisionism: The Aftermath of the Family International's Reboot." In *Radical Changes in Minority Religions*, edited by Eileen Barker and Beth Singler. Abingdon, Oxon; New York: Routledge, forthcoming.
Bringhurst, Newell G., and John C. Hamer, eds. *Scattering of the Saints: Schism within Mormonism.* Independence, MO: John Whitmer, 2007.
Bromley, David. "Conservatorships and Deprograming: Legal and Political Prospects." In *The Brainwashing/Deprogramming Controversy: Sociological, Psychological, Legal and Historical Perspectives*, edited by David G. Bromley and James T. Richardson, 267–94. New York: Edwin Mellen, 1983.
Bromley, David G., and Anson Shupe. "Organised Opposition to New Religious Movements." In *Religion and the Social Order: A Handbook on Cults and Sects in America*, edited by David G. Bromley and Jeffrey K. Hadden, 177–98. Greenwich, CT: JAI, 1993.
Bromley, David G., and James T. Richardson, eds. *The Brainwashing/Deprogramming Controversy: Sociological, Psychological, Legal and Historical Perspectives.* Studies in Religion and Society 5. New York: Edwin Mellen, 1983.
Brown, Charles Paul, Berna Deane, and James Russell Strole. *Together Forever: An Invitation to Physical Immortality* Scottsdale, AZ: Eternal Flame Foundation, 1990.
Bugliosi, Vincent. *Helter Skelter: The Manson Murders.* Harmondsworth: Penguin, 1977.
Bull, Malcolm, and Keith Lockhart. *Seeking a Sanctuary: Seventh-Day Adventism and the American Dream.* 2nd ed. San Francisco: Harper and Row, 2007.
Carter, Helen. "Jedi Religion Founder Accuses Tesco of Discrimination over Rules on Hoods: Daniel Jones Says He Was Humiliated and Victimised for His Beliefs Following Incident at Store in Wales." *The Guardian*, September 18, 2009. https://www.theguardian.com/world/2009/sep/18/jedi-religion-tesco-hood-jones.
Carter, Lewis F. *Charisma and Control in Rajneeshpuram: A Community without Shared Values.* Cambridge: Cambridge University Press, 1990.
Cashmore, Ernest Ellis. *The Rastafarian Movement in England.* London: Unwin, 1983.
Chancellor, James D. *Life in the Family: An Oral History of the Children of God.* Syracuse, NY: Syracuse University Press, 2000.
"Charitable purposes and public benefit." *Gov.uk*, September 16, 2013. https://www.gov.uk/government/collections/charitable-purposes-and-public-benefit.
Christian Church. "The Embassy of the Blessed Kingdom of God for All Nations." http://godembassy.com.
Church of the Flying Spaghetti Monster. "About." http://www.venganza.org/about.
Church of Moo. "Occult." http://www.textfiles.com/occult/MOOISM.
Church of the Subgenius. "Become an Ordained Minister Now." http://www.subgenius.com.
Coleman, Gabriella. *Hacker, Hoaxer, Whistleblower, Spy: The Many Faces of Anonymous.* London: Verso, 2014.
Côté, Jean. *Prophet without Permit: Father John of the Trinity.* St. Jovite, QC: Editions Magnificat, 1991.
Cusack, Carole M. *Invented Religions: Imagination, Fiction and Faith.* Aldershot: Ashgate, 2010.

Cusack, Carole M., and Alex Norman, eds. *Handbook of New Religions and Cultural Production*: Brill, 2012.
Cusack, Carole M., and Pavol Kosnáč, eds. *Fiction, Invention and Hyper-Reality: From Popular Culture to Religion*. Abingdon, Oxon: Routledge, 2017.
Dasa, Anuttama. "The Changing Perception of ISKCON: Ancient Faith or Dangerous Cult?" In *'Cult Wars' in Historical Perspective: New and Minority Religions*, edited by Eugene Gallagher, 134–51. Abingdon, Oxon: Routledge, 2017.
Dawson, Andrew. *Santo Daime: A New World Religion*. London: Bloomsbury, 2013.
Deutscher Bundestag Referat Öffentlichkeitsarbeit, ed. *Enquete Commission on "So-called Sects and Psychogroups": New Religious and Ideological Communities and Psychogroups in the Federal Republic of Germany*. Translated by Wolfgang Fehlberg and Monica Ulloa-Fehlberg. Bonn: Bonner Universitäts-Buchdruckerei, 1998.
Douglas, Mary. *Purity and Danger: An Analysis of Concepts of Pollution and Taboo*. London: Routledge & Kegan Paul, 1966.
———. *Natural Symbols: Explorations in Cosmology*. London: Barrie & Rockliff, 1970.
Duquesne, Antoine, and Luc Willems. *Enquete Parlementaire Visant À Élaborer Une Politique En Vue De Lutter Contre Les Pratiques Illégales Des Sectes Et Le Danger Qu'elles Représentent Pour La Société Et Pour Les Personnes, Particulièrement Les Mineurs D'âge*. Parliamentary Enquiry, 313/7 & 8–95/96. Brussels: Belgian House of Representatives, 1997.
Ebaugh, Helen Rose. *The Gülen Movement: A Sociological Analysis of a Civic Movement Rooted in Moderate Islam*. Dordrecht: Springer, 2010.
Enroth, Ronald. *The Lure of the Cults*. New York: Christian Herald, 1979.
Evans, Bette Novit. "Religious Freedom vs. Compelling State Interests." *Rabbi Myer and Dorothy Kripke Center for the Study of Religion and Society* 9.2 (1998). http://moses.creighton.edu/csrs/news/s98-1.html.
Fairholm, Adam. "Pope Michael: A Documentary Film." https://popemichaelfilm.com.
Family International. "Welcome." https://www.thefamilyinternational.org.
Festinger, Leon, Henry H. Rieken, and Stanley Schachter. *When Prophecy Fails*. Minneapolis: University of Minnesota Press, 1956.
First Church of Cannabis. "Home." http://www.cannaterian.org.
Fox, Judith M. *Osho Rajneesh*. Salt Lake City: Signature, 2000.
Fudge, Thomas A. *The Trial of Jan Hus: Medieval Heresy and Criminal Procedure*. New York: Oxford University Press, 2013.
Gallagher, Eugene V., ed. *'Cult Wars' in Historical Perspective: New and Minority Religions*. Abingdon, Oxon: Routledge, 2017.
———, ed. *Visioning New and Minority Religions: Projecting the Future*. Abingdon, Oxon: Routledge, 2017.
Giambalvo, Carol, Michael Kropveld, and Michael Langone. "Changes in North American Cult Awareness Organizations." In *Revisionism and Diversification in New Religious Movements*, edited by Eileen Barker, 227–45. Farnham: Ashgate, 2013.
Grabner, Barbara. "Slovakia: Religious Freedom only for the Big and Mighty?" *Forum for Religious Freedom Europe*, November 5, 2016. https://foref-europe.org/2016/11/05/1667.
Graebner, William. *Patty's Got a Gun: Patricia Hearst in 1970s America*. Chicago: University of Chicago Press, 2008.

Gregory, Richard L. *Seeing through Illusions: Making Sense of the Senses.* Oxford: Oxford University Press, 2009.
Guyard, Jacques, and Alain Gest. *Les Sectes En France.* Paris: Assemblée Nationale, 1995.
Hanegraaff, Wouter J. *Esotericism and the Academy: Rejected Knowledge in Western Culture* Cambridge: Cambridge University Press, 2012.
———. *New Age Religion and Western Culture: Esotericism in the Mirror of Secular Thought.* Albany, NY: State University of New York, 1998.
Harvey, Graham, ed. *Indigenous Religions: A Companion.* London: Cassell, 2000.
Hassan, Steven. *Combatting Cult Mind Control: Protection, Rescue and Recovery from Destructive Cults.* Wellingborough: Aquarian, 1988.
Henderson, Bobby. *The Gospel of the Flying Spaghetti Monster.* London: HarperCollins, 2006.
Her Majesty's Government. *Revised Prevent Duty Guidance: For England and Wales. Guidance for Specified Authorities in England and Wales on the Duty in the Counter-Terrorism and Security Act 2015 to Have Due Regard to the Need to Prevent People from Being Drawn into Terrorism.* London: HM Government, 2015.
Hill, Daniel G. *Study of Mind Development Groups, Sects and Cults in Ontario.* Ontario Government, Toronto, 1980.
Hobsbawm, Eric, and Terence Ranger, eds. *The Invention of Tradition.* Cambridge: Cambridge University Press, 1983.
Hubbard, L. Ron. *Dianetics: The Modern Science of Mental Health.* Copenhagen: New Era, 1950.
Inform (Information Network Focus on Religious Movements). "Home." www.inform.ac.
Ingvardsson, Margó, Sonja Wallbom, and Lars Grip. *I God Tro: Samhället Och Nyandligheten [In Good Faith: Society and the New Religious Movements].* Stockholm: Statens offentliga utredningar, Socialdepartementet, 1998.
Jedi Church. "Home." https://www.jedichurch.org.
Jehovah's Witnesses. "Jehovah's Witnesses Imprisoned for Their Faith—By Location." February 2109. https://www.jw.org/en/news/legal/by-region/world/jehovahs-witnesses-in-prison-2.
Jones, Kristina, Celeste Jones, and Juliana Buhring. *Not without My Sister.* London: HarperElement, 2007.
Kent, Stephen, and Deanna Hall. "Brainwashing and Re-Indoctrination Programs in the Children of God/the Family." *Cultic Studies Journal* 17 (2000) 56–78.
Kilduff, Marshall, and Ron Javers. *The Suicide Cult: The inside Story of the Peoples Temple and the Massacre in Guyana.* New York: Bantam, 1978.
King, Christine. *The Nazi State and the Nazi New Religions.* New York: Edwin Mellen, 1982.
King, George. *Cosmic Voice.* Vol. 1. 3rd ed. London: Aetherius Society, 1980.
King, George, and Richard Lawrence. *Contacts with the Gods from Space: Pathway to the New Millennium.* Hollywood: Aetherius Society, 1996.
Lambert, Malcolm. *The Cathars.* Oxford: Blackwell, 1998.
Langlais, Jean-Louis. *The 2004 Report to the Prime Minister: The Sectarian Risk.* Paris: MIVILUDES, 2005.
Lewis, James R., ed. *Encyclopedic Sourcebook of UFO Religions.* Amherst, NY: Prometheus, 2003.

Lheureux, N. L., et al. *Report on Discrimination against Spiritual and Therapeutical Minorities in France*. Paris: Coordination des Associations et Particuliers Pour la Liberté de Conscience, 2000.

Liebster, Max. *Crucible of Terror: A Story of Survival through the Nazi Storm*. New Orleans: Grammaton, 2003.

Lifton, Robert Jay. *Destroying the World to Save It: Aum Shinrikyo, Apocalyptic Violence, and the New Global Terrorism*. New York: Owl, 1999.

"LOI no 2001–504 du 12 juin 2001 tendant à reforcer la prevention et la repression des mouvements sectairs portant atteinte aux droits de l'homme et aux libertés fondamentales." *Journal Officiel de la République Française* 13 (2001) 9337.

MacLaine, Shirley. *Out on a Limb*. New York: Bantam, 1983.

Maher, Shiraz. "Change and Continuity: Hizb Ut Tahrir's Strategy and Ideology in Britain." In *Revisionism and Diversification in New Religious Movements*, edited by Eileen Barker, 155–70. Farnham: Ashgate, 2013.

Martin, Sean. *The Cathars: The Most Successful Heresy of the Middle Ages*. Harpenden, Herts: Pocket Essentials, 2005.

Martin, Walter. *The Kingdom of the Cults: An Analysis of the Major Cult Systems in the Present Christian Era*. Rev. ed. Minneapolis: Bethany House, 1985.

Matrixism. "Home." http://www.matrixism.org.

McFarland, H. Neill. *The Rush Hour of the Gods: A Study of New Religious Movements in Japan*. New York: Macmillan, 1967.

McGuire, Meredith B. *Religion: The Social Context*. 5th ed. Belmont, CA: Wadsworth, 2002.

Melton, J. Gordon. *Finding Enlightenment: Ramtha's School of Ancient Wisdom*. Hillsboro, OR: Beyond Words, 1998.

———. *Melton's Encyclopedia of American Religions*. 8th ed. Farmingron Hills, MI: Gale, 2009.

———. "Spiritualization and Reaffirmation: What Really Happens When Prophecy Fails." *American Studies* 26.2 (1985) 17–29.

Miller, Russell. *Bare-Faced Messiah: The True Story of L. Ron Hubbard*. London: Michael Joseph, 1987.

Miller, Timothy. *American Communes, 1860–1960: A Bibliography*. New York: Garland, 1990.

———, ed. *When Prophets Die: The Postcharismatic Fate of New Religious Movements*. Albany: SUNY Press, 1991.

Milne, Hugh. *Bhagwan: The God That Failed*. London: Caliban, 1986.

Moore, Rebecca. *Understanding Jonestown and Peoples Temple*: Praeger, 2009.

Muster, Nori, ed. *Child of the Cult*. Independently published, 2012.

Norman, Ruth. *Preparation for the Landing*. El Cajon, CA: Unarius Educational Foundation, 1987.

Office for National Statistics. "390,000 Jedi There Are." Census 2001, February 13, 2003. http://www.ons.gov.uk/ons/rel/census/census-2001-summary-theme-figures-and-rankings/390-000-jedis-there-are/jedi.html/

Osho. "Places To Meditate & Meditation Centers Around The World." https://www.osho.com/meditate/places-to-meditate/meditation-centers#countryLocations

Otherkin. "Welcome." https://www.otherkin.net.

Palmer, Susan J. *Aliens Adored: Raël's UFO Religion*. New Brunswick, NJ: Rutgers University Press, 2004.

Palmer, Susan J., and Charlotte E. Hardman, eds. *Children in New Religions*. New Brunswick, NJ: Rutgers University Press, 1999.
Partridge, Christopher, ed. *UFO Religions*. London: Routledge, 2003.
Patrick, Ted, with Tom Dulack. *Let Our Children Go*. New York: Ballantine, 1976.
Paulk, Rachel. "Falun Gong Protests China Policy." *Accuracy in Academia* 24 (2008). https://www.academia.org/falun-gong-protests-china-policy.
People Unlimited, Inc. "Super Longevity Community." https://www.peopleunlimitedinc.com.
Perkins, Rodney, and Forrest Jackson. *Cosmic Suicide: The Tragedy and Transcendence of Heaven's Gate*. Dallas, TX: Pentaradial, 1997.
Pieri, Zacharias. *Tablighi Jamaat*. London: Lapidomedia, 2012.
Possamai, Adam, ed. *Handbook of Hyper-Real Religions*. Leiden: Brill, 2012.
———. *Religion and Popular Culture*. Oxford: Peter Lang, 2005.
"Preston Down Trust." *Gov.uk*, January 9, 2014. https://www.gov.uk/government/publications/preston-down-trust.
"Principia Discordia." http://principiadiscordia.com/book/8.php.
Prophet, Erin. *Prophet's Daughter: My Life with Elizabeth Clare Prophet inside the Church Universal and Triumphant*. Guilford, CT: Lyons, 2009.
Rawlings, Helen. *The Spanish Inquisition*. Oxford: Blackwell, 2005.
Richardson, James T., ed. *Regulating Religion: Case Studies from around the Globe*. Dordrecht: Kluwer Academic/Plenum, 2004.
Richardson, James T., and François Bellanger, eds. *Legal Cases, New Religious Movements, and Minority Faiths*. Aldershot: Ashgate, 2014.
Richardson, James T., and Massimo Introvigne. "'Brainwashing' Theories in European Parliamentary and Administrative Reports on 'Cults' and 'Sects.'" *Journal for the Scientific Study of Religion* 40.2 (2001) 143–68.
Rochford, Burke E. *Hare Krishna in America*. New Brunswick, NJ: Rutgers University Press, 1985.
———. *Hare Krishna Transformed*. New York: New York University Press, 2007.
Ross, Rick Alan. *Cults inside Out: How People Get in and Can Get Out*. North Charleston, SC: CreateSpace, 2014.
Shakespeare, William. *Romeo and Juliet*. New York: Washington Square, 1964.
Shaw, Jane. *Octavia, Daughter of God: The Story of a Female Messiah and Her Followers*: Yale University Press, 2011.
Shields, Steven. *Divergent Paths of the Restoration*. 1975. Reprint, Las Vegas: Herald House, 2001.
Shupe, Anson D., and David G. Bromley. *The New Vigilantes: Deprogrammers, Anti-Cultists, and the New Religions*. Beverly Hills: Sage, 1980.
Shupe, Anson D., and Susan E. Darnell. *Agents of Discord: Deprogramming, Pseudo-Science, and the American Anticult Movement*. New Brunswick, NJ: Transaction, 2006.
Singer, Margaret Thaler. "Consulting with Families of Cultists." In *Systems Consultation: A New Perspective for Family Therapy*, edited by L. C. Wynne, et al., 270–83. New York: Guilford Press, 1986.
Singer, Margaret Thaler, and Janja Lalich. *Cults in Our Midst: The Hidden Menace in Our Everyday Lives*. San Francisco: Jossey-Bass, 1995.
Slotte, Pamela, and Helge Årsheim. "The Ministerial Exception—Comparative Perspectives." *Oxford Journal of Law and Religion* 4.2 (2015) 171–98.

Stark, Rodney, and William Sims Bainbridge. *A Theory of Religion*. New York: Peter Lang, 1987.

Sunday Assembly. "Celebrating Life Together." https://www.sundayassembly.com.

Tan, Chik Kaw. "Can One Be Christian and Buddhist at the Same Time?" *American Anglian Council*. https://www.americananglican.org/can-one-be-christian-and-buddhist-at-the-same-time.

Tillich, Paul, and B. MacKenzie. *Ultimate Concern: Tillich in Dialogue*. New York: Harper & Row, 1965.

Tumminia, Diane, and R. G. Kirkpatrick. "Unarius: Emergent Aspects of an American Flying Saucer Group." In *The Gods Have Landed*, edited by James R. Lewis, 85–104. Albany: SUNY Press, 1995.

Turner, Harold. "New Religious Movements in Primal Societies." In *A New Dictionary of Religions*, edited by John R. Hinnells, 350–51. Rev. ed. Oxford: Blackwell, 1995.

Underwood, Barbara, and Betty Underwood. *Hostage to Heaven: Four Years in the Unification Church by an Ex Moonie and the Mother Who Fought to Free Her*. New York, NY: Clarkson N. Potter, 1979.

Universal Church. "Jesus Cristo E O Senhor Universal." https://www.universal.org.

Urban, Hugh B. "The Church of Scientology." In *Revisionism and Diversification in New Religious Movements*, edited by Eileen Barker, 65–78. Farnham, Surry: Ashgate, 2013.

———. *The Church of Scientology: A History of a New Religion*. Princeton, NJ: Princeton University Press, 2011.

Van Eck Duymaer van Twist, Amanda. *Perfect Children: Growing up on the Religious Fringe*. Oxford: Oxford University Press, 2015.

Vivien, Alain. *Les Sectes En France: Expression De La Liberté*. Paris: La Documentation Française, 1985.

Vonck, Chris. *The Life and Legacy of Sun Myung Moon and the Unification Movement in Scholarly Perspective. Special Edition of Acta Comparanda Vi*. Wilrijk-Antwerp, Belgium: Faculty for Comparative Study of Religions and Humanism, 2017.

Wallis, Roy. "The Aetherius Society: A Case Study in the Formation of a Mystagogic Congregation." In *Sectarianism: Analysis of Religious and Non-Religious Sects*, edited by Roy Wallis, 17–34. London: Peter Owen, 1975.

———. *The Elementary Forms of the New Religious Life*. London: Routledge and Kegan Paul, 1984.

———. *The Road to Total Freedom: A Sociological Analysis of Scientology*. London: Heinemann, 1976.

Ward, Alan. "Judgement of Lord Justice Ward in the Matter of ST (a Minor) W 42 1992." *The High Court of Justice Family Division*, 19 October 1995. https://www.xfamily.org/index.php/Complete_Judgment_of_Lord_Justice_Ward.

Weber, Max. *The Theory of Social and Economic Organization*. Translated by A. M. Henderson and Talcott Parsons. New York: Free Press, 1947.

Wells, Simon. *Charles Manson Coming Down Fast*. London: Hodder and Stoughton, 2010.

Westboro Baptist Church. "God Hates Fags." http://www.godhatesfags.com.

"Why God Loves JuBus." *BeliefNet*, September 2003. https://www.beliefnet.com/faiths/judaism/2003/09/why-god-loves-jubus.aspx?.

Williams, Miriam. *Heaven's Harlots: My Fifteen Years as a Sacred Prostitute in the Children of God Cult*. New York: Eagle Brook, 1998.

Wilson, Bryan R. *Religious Sects: A Sociological Study*. London: Weidenfeld & Nicholson, 1970.
Witteveen, Tobias A. M. *Onderzoek Betreffende Sekten: Overheid En Nieuwe Religeuze Bewegingen*. The Hague: Tweede Kamer, 1984.
Wright, Lawrence. *Going Clear: Scientology, Hollywood, & the Prison of Belief*. New York: Knopf, 2013.
Wright, Stuart, ed. *Armageddon in Waco: Critical Perspectives on the Branch Davidian Conflict*. Chicago: University of Chicago Press, 1995.
———. *Leaving Cults: The Dynamics of Defection*. Washington, DC: Society for the Scientific Study of Religion, 1987.
Yamamoto, J. I. *The Puppet Master: An Inquiry into Sun Myung Moon and the Unification Church*. Downers Grove, IL: InterVarsity, 1977.
Yang, Fenggang. *Religion in China: Survival and Revival under Communist Rule*. Oxford: Oxford University Press, 2012.
York, Michael. *Pagan Theology: Paganism as a World Religion*. New York: New York University Press, 2003.

Chapter 11

Barth, Karl. "The Church—the Living Congregation of the Living Lord Jesus Christ." In *Man's Disorder and God's Design*, edited by The Amsterdam Assembly, 67–76. The Amsterdam Assembly 1. New York: Harper and Brothers, 1948.
Durnbaugh, Donald. *The Believers' Church: The History and Character of Radical Protestantism*. Eugene, OR: Wipf and Stock, 1968.
Eller, David B., ed. *Servants of the Word: Ministry in the Believers' Church*. Elgin, IL: Brethren, 1990.
Enns, Fernando. "Believers Church Ecclesiology: A Vital Alternative within the Ecumenical Family." In *New Perspectives in Believers Church Ecclesiology*, edited by Abe Dueck, et al., 107–24. Winnipeg, MB: CMU, 2010.
———. *The Peace Church and the Ecumenical Community. Ecclesiology and the Ethics of Nonviolence*. Geneva, CH: WCC, 2007.
European Baptist Press Service. *Newsletter*. Rüschlikon-Zürich, Switzerland, June 2, 1964.
Gagliardi, Mauro. "A Look at the Catechism's Presentation of Liturgy." *Zenit Daily Dispatch*, December 21, 2011. http://www.ewtn.com/library/Liturgy/zbelieving.htm.
Garrett, James Leo, Jr., ed. *The Concept of the Believers' Church: Addresses from the 1967 Louisville Conference*. Scottdale, PA: Herald, 1969.
Hindmarsh, Bruce. "Is Evangelical Ecclesiology an Oxymoron? A Historical Perspective." In *Evangelical Ecclesiology: Reality or Illusion?*, edited by John G. Stackhouse, 15–38. Grand Rapids, MI: Eerdmans, 2003.
Klaver, Miranda. "We are the World? Identity Politics and Congregational Transformation of Dutch Baptists." *American Baptist Quarterly* 31.4 (2012) 420–30.
Leer, Teun van der. "Which future Church(form)? A plea for a 'Believers Church' ecclesiology." *Journal of European Baptist Studies* 9.3 (2009) 40–51.

McClendon, James Wm, Jr. *Systematic Theology: Doctrine*. Nashville, TN: Abingdon, 1994.

———. *Systematic Theology: Ethics*. 2nd ed. Nashville, TN: Abingdon, 2002.

Murray, Stuart. *Church After Christendom*. Milton Keynes, UK: Paternoster, 2004.

Newbigin, Lesslie. *The Household of God: Lectures on the Nature of the Church*. London: SCM, 1953.

Pannabecker, S. F. "The Anabaptist Conception of the Church in the American Mennonite Environment." *The Mennonite Quarterly Review* 25.1 (1951) 34–46.

Verkuyl, J. *Preken en preekschetsen*. Kampen, NL: Kok, 1980.

Volf, Miroslav. *After Our Likeness: The Church as the Image of the Trinity*. Grand Rapids, MI: Eerdmans, 1998.

Vries, O. H. de. *De dynamiek tussen traditionele kerk en opwekkingsbeweging*. Utrechtse Theologische Reeks 23. Utrecht: Faculteit der Godgeleerdheid, Universiteit Utrecht, 1994.

Weber, Max. *The Protestant Ethic and the Spirit of Capitalism*. London/New York: Routledge Classics, 2001.

World Council of Churches. *Baptism, Eucharist, and Ministry*. Faith and Order Paper 111. Geneva, CH: WCC, 1982.

———. *The Church—Towards a Common Vision*. Faith and Order Paper 214. Geneva, CH: WCC, 2013.

Yoder, John Howard. "The Believers' Church Conferences in Historical Perspective." *The Mennonite Quarterly Review* 65.1 (1991) 5–19.

———. "Introduction." In *Baptism and Church: A Believers' Church Vision*, edited by Merle D. Strege, 3–7. Grand Rapids, MI: Sagamore, 1986.

———. *Real Christian Fellowship*. Harrisonburg, VA: Herald, 2014.

Zeman, Jarold K., and Walter Klaassen. *The Believers' Church in Canada: Adresses and Papers from the Study Conference in Winnipeg, May 15–18, 1978*. Brantford, ON: Baptist Federation of Canada; Winnipeg, MB: Mennonite Central Committee, 1979.

Index

Adelaja, Sunday, 186
Aetherius Society, 164
African-American Baptists, 102–16
Ahmadiyya Community, 187
All Canada Committee of the Churches of Christ (Disciples), 129
Alliance of Baptists, 30
Alline, Henry, 119
American Baptist Convention, 37
American Baptist Free Mission Society, 111
American Baptist Home Mission Society, 29
American Baptist Missionary Convention, 111
American Baptist Missionary Union, 33n38
American Baptist Publication Society, 122
American Christian Missionary Society, 125
American National Baptist Convention, 112
Amherstburg Association (Ont.), 111
Anabaptist Network, 48
The Anabaptist Vision of the Church, 23
Anabaptists, 21, 39, 72–82, 159
Ancient Order, 58
Antiburghers, 52
Antichrist, 5
Antitrinitarians, 18
The Apostles of the Infinite Love (Quebec), 187

Associate Synod of North America, 53
Association of Historic Baptists, 28
Atlantic Ecumenical Council, 129
Augsburg Confession (1530), 22

Baha'i, 187
Bainton, Roland, 23
Baker, Robert A., 33
Baptism, believers, 38–50
Baptists 20; 23–37; Baptist America, 32; ecclesiology, 36; importance of New Testament, 37; in Canada 27, 35; Sabbath-keeping 32
Baptist Association for Colored People, 110
Baptist Bible College (Mo.), 35
Baptist Bible Fellowship, 28n18
Baptist Federation of Canada, 129
Baptist Foreign Mission Convention, 112
Baptist World Alliance, 88
Barber, Edward, 25
Barltrop, Mabel, 178
Barnes, Kenneth S., 147
Barnes, W. A., 123
Barrowists, 24
Barth, Karl, 190, 195
Beachy Mennonites, 71
Beginning of a True Christian Life, 39
Believed Church, 192
The Believers' Church, 189
Believers Churches, 189–97; list of, Appendix

Bender, Harold, 23
Berends, Kurt O., 137–38
Berg, David, 162, 181
Bethel Theological Seminary (Minn.), 29n
Bethesda Mission, 139, 142, 147
Bhaktivedanta, A. C., Swami Prabhupada, 163
Bible of Kralice, 13
Biblical Concordance of the Swiss Brethren, 49
Black Baptists, 30. *See also* African American Baptists.
Black, William, 147n76, 148n77
Black Rock Resolutions (1832), 33n
Blackwood, Christopher, 25n
Bogard, Ben M., 33
Bohemian Brethren (Unity of Brethren), 10–14
Book of Mormon, 177
Booth, L. V., 34, 114
Booth, William, 147
Boyd, Richard H., 34
Boyd Baptist Convention, *See* National Baptist Convention of America.
Bracht, Thieleman Jansz van, 11, 81n34
Brandon College (Man.), 28
Branch Davidians, 162
Brisbane, William, 31
Broadmead Church, Bristol, 95
Broadmead Records, 91
Brown, Nathan, 31
Brown University, 27n15
Brownists, 24, 25–26
Bucer, Martin, 18
Buddhism, 186
Bullinger, Heinrich 71
Burroughs, Nannie Helen, 113
Busher, Leonard, 25n7

Caffyn, Matthew, 25n8, 27n14
Calvin, John, 18
Campbell, Alexander, 52, 53, 55, 57, 58, 59, 61, 120
Campbell, Thomas, 52, 53, 55, 58
Canadian Antislavery Baptist Association, 111

Canadian Association of Baptist Freedoms, 31n31
Canadian Bible Society, 129
Canadian Council of Churches, 129
Canadian Pentecostals, 153
Case, S. J., 28n17
Cathars, 10
Catholic Apostolic Church, 16
Charles V, Emperor, 40
Children of God, 163, 185
Chown, S. D., 150
Christadelphians, 158, 179
Christian Association, 53
Christie, Michael, 119
Christian and Missionary Alliance, 118
The Christian, 117n
The Christian Baptist, 56, 58
Christian Endeavour, 118
The Christian Gleaner, 120
The Church: Towards a Common Vision, 189
Church of Christ, 129–30
Church of God in Moravia, 16
Church of Ireland, 52
Church of Jesus Christ of Latter Day Saints, 158, 172
Church of Scientology, 164, 186
Church Universal and Triumphant, 178
Civil Rights Movement, 114–15
Clarke, William Newton, 28n17
Clearwaters, Richard, 35n
Colloquy of Thorn (1645), 14
Confessio Bohemica (1575), 14n24
Confession of Faith from a Mennonite Perspective, 69
Congregational autonomy, 115
Congregational Way, 190
Congregationalists, 119
Conservative Baptist Association, 35
Consolidated American Baptist Missionary Convention, 111
Cooperative Baptists, 30, 31–32
Coughlin, Lawrence, 133–34
Council of Bale (1531), 8
Council of the Evangelical Church in Germany, 3
Covenant life, 88
Cox, Benjamin, 98

Crawford, Donald, 124
Crawford, Tarlton P., 31
Crozer Theological Seminary, 28n17
Cults, 184–87

Daime, Santo, 186
David, Zdenek, 8
DeBaptiste, Richard, 111
Declaration and Address of the Christian Association of Washington, PA, 53, 62
Deleuze, Gilles, 77
Demarest, Victoria Booth-Clibborn, 147
Denk, Hans, 40
Dianetics: The Modern Science of Mental Health, 164
Dictionary of Pentecostal and Charismatic Movements, 139
Differences in the Churches of the Separation, 25
Diggers, 24
Disciples of Christ, 53, 117–30
Dissent, 24
Dixie, Quinton Hosford, 115
Donation of Constantine, 10
Druids, 186
Durnbaugh, Donald, 189, 191, 194
Dutch Mennonites, 72
Dutch Mennonite Seminary, 190
Dykes, Daniel, 98

Eddy, Myrtle Broomfield, 145
Edwards, Thomas, 86
Elijah the Prophet, 16
Elyett, Mary, 99
Embassy of the Blessed Kingdom of God for All Nations, 186
English, Robert C., 139–40, 144, 147
Enns, Fernando, 192
Erasmus, Desiderius, 41
Eschatology, 41–46
Estep, William R., 191
European Baptist Federation, 191
European Convention of Human Rights, 172
Evans, Milton G., 28n17
Evangelical Alliance, 118
Evangelical Anabaptism (EVANA), 71

Evangelical Christianity, 21, 100, 118
Experienced Church, 192

Faith and Order Commission, 191
Faithful Brethren, 9
Falon Gong, 182
Fellowship of Evangelical Baptist Churches, 32n, 35
Fenstanton Church, (England), 95
Fifth Monarchist Movement, 86, 93
Findings Summary, 199–200
Five Principle Calvinistic Baptists, 26
First Church of Cannabis, 186
Flirty fishing, 176
Ford, E. C., 123
Foreign Christian Missionary Society, 124
Forty, Henry, 98
Foster, A. H., 123
Foster, George B., 28n16
Founders Movement, 28
Foxe, John, 15
Franck, Sebastian, 71
Free Baptists 119
Free Church Movement, 23, 190
Free Communion Baptists, 27n12
Freewill Baptists, 27
Friends to Humanity, 110
Frustrated Fellowship: The Black Baptist Quest for Social Power, 108
Fundamentalism, 161
Fundamentalist Baptists, 35–36

Gangraena, 86
Garraty, George, 121
Garrigus, Alice Bell, 137–39, 140, 144, 146, 148, 152
Garrison, William Lloyd, 31
Gathered church, 88n
General Association of Regular Baptists, 35
General Conference of the Pentecostal Assemblies of Newfoundland, 133
General Conference Mennonite Church, 69
General Six Principle Baptists, 26

A Genetic History of Baptist Thought, 27n15
German Enquete Commission, 171
German Peasants War, 42, 46
German Reformation, 3
Glock, Paul 45
The Glory of a True Church and Its Discipline Display'd, 89
Goatley, David, 30
Gordon Conwell Theological Seminary (Mass.), 32n33, 72n17
Gospel Mission Movement, 30
Grantham, Thomas, 25
Grave(s), Ann, 94–95
Graves, James M., 33
Griffin, Sister, 95
Gülen, Fethullah, 187
Gunn, Murdoch, 130

Haldane, Robert, 120
Hari Krishna Movement, 163
Harper, William Rainey, 28n17
Heathens, 186
Helwys, Thomas, 25
Henry VIII, King of England, 15
Hewitt, James A., 139
Hicks, Thomas, 98
Hill, Rev. A., 136
Hollett, Calvin, 136, 143
Holiness Movement, 139
Holy dying, 97–101
Horsey, Esther, 99–100
Hubbard, L. Ron, 164
Hubmaier, Balthasar, 40, 43, 71
Hus, Jan, 6
Hussite Utraquists, 6–8
Hut, Hans, 39, 46
Hutter, Jakob, 15
Hutterites, 14–17, 45, 179
Hyper-Calvinist Baptists, 28

The Independent Church, 177
The Independent Communion, 149
International Society for Krishna Consciousness, 163, 182
Introvigne, Massimo, 171
Irving, Edward, 16

Jablonsky, Daniel Ernest, 14
Jackson, Joseph H., 34, 109, 114
Jackson, Mahalia, 113
Janes, Burton J., 137, 139
Jehovah's Witnesses, 158, 168, 179
Jemison, D. V., 114
Jessey, Henry, 92
Jesuits, 15
Jim Crow Laws, 112
"Justification on Freedom," 3–4

Keach, Benjamin, 89
Kelly, Dorothy, 94
Keswick Movement, 118n7
Ketcham, R. T., 35
Kierstead, E. M., 123
Kiffen, William, 94
King, Martin Luther, Jr., 34, 113, 114
Kingdom of God, 50
Klaver, Miranda, 196, 197
Komensky, Jan Amos, 14
Knollys, Hanserd, 92, 93, 98
Knox, John, 120
Koresh, David, 162
Krahn, Cornelius, 23
Kraus, Fred, 67
Krieder, Alan, 81–82
Kreitzer, Larry, 94n35

Lamb, Thomas, 25n
Landmarkists, 28, 33
Latourette, Kenneth Scott, 23
Liberal Baptists, 27–28
Littell, Franklin H., 23, 38, 190
Levellers, 24
Lipscomb, David, 65
London Confession (1644), 24, 26n9, 10, 85
London Confession (1677/1689), 85, 89
Loofs, Friedrich, 190
Lords Day Alliance, 118
Luther, Martin, 3, 4, 5, 64
Lutheran Reformation, 4, 18, 40, 174n68
Lyons, Mary, 137

Mainstream Baptists, 25
The Maritime Baptist, 126
Maritime Christian College, 122, 128

INDEX

Maritime Religious Education, 129
Martyrs Mirror, 11, 81
Mathews, Shailer, 28n17
McMaster University, 28
Massee, J. C., 35
McBeth, H. Leon, 33
McClendon, James Wm., 49, 190
McCormick, Roland, 119
McDonald, John, 121
McLean, Archibald, 124, 125
Melancthon, Philipp, 6
Memorial University of Newfoundland, 146
Mennonites, 66–82; doctrine of the church, as rhizome, 73–76; Seven Shared Convictions, 78; Global Mennonite History Shelf of Literature, 79; Global Anabaptist Profile, 80; Global Anabaptist Wiki, 80; Bearing Witnesses Stories Project, 81; Radical Patience, 82
Mennonite Church, Canada, 76
Mennonite Church USA, 66–67
Mennonite World Conference, 75–76, 78
Methodism, 148–54
Miell, Sarah, 99
Millennial Harbinger, 58, 62
Miller, William, 176
Moody, Dale, 191
Moon, Rev. Sun Myung, 162
Morgan, Edmund, 92n27
Mormonism. *See* Church of Jesus Christ of Latter Day Saints
Morris, Elias Camp, 109
Mount Holyoke Female Seminary, 137
Murray, James, 120
Murray, Stuart, 48
Mennonites, 19–21
Methodists 118, 133–50
Michael the Priest, 12
Midland Confession (1655), 26
Moody Bible Institute (Ill.), 143
Mountain States Conference (Mennonite), 70
Myers, Cortland, 35
Myles, John, 28

Nadler, Hans, 42–43, 46
National Baptist Convention in the USA, 30, 34, 109, 111–13, 115
National Baptist Educational Convention, 112
National Baptist Convention of America, 34
National Church of Cromwell, 24
Neo-Evangelicalism, 35
Nethway, Mrs., 95
New Age, 186
New Light Movement, 119
New Religious Movements, 157–88; characteristics of, 165–67
Newbigin, Leslie, 190
Newfoundland, 131–54
Norris, J. Frank, 35
North, S.N.D., 65
North American Baptist Conference, 29
North American Baptist Seminary, 29n23
Northwestern and Southern Baptist Convention, 111
Noseworthy, Jacob, 140–42
Nova Scotia, 120–21, 124, 131

Odinists, 186
O'Kelly, James, 52
Old Mennonite Church, 69
Old School Baptists, 33
On the Christian Baptism of Believers, 40
Oosterbaan, Johannes, 190, 191
Ordnung, 68
Orthodox Creed (1678), 26
Osho International Meditation Resort, 185

Packull, Werner O., 15
Panacea Society, 178
Pannabecker, S.F., 196
Parr, Susanna, 87
Particular Baptists, 85
Patient Ferment of the Church, 81
Pendleton, James M., 33
Pentecostal Assemblies of Newfoundland, 153
Pentecostal Evangel, 144
Pentecostalism, 132–54
Perkins, William, 92n26

INDEX

Pharepoint, Ann, 95
Philadelphia/Charleston Tradition, 30
Philips, Dirk, 40, 43–44
Pilgrim Church, 190
Plymouth Brethren, 158, 181
Poems on Subjects Chiefly Devotional, 96
Polish Brethren, 17–19
Poole, Elizabeth, 94,
Pope Michael, 187
Post, Albert, 31
Powell, Adam Clayton, Jr., 113
Premillennial Baptist Fellowship, 35
Presbyterians, 52–53, 118
Priesthood of all believers, 72
Prima donnaism, 34–36
Prince Edward Island, 120, 127–28, 130
Proctor, Samuel DeWitt, 113
Progressive National Baptist Convention, 114
Providence Association, 110
Puritans, 25, 34, 85, 92

Quakers, 16, 24, 110

Racial Prejudice, 102–6
Radical Reformation, 191
Rajneesh, Bagwan Shree, 163
Randall, Benjamin, 27
Rastafarians, 166, 186
Rauschenbusch, Walter, 28n17
Rawlyk, George, 119
Reformed Baptists, 28
Regular Baptists, 27, 120
Reiser, Friedrich, 9
Reiling Jannes, 190, 191
Resurgent Southern Baptists, 32n33
Revivalism, 21
Restoration Movement 51–65, 130
Rice, John R., 35
Richardson, James, 171
Ridemann, Peter, 40, 45
Riley, William Bell, 3
Riso, Mary, 100
Rite of Christian Initiation for Adults, 48
Roberson, Lee, 35
Rochester Bible Training School (NY), 143

Rollman, Hans, 146, 147, 150
Roman Catholics, 134, 182
Romney, Mitt, 158n4
Roseman Doreen, 100

Salvation Army, 151
Sanctuary Church, 185
Sandomierz Agreement (1575), 14
Sattler, Michael, 11
Schlaffer, Hans, 39
Schleitheim Confession (1527), 49
Schmidt, Nathaniel, 28n17
Schneider, Johannes, 191
Scott, Walter, 57
Second Coming of Christ, 38
Seekers, 24
Separate Baptists, 30, 31
Separationism, 46–47
Separatists, 24, 85
Servet, Miquel, 18
Seventh Day Adventists, 158
Shields, Thomas Todhunter, 35
Simons, Menno, 19, 40, 43
Slavery, 104–6
Smith, Gerald Birney, 28n17
Smyth, John, 24
Social Gospel, 28, 118
Socinianism, 18, 24, 27
Southern Baptist Theological Seminary (Ky), 32n33
Southern Baptists, 31–32, 33–34, 108;
  Home Mission Board, 108
Southwestern Baptist Theological Seminary, 35
Southwide Baptist Fellowship, 35
Sovereign Grace Baptists, 28
Spiritualist principle, 75
Spurgeon, Charles Haddon, 26n11, 34, 36
Stayer, James M., vii–xii
Steele, Ann, 96
Stevenson, John, 120
Stone, Barton W., 52, 59–60
Stone-Campbell Dialogue, 65n50
Stone-Campbell Movement, 51–55, 122;
  ecclesiology of, 55–56
Strict and Evangelical Baptists, 26n11

Sunday School movement, 117
Sutton, Katherine, 86, 93
Synod of Ulster, 52

Taylor, Gardner C., 34, 114
Torbet, Robert G., 37
Trapnel, Anna, 86, 92, 93
Trinity Evangelical Divinity School, 32n33
Troeltsch, Ernst, 23, 190
Turner, Jane, 86
Turner Thesis, 36
Two Seed in the Spirit Double Predestinarian Baptists 28, 33

Unarius Society Academy of Science, 164
Unification Church, 165, 176, 185
Union Baptist Antislavery Association, 110
United Baptist Convention of the Maritime Provinces, 119
United Church of Canada, 130, 148
Universal Church of the Kingdom of God, 186
Universal Declaration of Human Rights, 171–72
University of Chicago, 28n17
Upper Canada Baptist Missionary Society, 29

Valdesius, Peter, 8–9
Vaters, Eugene, 142, 143, 144, 149
Vatican II, 48
Vedder, Henry C., 28n17
Verge, Carl, 145
Verkuyl, Johannes, 197

Vick, G. Beauchamp, 35
Volf, Miroslav, 190
Vries, Olof de, 193

Waldensians, 8–11
Wallace, Roy, 161
Warren, Rick ,48
Washington, James Melvin, 108–111, 115
Watts, Michael, 92n26
Weber, Max, 194
Welsh Baptists, 28
Wentworth, Anne, 86
Wesley, John, 144
Westboro Baptist Church, 187
Whitefield, George, 31
Wicca, 186
Wight, Sarah, 86
Wilkinson, Michael, 153
Williams, L. K., 114
Winsor, Naboth 134
Wise, Lawrence, 98
Women, 85–101; roles of women in Baptist life, 90
Wood River Association (Ill.), 110
World Council of Churches, 189

Yoder, John Howard, 191, 193, 194, 197
Young Anabaptist Mennonite Exchange Network, 79
Young Women's Christian Association, 171

Zeman, Jarold K., 193n
Zinzendorff, Count Nicholas von, 14
Zwingli, Huldrych, 41, 64, 71, 72

www.ingramcontent.com/pod-product-compliance
Lightning Source LLC
Chambersburg PA
CBHW050439240426
43661CB00055B/2446